THE ITALIAN REGIONAL PASTA COOKBOOK

The ITALIAN REGIONAL PASTA COOKBOOK

250 Authentic Recipes from the North to the South of Italy

Gabriella Mari and Cristina Blasi

APPLE

First published in the UK by Apple Press in 2006
Apple Press
Sheridan House
114 Western Road
Hove
East Sussex BN3 1DD

www.apple-press.com

Isbn 1-84543-102-2

Printed in China

This book was conceived, edited and designed by McRae
Books Srl
Borgo Santa Croce, 8 – 50122 Florence, Italy
info@mcraebooks.com

Project Director: Anne McRae
Design Directors: Marco Nardi, Sara Mathews
Text: Scuola di Arte Culinaria Cordon Bleu, Florence
(Gabriella Mari, Cristina Blasi)
Project Editor: Helen Farrell
Editor: Osla Fraser
Photography: Marco Lanza, Walter Mericchi
Home Economists: Scuola di Arte Culinaria Cordon Bleu,
Florence
(Gabriella Mari, Cristina Blasi, Emilia Onesti)
Layouts and Cut-outs: Adina Stefania Dragomir,
Giampietro Bruno, Filippo delle Monache
Jacket design: Jane Waterhouse

CONTENTS

INTRODUCTION

Pasta—the flagship of Italian cuisine—is an essential part of almost every Italian meal. Since Italy's unification in 1861, a modern national heritage of regional cooking has been asserted and maintained, and its variety manifests itself even from city to city. In this book, we have compiled authentic regional recipes so you can enjoy the true taste of each of them in your own home. From the warming winter pasta recipes of the northern regions of Piedmont, Veneto, and Lombardy to the sun-kissed summer vegetable sauces of Sicily and Calabria, the wide range of pasta *fresca* (fresh) and *pastasciutta* (dried) recipes, plus all the filled pasta will please the entire family.

Italians are proud of their local ingredients and are masters of transforming their seasonal produce into mouthwatering and creative food. On the following two pages, you will find four basic recipes, from Béchamel to Vegetable stock, which will provide an authentic Italian foundation in your kitchen time and time again. With over 250 recipes, *Pasta Italia* is one of the most comprehensive, single-volume books specializing in Italian regional pasta available today.

Béchamel sauce

VEGETABLE STOCK

Brodo vegetale

- 4 tablespoons butter, cut up
- 2 onions
- 2 carrots
- 1 leek
- 2 stalks celery with leaves
- 3 tomatoes, halved
- 6 sprigs parsley
- 8 black peppercorns
- 1 clove
- 1 bay leaf (optional)
- $^1/_2$ teaspoon salt
- 4 quarts/4 liters water

Melt the butter in a large saucepan and add all the vegetables. • Cover and simmer over low heat for 10 minutes, stirring occasionally. • Add the parsley, peppercorns, clove, bay leaf, if using, and salt. • Add the water and simmer over low heat for 1 hour, skimming off the froth. • Strain the stock, discarding the vegetables.

Makes 3 quarts/3 liters • Prep: 15 min • Cooking: 1 hr 15 min • Level: 1

LIGHT CHICKEN STOCK

Brodo di pollo

Clean and firmly tie the chicken with kitchen string. Place in a large cooking pot with the water. • Bring to a boil and skim off the froth. • Add the vegetables and salt. Simmer, uncovered, for about 2 hours. • Strain the stock and use as required.

Makes 2 quarts/2 liters • Prep: 40 min • Cooking: 2 hr • Level: 1

- 1 medium chicken, weighing about 3 lb/ 1.5kg, or 2 carcasses
- 4 quarts/4 liters water
- 1 white onion, peeled
- 1 stalk celery
- 1 small carrot
- 1 clove garlic
- 1 bay leaf
- 4 sprigs fresh parsley
- salt

FISH STOCK

Brodo di pesce

- 1 lb/500 g fish heads and bones (such as sea-bass, turbot, sole, and grouper)
- 3 quarts/3 liters cold water
- 1 carrot, coarsely chopped
- 1 stalk celery, coarsely chopped
- 1 white onion, coarsely chopped
- 1 shallot, coarsely chopped
- 1 clove garlic
- 4 sprigs fresh parsley
- 1 sprig fresh thyme
- 1 bay leaf
- 4 white peppercorns
- 1 tablespoon coarse salt
- scant $^1/_2$ cup/100 ml dry white wine

Soak the fish heads and bones in cold water for 1 hour. This will cleanse the bones of any left-over blood. Drain and transfer to a large saucepan. Pour in the water and bring to a boil over low heat. • Skim off the froth and add the carrot, celery, onion, shallot, garlic, parsley, thyme, bay leaf, peppercorns, salt, and wine. Simmer, uncovered, for about 1$^1/_2$ hours. • Strain the stock. The stock will keep in the refrigerator for about 4–5 days or about 3 months in the freezer.

Makes 2 quarts/2 liters • Prep: 40 min + 1 hr to soak the fish bones • Cooking: 1$^1/_2$ hr • Level: 1

BÉCHAMEL SAUCE

Besciamella

Béchamel sauce is a vital base for Italian cuisine.

Melt the butter in a saucepan, add the flour and stir over medium heat until a light paste (or roux) is achieved. Pour in a dash of the milk to dissolve the roux. • Pour in the remaining milk and stir, making sure no lumps have formed. • Season with salt, white pepper, and freshly grated nutmeg to taste. Bring to a boil and simmer over low heat for 20 minutes. There is no need to stir continuously as the flour has already cooked through. If you are using the Béchamel in a baked dish, the cooking time of the sauce can be reduced to 10 minutes.

Makes 2 cups/500 ml • Prep: 10 min • Cooking: 10–20 min • Level: 2

- 3 tablespoons butter, cut up
- 3 tablespoons all-purpose/plain flour
- 2 cups/500 ml milk
- salt and freshly ground white pepper
- freshly grated nutmeg

LIGURIA

From this region of steep cliff-top villages sweeping up to the French border comes a cuisine of varied herb- and vegetable-based dishes. For a special occasion, create delectable *pansôti* with one of the numerous featured sauces. The world-famed *pesto alla genovese*, from the region's capital of Genoa, was invented to highlight Liguria's uniquely flavored basil, the best-tasting basil in Italy. To recreate authentic Ligurian cuisine in your kitchen, be sure to always use the freshest herbs available.

Rustic tagliatelle
(see page 21)

Potato gnocchi with
mushroom and shallot sauce

POTATO GNOCCHI WITH MUSHROOM AND SHALLOT SAUCE

Bacialli con sugo di funghi

Gnocchi
- 3¹/₂ lb/1.5 kg baking/ floury potatoes
- salt
- 2²/₃ cups/400 g all-purpose/plain flour

Sauce
- 1¹/₂ oz/40 g dried mushrooms, soaked in warm water for 15 minutes
- 3 shallots, finely chopped
- 1 onion, finely chopped,
- ¹/₄ cup/60 ml extra virgin olive oil
- ¹/₄ cup/60 ml dry white wine
- 3 tablespoons tomato paste/puree
- salt and freshly ground black pepper
- 1 quart/1 liter vegetable stock or broth
- 6 tablespoons freshly grated Parmesan cheese

Gnocchi: Cook the potatoes in salted, boiling water for 15–20 minutes, or until tender. Drain and peel them. Use a potato masher or fork to mash them and spread them on a surface to cool. • Season with salt and add the flour. Knead the mixture into a ball. Pull off 1-inch (3-cm) pieces of dough and form into ¹/₂-inch (1-cm) thick logs. Cut the logs into 1-inch (3-cm) lengths and press against the tines of a fork or slide along a floured ridged board (see pages 130–131), making sure they are not too close together. • Sauce: Drain the mushrooms, straining the water through a coffee filter or paper towel to remove grit. Finely chop the mushrooms. • Sauté the shallots, onion, and mushrooms in the oil in a saucepan over medium heat for about 5 minutes. • Increase the heat and pour in the wine. Mix the tomato paste into ¹/₄ cup of the filtered mushroom water. Add to the saucepan. Season with salt and pepper and simmer over medium heat for 20 minutes, adding the stock as the sauce starts to thicken and stick to the bottom of the pan. • Cook the gnocchi in small batches in a large pot of salted boiling water until they rise to the surface, about 2 minutes. • Use a slotted spoon to remove the gnocchi and transfer to the sauce. Sprinkle with Parmesan and serve.

Serves 6–8 • Prep: 60 min + time to soak the mushrooms • Cooking: 60 min • Level: 2

GNOCCHI WITH MEAT SAUCE

Bacialli con sugo di carne

Gnocchi: Prepare the gnocchi dough. Shape it into a ball, wrap in plastic wrap, and let rest for 1 hour. • Roll the dough out into a thin, rectangular sheet measuring 12 x 16 inches (30 x 40 cm) and cover with a clean cloth or plastic wrap to prevent it from drying out. • Filling: Wash the spinach leaves and place in a saucepan. Cook until tender with just the water left clinging to the leaves, about 5 minutes. • Squeeze out excess moisture, then chop coarsely. • Sauté the spinach in 2 tablespoons of butter in a medium saucepan over high heat for 2 minutes, or until the spinach is coated all over with butter. • Sprinkle with 1 tablespoon of Parmesan. • Sauté the mushrooms in 2 tablespoons of butter in a small saucepan over medium heat for 4–5 minutes, or until tender. • Poach the chicken livers in water to cover for 3 minutes. Drain and chop finely. • Melt 4 tablespoons of butter in a frying pan over low heat and begin to sauté the sausage meat, chicken livers, and beef. Season with salt and cook for 10 minutes, moistening with a little water if the meat sticks to the bottom of the pan. • Spread this mixture over the sheet of gnocchi dough, leaving a ³/₄-inch (2-cm) border. Cover with the spinach in an even layer. • Fold over the edge of one of the longer sides and roll up, forming a long sausage. • Wrap firmly in a large piece of cheesecloth. Tie the gathered ends of the cloth with string. • Place the roll in boiling water in an oval Dutch oven or fish kettle. Simmer gently for 50 minutes. • Carefully remove from the water and set aside to cool. Untie and remove the cloth. • Preheat the oven to 450°F/220°C/gas 8. • Cut into ¹/₂-inch (1-cm) thick slices and place in a lightly buttered ovenproof dish. Melt the remaining butter and pour over the slices. Sprinkle with the remaining Parmesan. • Bake for 5–10 minutes, or until lightly browned. • Serve hot.

Serves 6–8 • Prep: 60 min + 60 min to rest the dough • Cooking: 90 min • Level: 3

Gnocchi
- Gnocchi dough (see recipe left)

Filling
- 2 lb/1 kg spinach leaves, tough stalks removed
- ³/₄ cup/180 g butter
- ³/₄ cup/90 g freshly grated Parmesan cheese
- 8 oz/200 g fresh mushrooms, thinly sliced, or 1 oz/30 g dried porcini mushrooms, soaked in warm water for 15 minutes and drained
- 8 oz/200 g chicken livers, trimmed
- 4 oz/125 g fresh sausage meat, crumbled
- 8 oz/200 g finely ground/minced lean beef
- salt
- water (optional)

WALNUT SAUCE

Salsa alle noci

- 3 tablespoons butter
- 2 cloves garlic, finely chopped
- 40 walnuts, coarsely crushed
- 1 cup/250 ml heavy/double cream
- salt and freshly ground white pepper

This sauce is best served with short pasta and sprinkled with freshly grated Parmesan cheese.

Melt the butter with the garlic in a frying pan over medium heat. Sauté for 1 minute, then add the walnuts. • Continue cooking for 2 minutes and mix in the cream. • Cook over low heat until the sauce thickens, about 12 minutes. Season with salt and pepper.

Serves 4 • Prep: 15 min • Cooking: 15 min • Level: 1

GENOESE PESTO

Pesto alla genovese

Process the basil, pine nuts, garlic, olive oil, and salt in a food processor until smooth. Transfer the mixture to a large serving bowl and stir in the cheeses. • Add the water and butter and stir well. Serve at room temperature.

Serves 4 • Prep: 10 min • Level: 1

- 2 cups/60 g fresh basil leaves
- 2 tablespoons pine nuts
- 2 cloves garlic
- 1/2 cup/125 ml extra-virgin olive oil
- salt
- 2 tablespoons freshly grated Parmesan cheese
- 2 tablespoons freshly grated Peccrino cheese
- 2 tablespoons pasta cooking water
- 2 tablespoons butter, to serve

Walnut sauce

Artichoke sauce

ARTICHOKE SAUCE

Sugo di carciofi

- 3 medium artichokes
- 1 lemon
- $^1/_4$ cup/60 ml extra-virgin olive oil
- 1 onion, finely chopped
- $^1/_2$ oz/15 g dried mushrooms, soaked in warm water for 15 minutes, drained, and coarsely chopped
- 2 cloves garlic, finely chopped
- 1 tablespoon finely chopped fresh parsley
- $^1/_4$ cup/60 ml dry white wine
- 3 tablespoons unseasoned store-bought tomato sauce
- 1 tablespoon butter, cut up
- salt and freshly ground black pepper

This sauce is perfect with all pasta types.

Remove the tough outer leaves from the artichokes by snapping them off at the base. Cut off the top third of the remaining leaves. Cut the artichokes in half, removing any fuzzy choke with a sharp knife. Rub with the lemon. • Thinly slice the artichokes vertically and put them in a Dutch oven (saucepan) with the oil and onion. Cover and cook over medium heat for 10 minutes. • Add the mushrooms, garlic, and parsley and sauté for 3 minutes. • Increase the heat and pour in the wine and tomato sauce. Bring to a boil and cook until the sauce is creamy, about 10 minutes. • Stir in the butter and season with salt and pepper.

Serves 6 • Prep: 30 min • Cooking: 20 min • Level: 1

LIGURIAN MEAT SAUCE

Sugo di carne

Serve with long pasta types, such as trenette.

Sauté the beef in the oil in a large frying pan over high heat until browned all over, about 3 minutes. • Add the onion, celery, carrot, garlic, and rosemary and cook for 5 minutes. • Season with salt and pepper. Pour in the wine and let it evaporate. • Stir in the tomatoes and simmer over medium-low heat for at least 2 hours, adding stock as soon as the sauce begins to thicken and stick to the bottom of the pan. • Remove the rosemary and serve the sauce hot.

Serves 6–8 • Prep: 40 min • Cooking: 2 hr 10 min • Level: 1

- 1 lb/500 g ground/minced beef
- 6 tablespoons extra-virgin olive oil
- 1 onion, finely chopped
- $^1/_2$ stalk celery, finely chopped
- $^1/_2$ carrot, finely chopped
- 1 clove garlic, finely chopped
- 1 sprig fresh rosemary
- salt and freshly ground black pepper
- $^1/_2$ cup/125 ml dry red wine
- 3 large firm-ripe tomatoes, peeled, seeded, and coarsely chopped
- 1–2 cups/250–500 ml beef stock or broth

Soups

GENOESE GARBANZO BEAN SOUP

Minestra genovese di ceci

- 4 quarts/4 liters water, + more as needed
- 3 cups/300 g dried garbanzo beans/ chickpeas, soaked overnight and drained
- salt
- 1 lb/500 g cardoons or tender green celery stalks, tough strings removed and coarsely chopped
- 1 oz/30 g dried mushrooms, soaked in warm water for 15 minutes and drained
- 2 Italian sausages, crumbled
- 6 tablespoons extra-virgin olive oil
- 1 teaspoon all-purpose/plain flour
- freshly ground black pepper
- 12 oz/350 g small dried soup pasta, such as ditalini

Bring the water with the beans to a boil in a large saucepan over medium-low heat. Skim off the froth. Cook over low heat for about 3 hours, or until the beans are very soft. • Season with salt and remove from the heat (there should still be plenty of cooking water). Drain. • Cook the cardoons in salted boiling water for 25–35 minutes, or until tender. • Drain and set aside. • Sauté the mushrooms and sausage in the oil in a Dutch oven (casserole) over medium heat until the sausage is browned all over, about 10 minutes. • Sprinkle with the flour and season with salt and pepper. Pour in 1 quart (1 liter) of the cooking water from the beans. Cook, covered, over medium heat for 30 minutes. • Stir in the cooked garbanzo beans and cardoons. • Add the pasta and cook until al dente, about 5 minutes. • Serve in individual serving bowls.

Serves 6 • Prep: 40 min + overnight to soak the beans • Cooking: 4 hr 15 min • Level: 1

VEGETABLE SOUP WITH PASTA AND PESTO

Minestrone col pesto

Bring the water to a boil with the beans in a large pot over low heat. Add the yellow squash, potatoes, zucchini, green beans, peas, tomato, eggplant, celery, parsley, garlic, carrot, and onion. Season with salt and drizzle with oil. • Cook over low heat for 1 hour. • Add the Parmesan rinds and continue cooking for 30 minutes until the beans are tender. • Use a wooden spoon to crush the beans and potatoes against the sides of the pot to make a dense soup. Add the pasta and cook until al dente, about 7 minutes. • Ladle the soup into individual bowls and top with 1 tablespoon pesto.

Serves 6–8 • Prep: 90 min + overnight to soak the beans • Cooking: 97 min • Level: 1

- 2 quarts/2 liters cold water
- 1/2 cup/100 g dried cannellini or borlotti beans, soaked overnight and drained
- 10 oz/300 g winter squash or pumpkin, peeled and cut into cubes
- 14 oz/400 g waxy or all-purpose potatoes, peeled and cut into cubes
- 4 zucchini/courgettes, cut into cubes
- 4 oz/150 g green beans, cut into short lengths
- 3/4 cup/90 g fresh or frozen peas
- 1 firm-ripe tomato, coarsely chopped
- 1 eggplant/aubergine, peeled and cut into cubes
- 1 stalk celery, finely chopped
- 1 sprig parsley, finely chopped
- 2 cloves garlic, finely chopped
- 1 carrot, peeled and finely chopped
- 1 onion, finely chopped
- salt
- 1 tablespoon extra-virgin olive oil
- 2 rinds of Parmesan cheese
- 4 oz/150 g dried egg tagliatelle, broken up into pieces
- 6–8 tablespoons Genoese Pesto (see page 16)

Fresh Pasta & Sauces

PASTA RAVIOLI WITH WALNUT SAUCE

Pansôti al preboggion con salsa di noci

Pasta Dough
- 2 cups/300 g all-purpose/plain flour
- ¼ teaspoon salt
- 2 tablespoons extra-virgin olive oil
- 2–3 tablespoons dry white wine
- 1 tablespoon water + more as needed

Filling
- 10 oz/300 g wild spring greens, such as dandelion greens, beet greens, wild chicory, borage, burnet, wild greens, or cress
- 8 oz/200 g Prescinsena or Ricotta cheese
- 1 large egg, lightly beaten
- ¼ cup/30 g freshly grated Parmesan cheese
- 1 tablespoon finely chopped fresh marjoram
- salt and freshly ground black pepper

Preboggion is a mixture of herbs and greens not found outside of Liguria. Prescinsena is slightly curdled whole milk, with some of the whey left in.

Pasta Dough: Sift the flour and salt onto a work surface and make a well in the center. Mix in the oil, wine, and enough water to make a smooth dough. Knead for 15–20 minutes, until smooth and elastic. • Shape the dough into a ball, wrap in plastic wrap (cling film), and let rest for 30 minutes. • Filling: Blanch the greens in salted boiling water for 5 minutes. Drain, squeezing out excess moisture, and coarsely chop. • Mix with the Prescinsena, egg, Parmesan, and marjoram in a large bowl. Season with salt and pepper. • Roll out the dough on a lightly floured surface until paper-thin. • Cut into pansôti, triangular shapes, 1½ inches (4 cm) on each side, with smooth edges, or into 1½-inch (4-cm) squares. • Drop small heaps of the filling into the center of each triangle and seal the edges. • Walnut Sauce: Crush the walnuts, bread crumbs, garlic, and salt in a pestle and mortar until creamy. • Mix in the Prescinsena until well blended. • Cook the pasta in small batches in a large pot of salted boiling water for 3–4 minutes, or until al dente. • Drain and serve with the sauce.

Serves 6 • Prep: 50 min + 30 min to rest the dough • Cooking: 15 min • Level: 3

Walnut Sauce
- ½ cup/50 g coarsely chopped walnuts
- 2 tablespoons fresh bread crumbs, soaked in milk and squeezed dry
- 1 tablespoon finely chopped garlic
- ⅛ teaspoon coarse salt
- 3 tablespoons Prescinsena or Ricotta cheese

Pasta ravioli with walnut sauce

Clam and mussel sauce

RUSTIC TAGLIATELLE

Picagge verdi

Sauce

- 1 large red onion, finely chopped
- 1 stalk celery, finely chopped
- 1 carrot, finely chopped
- $^1/_4$ cup/60 ml extra-virgin olive oil
- 1 lb/400 g stew beef, cut into large chunks
- $^1/_2$ oz/15 g dried porcini mushrooms, soaked in warm water for 15 minutes, drained, and finely chopped
- 1 tablespoon finely chopped fresh parsley
- 1 tablespoon all-purpose/plain flour
- $^1/_2$ cup/125 ml dry white wine
- $1^1/_3$ cups/310 g crushed tomatoes
- salt and freshly ground black pepper
- water (optional)

Pasta Dough

- $2^2/_3$ cups/400 g all-purpose/plain flour
- 2 large eggs
- 2 tablespoons wild herbs
- 1 tablespoon Italian sausage meat, crumbled
- 1 tablespoon freshly grated Parmesan cheese
- $^1/_4$ cup/60 ml dry white wine, + more as needed

Picagge are country tagliatelle. The version below includes a classic mixture of wild spring herbs (preboggion) but they can also be made with chestnut or whole-wheat flour.

Sauce: Sauté the onion, celery, and carrot in the oil in a Dutch oven (casserole) over high heat for 5 minutes. • Add the beef and cook until browned all over, about 10 minutes. • Add the mushrooms and parsley and cook for 3 minutes. • Stir in the flour, letting it soak up the oil. • Pour in the wine and let it evaporate. • Stir in the tomatoes, season with salt and pepper, and bring to a boil. Cover and simmer over low heat, stirring occasionally, for about 1 hour, or until the meat is tender, adding water if the sauce begins to stick to the bottom of the pan. • Pasta Dough: Place the herbs in a small bowl. Pour in enough boiling water to cover and let stand until wilted, 5 minutes. • Sift the flour onto a surface and make a well in the center. Break the eggs into the well. Mix in with the herbs, sausage meat, Parmesan, and enough wine to make a smooth dough. Knead for 15–20 minutes, until smooth and elastic. • Shape the dough into a ball, wrap in plastic wrap (cling film), and let rest for 30 minutes. • Roll out the dough until thin, cover with a cloth, and let rest for 30 minutes more. Cut into 8 x $^1/_2$-inch (20 x 1-cm) wide strips. • Cook the pasta in a large pan of salted boiling water until al dente, about 5 minutes. • Drain and add to the pan with the meat sauce. Serve hot.

Serves 6 • Prep: 60 min + 60 min to rest the dough • Cooking: 70 min • Level: 2

CLAM AND MUSSEL SAUCE

Sugo di vongole e cozze

Soak the clams and mussels in separate large bowls of warm salted water for 1 hour. • Transfer the clams to a large saucepan with half the wine. Cover and cook until they open up, about 5 minutes. • Discard any that do not open. • Pull off the beards from the mussels. • Cook the mussels in the remaining wine until they open up, about 5 minutes. Discard any that do not open. Strain the liquids and set aside. • Remove the shellfish from their shells. Coarsely chop the mussels. • Sauté the garlic in the oil in a large frying pan over medium heat until pale gold, about 2 minutes. • Add the tomatoes and cook for 3 minutes over medium heat. • Add the shellfish and $^1/_4$ cup (60 ml) of the strained cooking liquid. • Season with salt and pepper. Cook for 1 minute and remove from the heat. • Sprinkle with the basil and parsley.

Serves 6 • Prep: 20 min + 60 min to soak the clams and mussels • Cooking: 20 min • Level: 2

- 2 lb/1 kg clams, in shell
- 2 lb/1 kg mussels, in shell
- generous $^3/_4$ cup/ 200 ml dry white wine
- 2 cloves garlic, finely chopped
- 5 tablespoons extra-virgin olive oil
- 5 firm-ripe tomatoes, peeled, seeded, and coarsely chopped
- salt and freshly ground white pepper
- Leaves from 1 bunch fresh basil, torn
- 2 tablespoons finely chopped fresh parsley

Fresh Pasta

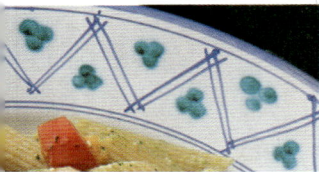

GREENS-FILLED RAVIOLI, GENOESE STYLE

Ravioli verdi alla Genovese

Pasta Dough
- 4 cups/600 g all purpose/plain flour
- ¼ teaspoon salt
- 2 large eggs
- 1 cup/250 ml water + more as needed

Filling
- 1 onion, finely chopped
- 6 tablespoons butter
- 10 oz/300 g lean veal or beef, cut into small chunks
- salt
- 1 tablespoon water
- 2 cups/250 g cooked, drained spinach
- ¾ cup/100 g cooked, drained Swiss chard
- 1 sprig fresh parsley, finely chopped
- 6 leaves fresh basil, torn
- 1 large egg, lightly beaten
- freshly ground black pepper
- cooking juices from roast meat (optional)
- 2 tablespoons butter, melted
- 2 tablespoons freshly grated Parmesan cheese

Pasta Dough: Sift the flour and salt onto a work surface and make a well in the center. Break the eggs into the well and mix in with enough water to make a smooth dough. Knead for 15–20 minutes, until smooth and elastic. • Shape the dough into a ball, wrap in plastic wrap (cling film), and let rest for 30 minutes. • <u>Filling</u>: Sauté the onion in 3 tablespoons butter in a large frying pan over medium heat until softened, about 5 minutes. • Add the veal and cook until browned all over, about 8 minutes. • Season with salt and add the water. • Cook, covered, over low heat for 90 minutes. • Transfer to a cutting board and coarsely chop. • Sauté the spinach and Swiss chard in the remaining 3 tablespoons butter in a separate frying pan over high heat for 3 minutes. Sprinkle with parsley and basil. Remove from the heat, let cool, and add the chopped meat. • Mix in the egg and season with salt and pepper. • Roll out the dough on a lightly floured surface until paper-thin. Cut into 3–4-inch (8–10-cm) wide strips and arrange small heaps of filling near one edge, about ¾ inch (2 cm) apart. Fold each strip of dough lengthwise to cover the filling. Seal, after making sure no air pockets remain, then cut into squares with a saw-toothed ravioli cutter. • Cook the pasta in small batches in a large pot of salted boiling water for 4–5 minutes until al dente. • Drain and drizzle with the cooking juices and butter. Sprinkle with Parmesan and serve.

Serves 4 • Prep: 1 hr + 30 min to rest the dough • Cooking: 2 hr • Level: 3

RAVIOLI FILLED WITH FISH AND WILD GREENS

Ravioli di magro

This dish is particularly delicious served with a clam sauce (see page 21) or drizzled with marjoram-infused olive oil.

<u>Pasta Dough</u>: Sift the flour and salt onto a work surface and make a well in the center. Break the eggs into the well and mix in with enough water to make a smooth dough. Knead for 15–20 minutes, until smooth and elastic. • Shape the dough into a ball, wrap in plastic wrap (cling film), and let rest for 30 minutes. • <u>Filling</u>: Place the fish in a large Dutch oven or fish kettle with the parsley, oil, and the whole clove of garlic. Season with salt and pepper. Pour in the water and cover with waxed (grease-proof) paper. • Bring to a boil over low heat and simmer for 20 minutes, turning the fish halfway through the cooking. Remove from the heat, discard the paper, and bone the fish. • Transfer the fish to a large bowl and mix in the spring greens, Ricotta, chopped garlic, egg, and Parmesan. Season with salt and pepper. • Roll out the dough on a lightly floured surface until paper-thin. Cut into 3–4-inch (8–10-cm) wide strips and arrange small heaps of filling near one edge, about ¾ inch (2 cm) apart. Fold each strip of dough lengthwise to cover the filling. Seal, after making sure no air pockets remain, then cut into squares with a saw-toothed ravioli cutter. The ravioli should be smooth on one side and crimped on three sides. • Cook the pasta in small batches in a large pot of salted boiling water for 4–5 minutes, or until al dente. • Use a slotted spoon to transfer to a serving dish and drizzle with oil.

Serves 6 • Prep: 2 hr + 30 min to rest the dough • Cooking: 45 min • Level: 3

Pasta Dough
- 2⅔ cups/400 g all-purpose/plain flour
- ⅛ teaspoon salt
- 2 large eggs
- ½ cup/125 ml water + more as needed

Filling
- 2 lb/1 kg white firm-textured fish (such as grouper or sea bass)
- 1 bunch fresh parsley, coarsely chopped
- 2 tablespoons extra-virgin olive oil
- 1 clove garlic, lightly crushed but whole + 1 clove garlic, finely chopped
- salt and freshly ground white pepper
- 2 cups/500 ml water
- 10 oz/300 g spring greens, such as dandelion greens, beet greens, wild chicory, borage, burnet, wild greens, or cress, finely chopped
- generous ⅓ cup/100 g Ricotta cheese
- 1 large egg
- ½ cup/60 g freshly grated Parmesan cheese
- best-quality olive oil, to drizzle

PIEDMONT
& VALLE D'AOSTA

Sustaining and warming, Piedmontese cuisine reflects its historical French influence. The mountainous terrain is home to one of the greatest culinary delights, the white Alba truffle. The long winters in this region have led to the creation of filling pasta dishes, such as agnolotti, stuffed with meat, drizzled with butter, and served with cheese. Valle d'Aosta, the smallest region, specializes in winter-warming dishes with strong French overtones.

Spinach agnolotti
(see page 30)

LEEK, POTATO, AND MUSHROOM PASTA

S-ciancun

Pasta Dough
- 2²/₃ cups/400 g all purpose/plain flour
- ¹/₈ teaspoon salt
- ¹/₄ cup/60 ml water + more if needed

Sauce
- 3 medium leeks, white and tender green parts only, thinly sliced
- ¹/₄ cup/60 g butter
- 3 medium porcini mushrooms, or other variety of mushrooms, rinsed and thinly sliced
- 6 tablespoons milk
- ²/₃ cup/150 ml heavy/double cream
- salt and freshly ground black pepper
- 1 lb/500 g waxy potatoes, peeled and cut into small cubes

Pasta Dough: Sift the flour and salt onto a work surface and make a well in the center. Mix in enough water to make a smooth dough. Knead for 15–20 minutes, until smooth and elastic. • Shape the dough into a ball, wrap in plastic wrap (cling film), and let rest for 30 minutes. • Roll out the dough, by hand on a lightly floured surface, or with a pasta machine, to a thickness of ¹/₈ inch (3 mm). Cut into ¹/₄-inch (5-mm) wide strips and then into 4-inch (10-cm) lengths with a knife or by hand, tearing the dough. Place on a floured cloth until ready to cook. • Sauce: Sauté the leeks in the butter in a large frying pan over high heat for 5 minutes. • Add the mushrooms and season with salt. Cook over high heat for 5 minutes. • Pour in the milk and cream and season with salt and pepper. • Continue cooking until the mushrooms are tender, about 10 minutes. • Cook the potatoes in 2 quarts (2 liters) of salted boiling water for 10 minutes. • Add the pasta and cook until al dente. • Drain and transfer to a serving dish. Serve with the sauce.

Serves 4–6 • Prep: 90 min + 30 min to rest the dough • Cooking: 30 min • Level: 2

Leek, potato, and mushroom pasta

Pasta and beans

POTATO AND NETTLE GNOCCHI

Cabiette

Cook the nettles in salted boiling water for 5–7 minutes, or until wilted. • Drain well. • Cook the potatoes in salted boiling water for 15–20 minutes, or until tender. • Slip off the skins and use a fork or potato masher to mash them. Spread out the potatoes on a clean surface. Let cool to lukewarm. • Use a fork to work in the nettles, flour, and the eggs. Season with salt and mix to make a smooth dough. • Form into 1-inch (3-cm) pellets and set aside on a floured work surface. • Filling: Sauté the onions in the butter in a large frying pan over low heat for 30 minutes, or until the onions have broken down completely. • Preheat the oven to 400°F/200°C/gas 6. • Butter a baking dish. • Arrange half the onions in a layer in the dish. • Cook the gnocchi in small batches in a large pot of salted boiling water until they rise to the surface, about 2 minutes. • Use a slotted spoon to remove them and arrange on top of the onions. • Cover with the remaining onions and sprinkle with the bread crumbs. • Bake for 20–25 minutes, or until lightly toasted. • Arrange the pieces of Toma cheese on top and serve piping hot.

Serves 4 • Prep: 1 hr • Cooking: 1 hr • Level: 2

- 4 oz/100 g young nettles, finely chopped
- 2 lb/1 kg baking/floury potatoes
- 1¼ cups/200 g rye flour
- 2 large eggs, lightly beaten
- salt

Filling

- 4 onions, thinly sliced
- 6 tablespoons butter
- 2 tablespoons fresh rye bread crumbs
- 4 oz/100 g Toma (a specialty cheese from Piedmont) or Emmental, cut into small cubes

PASTA AND BEANS

Tajarin e fagioli

Pasta Dough

- 1²/₃ cups/250 g all-purpose/plain flour
- 3–4 large egg yolks, lightly beaten
- ¹/₄ cup/60 ml water + more as needed

Soup

- ¹/₄ cup/60 g lard or butter
- 1 medium onion
- 3 cloves garlic
- 1 stalk celery
- 2 quarts/2 liters water
- salt
- 5 cups/500 g cannellini or borlotti beans
- 1 bunch fresh basil, torn
- 2 firm-ripe tomatoes, peeled and chopped
- 2 waxy potatoes, chopped
- 3 tablespoons extra-virgin olive oil

This is the classic pasta e fagioli. *It is customary to serve this dish on the second day, diluted with Barbera wine.*

Pasta Dough: Sift the flour onto a work surface and make a well in the center. Stir in enough egg yolk and water to make a smooth dough. Knead for 15–20 minutes until smooth and elastic. Shape into a ball, wrap in plastic wrap (cling film), and let rest for 30 minutes. • Roll out the dough on a lightly floured work surface until paper-thin. Cut into strips, about ¹/₄ inch (4 mm) wide. • Make the pasta into "nests" and let dry on a floured cloth until ready to cook. • Soup: Chop together the lard, onion, garlic, and celery in a food processor. • Bring the water to a boil in a large pot. • Season with salt and add the beans, the lard mixture, basil, tomatoes, potatoes, and oil. • Simmer over low heat for 40 minutes, or until the beans are tender. • Season with salt. • Add the pasta and cook until al dente. • Serve hot.

Serves 4–6 • Prep: 2 hr + 30 min to rest the dough • Cooking: 45 min • Level: 2

Fresh Pasta

BUCKWHEAT TAGLIATELLE

Tagliatelle di frumentin

Pasta Dough
- 3¹/₃ cups/500 g buckwheat flour
- ¹/₈ teaspoon salt
- 3 large eggs
- generous ¹/₃ cup/100 ml lukewarm water + more as needed

Sauce
- 4 waxy potatoes, peeled and cut into small cubes
- ¹/₂ onion, finely chopped
- 3 cloves garlic, finely chopped
- ¹/₄ cup/60 g butter
- 2 tablespoons freshly grated Testun (a specialty cheese from Piedmont) or Parmesan cheese

Pasta Dough: Sift the buckwheat flour and salt onto a work surface and make a well in the center. Break the eggs into the well and mix in with enough water to make a smooth dough. Knead for 15–20 minutes, until smooth and elastic. Shape the dough into a ball, wrap in plastic wrap (cling film), and let rest for 30 minutes. • Roll out the dough on a lightly floured surface until paper-thin. Cut into 8 x ¹/₂-inch (20 x 1-cm) wide strips. • Sauce: Cook the potatoes in a large pot of salted boiling water for 10 minutes. • Meanwhile, sauté the onion and garlic in the butter in a large frying pan until the onion has softened, about 10 minutes. • Cook the pasta in the pot with the potatoes until al dente, about 8 minutes. • Drain and transfer to a serving bowl. Top with the onions and garlic. • Sprinkle with Testun and serve hot.

Serves 6 • Prep: 90 min + 30 min to rest the dough • Cooking: 30 min • Level: 1

SAUSAGE-FILLED AGNOLOTTI

Agnolotti alla marengo

Filling: Marinate the meat in a large bowl with the wine, carrot, onion, celery, the garlic, cinnamon, clove, sage, rosemary, bay leaf, and peppercorns. • Cover with plastic wrap and refrigerate for 12 hours. • Pasta Dough: Sift the flour and salt onto a work surface and make a well in the center. Mix in the eggs and egg yolks and water, if needed, to make a dough. Knead for 15–20 minutes, until smooth and elastic. Shape the dough into a ball, wrap in plastic wrap (cling film), and let rest for 30 minutes. • Drain the meat and vegetables, reserving the liquid. • Sauté the pancetta in the butter in a large frying pan over low heat until crispy, about 3 minutes. • Add the marinated meat and vegetables and sausage meat and cook over high heat for 5 minutes, or until browned all over. • Add the cabbage and the marinade liquid and cook until evaporated, about 5 minutes. • Season with salt. Cover and cook over low heat for 45 minutes, stirring occasionally and gradually adding stock during the cooking. • Remove from the heat and let cool completely. • Remove the sage, rosemary, cinnamon, clove, and bay leaf. Reserve the cooking juices. • Process the meat in a food processor or blender until finely chopped. Transfer to a large bowl and mix in the Parmesan, eggs, and nutmeg. • Roll out the dough on a lightly floured work surface until paper-thin. Cut into 1¹/₂-inch (4-cm) wide strips and arrange small heaps of filling near one edge, about ³/₄ inch (2 cm) apart. Cover with remaining plain pasta strips. Seal, after making sure no air pockets remain, then cut into 1¹/₂-inch (4-cm) squares with a saw-toothed ravioli cutter. • Melt the butter in a small saucepan and add the reserved juices. • Cook the pasta in small batches in a large pot of salted boiling water until al dente, about 5 minutes. • Use a slotted spoon to transfer to a serving dish and drizzle with butter. • Sprinkle with Parmesan and serve hot.

Serves 8–10 • Prep: 60 min + 30 min to rest the dough + 12 hr to marinate the meat • Cooking: 80 min • Level: 3

Filling
- 8 oz/250 g beef, cut into chunks
- 8 oz/250 g pork, cut into chunks
- 2 cups/500 ml dry red wine
- ¹/₂ carrot, chopped
- ¹/₂ onion, chopped
- ¹/₂ stalk celery, chopped
- 1 clove garlic, finely chopped
- 1 stick cinnamon
- 1 clove
- 1 sprig fresh sage
- 1 sprig fresh rosemary
- 1 bay leaf
- 5 black peppercorns

Pasta Dough
- 3¹/₃ cups/500 g all-purpose/plain flour
- ¹/₈ teaspoon salt
- 2 large eggs + 4 large egg yolks, lightly beaten
- water (optional)

To serve
- ¹/₂ cup/60 g diced pancetta
- 5 tablespoons butter
- 4 oz/100 g fresh Italian sausage meat, crumbled
- 8 oz/200 g Savoy cabbage, shredded
- salt
- 1 cup/250 ml beef stock or broth (optional)
- ¹/₂ cup/60 g freshly grated Parmesan cheese
- 2 large eggs
- ¹/₈ teaspoon freshly grated nutmeg
- 5 tablespoons butter
- 1³/₄ cups/215 g freshly grated Parmesan cheese

Fresh Pasta

FOLDED AGNOLOTTI

Agnolotti col plin

Pasta Dough

- 2²/₃ cups/450 g all-purpose/plain flour
- ¹/₈ teaspoon salt
- 4 large eggs, lightly beaten

Filling

- 8 oz/200 g Savoy cabbage
- 1 head butterhead lettuce
- 1 lb/400 g veal or beef, in a single cut
- ¹/₄ cup/60 g butter
- ¹/₂ onion
- 1 bay leaf
- 1 stalk celery
- 2 cups/500 ml meat stock or broth
- 2 cloves garlic, finely chopped
- 1 sprig fresh rosemary
- 1 sprig fresh parsley, finely chopped
- 2 tablespoons extra-virgin olive oil
- 1 large egg
- ¹/₂ cup/60 g freshly grated Parmesan cheese
- salt and freshly ground black pepper
- ¹/₂ teaspoon freshly grated nutmeg
- ¹/₂ cup/125 g butter, melted
- 3 sprigs marjoram, finely chopped
- ¹/₂ cup/60 g freshly grated Parmesan cheese

These agnolotti are unusual in that they are sealed with a plin, a little pinch that joins the edges, giving the pasta a special shape.

Pasta Dough: Sift the flour and salt onto a surface and make a well in the center. Break the eggs into the well and mix in to make a dough. Knead for 15–20 minutes, until smooth and elastic. Shape the dough into a ball, wrap in plastic wrap, and let rest for 30 minutes. • Filling: Cook the cabbage and lettuce in salted boiling water for 5–7 minutes, or until wilted. • Drain, chop them finely, and set aside. • Braise the veal in 2 tablespoons of butter with the onion, bay leaf, and celery over medium heat until the meat is tender, gradually adding all the stock as the meat begins to dry. • Discard the onion, bay leaf, and celery and chop the veal in a food processor until finely ground. • Sauté the garlic, rosemary, and parsley in the remaining 2 tablespoons of butter and oil in a large frying pan over medium heat until the garlic is pale gold, about 1 minute. • Add the ground meat and sauté over high heat for 5 minutes, or until browned all over. • Add the cabbage and lettuce and cook for 3 minutes. • Remove from the heat and let cool to warm. • Mix in the egg and Parmesan and season with salt, pepper, and nutmeg. • Roll out the dough on a lightly floured surface until paper-thin. Cut into 4¹/₂-inch (10-cm) wide strips and arrange small heaps of filling near one edge, about ³/₄ inch (3 cm) apart. • Fold each strip of dough lengthwise to cover the filling. Seal, after making sure no air pockets remain, then cut into squares with a ravioli cutter. Pinch as it you were going to fold it in half. • Cook the pasta in small batches in a large pot of salted boiling water until al dente, about 4 minutes. • Use a slotted spoon to transfer to a serving dish and drizzle with butter. Sprinkle with marjoram and Parmesan and serve.

Serves 6–8 • Prep: 2 hr + 30 min to rest the dough • Cooking: 60 min • Level: 3

SPINACH AGNOLOTTI

Agnolotti di spinaci

These agnolotti are good served with a liver or roast-meat sauce. You could also serve them simply in stock.

Filling: Marinate the beef and pork in a large bowl with the onion, carrot, celery, garlic, cloves, and peppercorns. Pour in the oil and wine. Refrigerate for 12 hours. • Transfer the marinated meat and vegetables with the liquid to a large deep frying pan. Season with salt. Add the pancetta, cover, and cook over low heat for 4 hours, until the meat is tender, adding stock or water if the meat starts to dry. • Cook the rice in the milk in a saucepan over medium heat for 15–20 minutes, or until the rice is tender. Season with salt. Drain well. • Chop the meat in a food processor until finely ground. • Transfer to a large bowl and mix in the rice, spinach, Parmesan, and eggs. Season with salt and nutmeg. • Pasta Dough: Sift the flour and salt onto a work surface and make a well in the center. Mix in the eggs, egg yolks, and enough water to make a smooth dough. Knead for 15–20 minutes, until smooth and elastic. Shape the dough into a ball, wrap in plastic wrap (cling film), and let rest for 30 minutes. • Roll out the dough on a lightly floured work surface until paper-thin. Cut into 1¹/₂-inch (4-cm) strips. Arrange small pellets of filling at 1-inch (2.5-cm) intervals along the strip and cover with another strip of dough. Seal, after making sure no air pockets remain, then cut into 1¹/₄-inch (3 cm) squares with a ravioli cutter. • Cook the pasta in small batches in a large pot of salted boiling water until al dente, about 4–5 minutes. • Use a slotted spoon to transfer to a serving dish and drizzle with the melted butter mixed with the sage and/or rosemary. Season with salt. • Sprinkle with Parmesan and serve.

Serves 8–10 • Prep: 2 hr + 30 min to rest the dough • Cooking: 4 hr 15 min + 12 hr to marinate the meat • Level: 3

Filling

- 8 oz/250 g lean beef
- 4 oz/150 g lean pork
- ¹/₂ onion, thinly sliced
- 1 carrot, cut into rounds
- 1 stalk celery, chopped
- 1 clove garlic, lightly crushed but whole
- 2 cloves
- 5 black peppercorns
- 3 tablespoons extra-virgin olive oil
- 1¹/₃ cups/310 ml dry red wine
- salt
- 2 oz/50 g pancetta, sliced
- ¹/₄ cup/60 ml meat stock or water (optional)
- ¹/₄ cup/50 g long-grain rice
- ²/₃ cup/150 ml milk
- 2 cups/200 g cooked, drained spinach
- 2 tablespoons freshly grated Parmesan cheese
- 2 large eggs
- ¹/₂ teaspoon nutmeg

Pasta Dough

- 3¹/₃ cups/500 g all-purpose/plain flour
- ¹/₈ teaspoon salt
- 2 large eggs – 4 large egg yolks, lightly beaten
- 1 tablespoon water + more as needed

To serve

- ²/₃ cup/150 g butter, melted
- 2 small bunches fresh sage and/or 1 sprig fresh rosemary
- salt
- ¹/₂ cup/60 g freshly grated Parmesan cheese

Spinach gnocchi

SPINACH GNOCCHI

Chicche al verde

- 2 lb/1 kg baking/floury potatoes
- ¹/₄ cup/50 g cooked, drained spinach, finely chopped
- 2 cups/300 g all-purpose/plain flour
- 2 large egg yolks, lightly beaten
- salt
- 1 tablespoon finely chopped fresh parsley

Cook the potatoes in salted boiling water for 15–20 minutes, or until tender. • Slip off the skins and use a fork or potato masher to mash them and spread out the potatoes on a surface. Let cool to lukewarm. • Use a fork to work in the spinach, 1²/₃ cups (250 g) flour, and egg yolks. • Season with salt, sprinkle with parsley, and mix to form a smooth dough. • Form into ¹/₂-inch (1-cm) diameter lengths and cut into 1-inch (3-cm) long pieces. • Roll in the remaining ¹/₃ cup (50 g) flour, giving them a slightly tapered shape. • Cook the gnocchi in small batches in a large pot of salted boiling water until they rise to the surface, about 2 minutes. • Use a slotted spoon to transfer to serving plates. Serve, piping hot, in a meat sauce or any other sauce you like.

Serves 4 • Prep: 40 min • Cooking: 45 min • Level: 1

HOMEMADE LASAGNA COOKED IN MILK AND BUTTER

Lasagne al latte

<u>Pasta Dough</u>: Sift the flour and salt onto a work surface and make a well in the center. Mix in the egg white, milk, and water to make a smooth dough. Knead for 15–20 minutes, until smooth and elastic. Shape the dough into a ball, wrap in plastic wrap (cling film), and let rest for 30 minutes. • Roll out the dough on a lightly floured surface into a paper-thin circle (or into rectangles if you are using a pasta machine). Cut into 2-inch (5-cm) wide strips, as long as you like. • Tear the dough with your hands to form irregular "rags." Allow them to dry on a flour-dusted surface, about 1 hour. • <u>Sauce</u>: Bring the milk and water to a boil in a large saucepan. Add the salt. • Cook the pasta until al dente, about 3 minutes. • Drain, but not thoroughly, and serve in layers with the melted butter and pepper.

Serves 4 • Prep: 60 min + 1 hr 30 min to rest the dough • Cooking: 15 min • Level: 2

Pasta Dough
- 2²/₃ cups/400 g all-purpose/plain flour
- ¹/₈ teaspoon salt
- 1 large egg white
- generous ¹/₃ cup/ 100 ml milk
- ¹/₄ cup/60 ml water
- 1 quart/1 liter milk

Sauce
- 2 cups/500 ml water
- ¹/₈ teaspoon salt
- 3 tablespoons butter, melted
- freshly ground black pepper

Gnocchi cooked in milk

Gnocchi al latte

- 2 lb/1 kg baking/floury potatoes
- 2 tablespoons extra-virgin olive oil
- 2²/₃ cups/450 g all-purpose/plain flour
- 2 quarts/2 liters milk
- salt
- 1²/₃ cups/400 g Ricotta cheese

Cook the potatoes in salted boiling water for 15–20 minutes, or until tender. • Slip off the skins and use a fork or potato masher to mash them and spread out the potatoes on a surface. Let cool to lukewarm. • Use a fork to work in the oil and 2¹/₃ cups (400 g) flour. • Season with salt and mix to form a smooth dough. • Roll into thin ¹/₂ inch (1 cm) lengths and cut into pieces. • Roll the gnocchi in the remaining ¹/₃ cup (50 g) flour. Press them with one thumb against the tines of a fork to create ridges. • Bring the milk to a boil in a large saucepan. Season with salt. • Cook the gnocchi in small batches until they rise to the surface, about 2 minutes. • Use a slotted spoon to remove them from the milk and place on plates with the Ricotta.

Serves 6–8 • Prep: 45 min • Cooking: 45 min • Level: 2

Gnocchi cooked in milk

Beef-filled agnolotti

Agnolotti canavesani

Filling
- 8 oz/250 g stew beef, cut into chunks
- 1–1¹/₂ cups/250–375 ml dry red wine

Pasta Dough
- 3¹/₃ cups/500 g all-purpose/plain flour
- ¹/₈ teaspoon salt
- 2 large eggs + 4 large egg yolks, lightly beaten
- water (optional)

Filling (continued)
- ¹/₄ cup/60 g butter
- salt
- ¹/₂–1 cup/125–250 ml beef stock or broth
- 1¹/₄ cups/150 g diced ham
- ¹/₂ cup/60 g freshly grated Parmesan cheese
- 2 large eggs
- ¹/₈ teaspoon freshly grated nutmeg
- scant 1 cup/200 ml milk
- ¹/₃ cup/80 g long-grain rice
- 4 oz/100 g fresh Italian sausage meat, crumbled
- 4 oz/100 g Savoy cabbage, finely shredded
- 1 clove garlic, lightly crushed but whole
- 1 tablespoon finely chopped fresh parsley

To serve
- ¹/₄ cup/60 g butter, melted
- 2 sprigs fresh sage and/or 1 sprig fresh rosemary
- 1³/₄ cups/215 g freshly grated Parmesan cheese

Filling: Marinate the meat with the wine in a small bowl. • Cover with plastic wrap and refrigerate for at least 12 hours. • Pasta Dough: Sift the flour and salt onto a surface and make a well in the center. Mix in the eggs and egg yolks and enough water to make a dough. Knead for 15–20 minutes, until smooth and elastic. Shape the dough into a ball, wrap in plastic wrap, and let rest for 30 minutes. • Brown the beef in 2 tablespoons of butter in a medium saucepan over high heat for 5 minutes. • Add the marinade liquid and let it evaporate, about 5 minutes. Season with salt. • Cover and cook over low heat for 1 hour, turning occasionally, adding stock if the mixture starts to dry. • Remove from the heat and let cool completely. Reserve the cooking juices. • Chop the beef and ham in a food processor until finely ground. Transfer to a large bowl and mix in the Parmesan, eggs, and nutmeg. Season with salt. • Bring the milk to a boil in a medium saucepan over low heat and season with salt. • Add the rice and cook for 15–20 minutes, or until tender. • Drain and transfer to the meat. Melt the remaining 2 tablespoons of butter in a frying pan over medium heat. Sauté the sausage meat, cabbage, and garlic for 5 minutes, or until the cabbage has softened, adding stock if the mixture starts to dry. • Discard the garlic and add the parsley. • Remove from heat and let cool completely. • Transfer to the meat and mix well. • Roll out the dough on a lightly floured surface until paper-thin. Cut into 1¹/₂-inch (4-cm) wide strips and arrange small heaps of filling near one edge, about ³/₄ inch (2 cm) apart. Cover with remaining plain pasta strips. Seal, after making sure no air pockets remain, then cut into 1¹/₂-inch (4-cm) squares with a fluted pastry wheel. • Melt the butter in a small saucepan and add the reserved cooking juices, sage, and/or rosemary. • Cook the pasta in small batches in a large pot of salted boiling water until al dente, about 4 minutes. • Use a slotted spoon to transfer to a serving dish and drizzle with the butter mixture. Sprinkle with Parmesan and serve hot.

Serves 8–10 • Prep: 2 hr + 30 min to rest the pasta • Cooking: 2 hr + 12 hr to marinate the meat • Level: 3

Fresh Pasta

RICE AND CABBAGE RAVIOLI

Ravioli di riso e cavolo

Pasta Dough
- 2²/₃ cups/400 g all-purpose/plain flour
- ¹/₈ teaspoon salt
- 4 large eggs

Filling
- ¹/₂ cup/100 g long-grain rice
- 1 Savoy cabbage, finely shredded
- 1 onion, finely chopped
- 3 tablespoons butter
- ¹/₈ teaspoon salt
- 2 cloves garlic, finely chopped
- salt and freshly ground white pepper
- 5 tablespoons freshly grated Parmesan cheese
- 1 large egg

To serve
- ¹/₂ cup/125 g butter, melted
- 1 cup/125 g freshly grated Parmesan cheese

Pasta Dough: Sift the flour and salt onto a surface and make a well in the center. Break the eggs into the well and mix in to make a smooth dough. Knead for 15–20 minutes, until smooth and elastic. Shape the dough into a ball, wrap in plastic wrap (cling film), and let rest for 30 minutes. • Filling: Cook the rice in salted boiling water and milk for 12–15 minutes, or until firm to the bite. • Cook the cabbage in a large saucepan of salted boiling water for 5–7 minutes, or until tender. Drain well, squeezing it dry, and chop finely. • Sauté the onion in the butter in a medium frying pan over high heat for 5 minutes until browned. Season with salt. Cook over low heat for 15 minutes. • Add the cabbage and simmer for 5 minutes. • Add the garlic and rice and season with salt and pepper. • Remove from the heat and transfer to a large bowl. Mix in the Parmesan and egg and let cool to lukewarm. • Roll out the dough on a lightly floured surface until paper-thin. Cut into 4-inch (10-cm) wide strips and arrange pellets of filling near one edge, about ³/₄ inch (2 cm) apart. Fold each strip of dough lengthwise to cover the filling. Seal, after making sure no air pockets remain, then cut into 2-inch (5-cm) squares with a saw-toothed ravioli cutter. The ravioli should be smooth on one side and crimped on three sides. • Lay the pasta on a kitchen cloth dusted with flour. • Cook the pasta in small batches in a large pot of salted boiling water until al dente, about 4–5 minutes. • Use a slotted spoon to transfer to a serving dish and drizzle with butter. Sprinkle with Parmesan and serve.

Serves 6 • Prep: 60 min + 30 min to rest the dough • Cooking: 60 min • Level: 3

AGNOLOTTI WITH TRUFFLE

Agnolotti con tartufo

Pasta Dough: Sift the flour and salt onto a work surface and make a well in the center. Break the eggs into the well and mix in enough water to make a smooth dough. Knead for 15–20 minutes, until smooth and elastic. Shape the dough into a ball, wrap in plastic wrap (cling film), and let rest for 30 minutes. • Filling: Sauté the veal and pork in the butter in a medium frying pan over high heat for 5 minutes, or until browned all over. • Pour in the stock and season with salt. • Cook over low heat until the liquid has evaporated, about 5 minutes. • Remove from the heat and let cool. • Process the meat and prosciutto in a food processor or blender until finely ground. Transfer to a large bowl. • Chop one-third of the truffle coarsely. • Add the eggs, Parmesan, and the chopped truffle. • Season with salt, cover with plastic wrap, and refrigerate while preparing the pasta. • Roll out the dough on a lightly floured surface until paper-thin. Cut into 1-inch (3-cm) wide strips and arrange pellets of filling near one edge, about ³/₄ inch (2 cm) apart. Cover with remaining plain pasta strips. Seal, after making sure no air pockets remain, then cut into 1-inch (3-cm) squares with a fluted pastry wheel. • Arrange the pasta on a dry cloth sprinkled with flour. • Cook the pasta in small batches in a large pot of salted boiling water until al dente, about 4–5 minutes. • Use a slotted spoon to transfer to a serving bowl and drizzle with the melted butter and a pinch of salt. • Sprinkle with Parmesan and serve hot with flakes of the remaining truffle on top.

Serves 8–10 • Prep: 1 hr 15 min + 30 min to rest the dough • Cooking: 30 min • Level: 3

Pasta Dough
- 3¹/₃ cups/500 g all-purpose/plain flour
- ¹/₈ teaspoon salt
- 3 large eggs
- ¹/₂ cup/125 ml water, + more as needed

Filling
- 8 oz/250 g veal or beef, cut into chunks
- 8 oz/250 g pork, cut into chunks
- ¹/₂ cup/125 g butter, cut up
- ¹/₄ cup/60 ml beef stock or broth
- salt
- 4 oz/150 g prosciutto/Parma ham, finely sliced
- 1–2 oz/30–50 g white truffle, preferably Alba
- 2 large eggs
- 1 cup/125 g freshly grated Parmesan cheese

To serve
- ²/₃ cup/150 g butter, melted
- salt
- ¹/₂ cup/60 g freshly grated Parmesan cheese

Polenta & Fresh Pasta

POLENTA GNOCCHI, PIEDMONT-STYLE

Gnocchi di polenta piemontesi

- 1 quart/1 liter + 2 tablespoons milk
- salt and freshly ground white pepper
- $1/4$ teaspoon freshly grated nutmeg
- 6 tablespoons butter
- 1 cup/150 g coarsely ground cornmeal
- $2/3$ cup/100 g finely ground cornmeal
- 2 large egg yolks
- 4 oz/150 g Swiss cheese, such as Gruyère, cut into small cubes
- $1/4$ cup/30 g freshly grated Parmesan cheese
- 1 small white truffle, cut into thin flakes (optional)

Bring 1 quart (1 liter) of milk almost to a boil in a saucepan (copper if available). Season with salt, pepper, and nutmeg and mix in 2 tablespoons butter. • Carefully whisk in the coarsely and finely ground cornmeal, making sure it does not come to a boil. • Cook over low heat for 20 minutes, stirring occasionally to prevent any lumps from forming and making sure that the mixture does not stick to the pan bottom. • Remove from the heat and let cool. • Lightly beat the egg yolks and the remaining 2 tablespoons of milk in a small bowl. • Mix the Swiss cheese and egg yolk mixture into the cornmeal. • Season with salt and pepper and spread out onto a buttered surface. Roll out with a buttered rolling pin and let cool completely. • Preheat the oven to 400°F/200°C/gas 6. • Butter a baking dish. • Cut into $1/2$-inch (1-cm) thick slices and arrange the slices in the prepared baking dish, overlapping them slightly. • Dot with the remaining 4 tablespoons of butter and sprinkle with Parmesan. • Bake for 15–20 minutes, or until the cheese is bubbling. • Serve hot and with thin flakes of white truffle sprinkled over, if available.

Serves 6 • Prep: 30 min + 60 min to cool • Cooking: 40 min • Level: 2

TRADITIONAL AGNOLOTTI

Agnolotti

Pasta Dough: Sift the flour and salt onto a surface and make a well in the center. Mix in the eggs, egg yolks, and water, if needed, to make a dough. Knead for 15–20 minutes, until elastic. Shape into a ball, wrap in plastic wrap, and let rest for 30 minutes. • Filling: Process the meat and mortadella in a blender until ground. Transfer to a large bowl and mix in the Parmesan, egg, cream, bread crumbs, and nutmeg. Season with salt and pepper. The mixture should be fairly soft. • Roll out the dough on a lightly floured surface until paper-thin. Cut into $2 1/2$-inch (6-cm) wide strips and arrange filling near one edge, about $3/4$ inch (2 cm) apart. Fold each strip of dough lengthwise to cover the filling. Seal, after making sure no air pockets remain, then cut into squares with a saw-toothed ravioli cutter. The agnolotti should be smooth on one side and crimped on three sides. • Lay the pasta on a kitchen cloth dusted with flour. • Cook the pasta in small batches in a large pot of salted boiling water for 4–5 minutes, or until al dente. • Arrange in layers, drizzling with the cooking juices, if using, butter, and Parmesan in between the layers.

Serves 6 • Prep: 60 min + 30 min to rest the dough • Cooking: 20 min • Level: 3

Pasta Dough
- $3 1/3$ cups/500 g all-purpose/plain flour
- $1/8$ teaspoon salt
- 2 eggs + 5 egg yolks
- $1/4$ cup/60 ml water + more as needed

Filling
- $1 1/4$ cups/310 g cubed roasted lean meat
- 4 oz/100 g mortadella
- $3/4$ cup/90 g freshly grated Parmesan cheese
- 1 large egg
- generous $1/3$ cup/100 ml heavy/double cream
- 1 cup/60 g fresh bread crumbs, soaked in 1 cup/250 ml milk and squeezed cry
- $1/8$ teaspoon freshly grated nutmeg
- salt and freshly ground black pepper
- $2/3$ cup/150 ml cooking juices from a roasted meat (optional)
- 3 tablespoons butter, melted
- 1 cup/125 g freshly grated Parmesan cheese

MAKING CORNMEAL GNOCCHI

1. Bring the milk to a boil over low heat and use a balloon whisk to beat in the cornmeal.

2. Continue cooking for about 20 minutes, stirring with a wooden spoon.

3. After adding the eggs and cheese to the cornmeal mixture, spread out the mixture on a lightly oiled marble surface to a thickness of about $2/3$ inch (1.5 cm). Let cool completely.

4. Use 1½-inch (4-cm) round cutters to cut out the gnocchi. Lay the gnocchi in a greased baking dish, over the scraps of dough. Bake until lightly golden.

To make gnocchetti (small gnocchi): With this dough, you can make ½-inch (0.5-cm) gnocchetti starting from 1-inch (2.5-cm) cylinders cut into sections.

An alternative way to serve: Sauté the gnocchetti in butter or oil in a frying pan over high heat until lightly golden. Serve with a sauce of your choice.

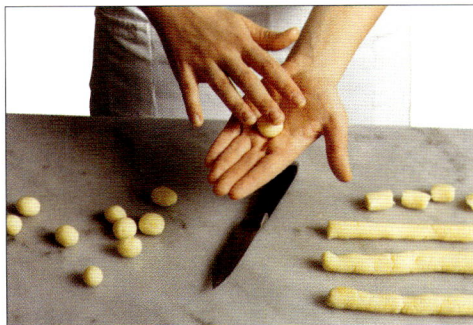

Gnocchi & Baked Pasta

Toma gnocchi with tomato and basil sauce

Raviöl

Gnocchi

- 3$\frac{1}{3}$ cups/500 g all-purpose/plain flour
- 1 large egg
- 5 oz/150 g Toma (a specialty cheese from Piedmont), crumbled, or Emmental cheese, coarsely grated
- $\frac{1}{4}$ cup/60 ml heavy/double cream
- $\frac{1}{4}$ cup/60 ml water + more as needed

Gnocchi: Sift the flour onto a surface and make a well in the center. Break the egg into the well and mix in with the Toma, cream, and enough water to make a stiff dough. Knead for 15–20 minutes until smooth and form into $\frac{1}{2}$ x 1-inch (1 x 3-cm) lengths. • Tomato and Basil Sauce: Melt the butter in a medium saucepan over low heat. • Stir in the tomatoes and cook for about 10 minutes until they have broken down. • Season with salt. Add the basil and cook for 1 minute. • Remove from the heat and set aside. • Cook the gnocchi in small batches in a large pot of salted boiling water for 4–5 minutes until they rise to the surface. • Remove with a slotted spoon and arrange on the serving dish. Pour the sauce over the cooked gnocchi.

Serves 6 • Prep: 40 min • Cooking: 20 min • Level: 2

Tomato and Basil Sauce

- $\frac{1}{4}$ cup/60 g butter
- 1$\frac{1}{2}$ lb/700 g tomatoes, peeled, seeded, and coarsely chopped
- salt
- Leaves from 1 sprig fresh basil, torn

Toma gnocchi
with tomato and basil sauce

Making gnocchi stuffed with prunes (or other filling)

1. Roll out the dough for the gnocchi (see recipe above) with more flour and cut out the disks to the size you like.

2. Stuff with a prune or your chosen filling.

3. Fold over and shape to make a large, round gnocco.

Cannelloni

CANNELLONI

Pasta Dough
- 2 cups/300 g all-purpose/plain flour
- 1/8 teaspoon salt
- 3 large eggs

Filling
- 14 oz/400 g roasted veal or beef
- 1/2 cup/100 g cooked, drained spinach
- 4 oz/150 g prosciutto/Parma ham
- 2 large eggs
- 1/4 cup/30 g freshly grated Parmesan cheese
- salt and freshly ground black pepper
- 1/4 teaspoon nutmeg

To serve
- 3/4 cup/180 ml Tuscan Ragù (page 103)
- 2 cups/500 ml Béchamel sauce (see page 10)
- 1 tablespoon butter
- 1/4 cup/30 g freshly grated Parmesan cheese

Pasta Dough: Sift the flour and salt onto a work surface and make a well in the center. Break the eggs into the well and mix in to make a smooth dough. Knead for 15–20 minutes until elastic. Shape into a ball, wrap in plastic wrap, and let rest for 30 minutes. • Preheat the oven to 400°F/200°C/gas 6. • Butter a baking dish. • Roll out the dough on a lightly floured surface until paper-thin. Cut the sheet of dough into 4 x 5-inch (10 x 12-cm) rectangles. • Blanch the dough in a large pot of salted boiling water for 1 minute. Drain and lay it out on a damp cloth (see pages 222). • Filling: Finely chop the veal, spinach, and prosciutto and transfer to a bowl. Mix in the eggs and Parmesan. Season with salt, pepper, and nutmeg. • Spread the filling onto the dough, leaving a border at the edges. • Roll up and arrange in the prepared baking dish, no more than two layers deep. Cover with meat sauce and top with Béchamel. Dot with the butter and sprinkle with Parmesan. • Bake for 15–20 minutes, or until bubbling. • Serve warm.

Serves 6 • Prep: 90 min + 30 min to rest the dough • Cooking: 25–30 min • Level: 2

MAKING CANNELLONI

1. Spread rectangles of pasta dough, measuring about 4 x 5 inches (10 x 12 cm), with your chosen filling (for example, Ricotta and spinach), and begin to roll them up lengthwise.

2. Continue rolling up, sufficiently tightly to make the pasta hold their shape. Take care not to roll too tightly or the filling will ooze out.

LOMBARDY

Polenta, saffron risotti, panettone—Lombards are a people who know how to eat well. Blue-veined Gorgonzola and sumptuous Mascarpone are just two of the excellent cheeses from this region. *Pizzoccheri*, a hearty pasta made with buckwheat flour and boiled until al dente with cabbage and potatoes, is the area's classic pasta dish. Milan, Italy's fashion and economic capital, accentuates the culinary excellence of the Lombardy region with its varied and sophisticated restaurant scene.

Penne with Gorgonzola (see page 42)

SOUP PASTA WITH BEAN STOCK

Pasta rasa o minestra rasida

- 2 liters/2 quarts cold water
- 3 cups/300 g dried borlotti beans, soaked overnight and drained
- 1/2 onion
- salt

Pasta Dough
- 5 cups/300 g fresh bread crumbs
- 2 large eggs
- 2 tablespoons freshly grated Parmesan cheese
- 1/8 teaspoon freshly grated nutmeg
- salt

Stock
- 1/4 cup/60 g finely chopped lard or butter
- 1 clove garlic, finely chopped
- 1 tablespoon finely chopped fresh parsley
- 12 oz/300 g firm-ripe tomatoes, peeled, seeded, and coarsely chopped
- salt and freshly ground black pepper
- 3/4 cup/90 g freshly grated Parmesan cheese

This is a type of pastina da brodo *(fine pasta for soup) that is found, with different dialect names, in both Piedmont and Emilia-Romagna. It goes very well with meat stock and strong-flavored soups.*

Bring the water to a boil with the drained beans and the onion. Cook over low heat for 1 hour. • Season with salt. • Drain the beans, reserving the cooking liquid. • Pasta Dough: Mix the bread crumbs, eggs, Parmesan, nutmeg, and salt in a large bowl to make a stiff dough. • Grate the dough coarsely onto a floured surface and let it dry until you are ready to cook it. • Stock: Melt the lard in a Dutch oven (casserole) with the garlic and parsley and sauté over low heat for 5 minutes until the garlic is pale gold. • Stir in the tomatoes and cook for about 10 minutes, or until the tomatoes begin to break down. • Add the beans and pour in 1 1/2 quarts (1.5 liters) of the cooking water from the beans. Season with salt and pepper and cook for 30 minutes. • Add the pasta to the stock and cook for 1–2 minutes until al dente. • Sprinkle with Parmesan and serve.

Serves 6 • Prep: 60 min + overnight to soak the beans• Cooking: 2 hr • Level: 2

PENNE WITH GORGONZOLA

Penne al Gorgonzola

This simple recipe can serve as the foundation for the thousands of variations on the quattro formaggi *(four cheeses) sauce, a classic* primo piatto *that is easy to make. Follow the recipe, melting the cheeses into a soft paste and adding the cubes of cheese to the paste before mixing in the pasta. If you use Mozzarella, add it just before you serve, otherwise it will be difficult to make equal portions!*

Melt the butter and Gorgonzola in the cream in a double boiler over barely simmering water until the cheese has melted. Season with salt. • Cook the pasta in a large pot of salted boiling water for about 10 minutes until al dente. • Drain and mix into the cheese mixture. Sprinkle with Parmesan. • Serve piping hot.

Serves 4 • Prep: 5 min • Cooking: 10 min • Level: 1

- 1 tablespoon butter
- 6 oz/180 g creamy Gorgonzola cheese, crumbled
- 2/3 cup/150 ml heavy/double cream
- salt
- 12 oz/350 g dried penne
- 5 tablespoons freshly grated Parmesan cheese

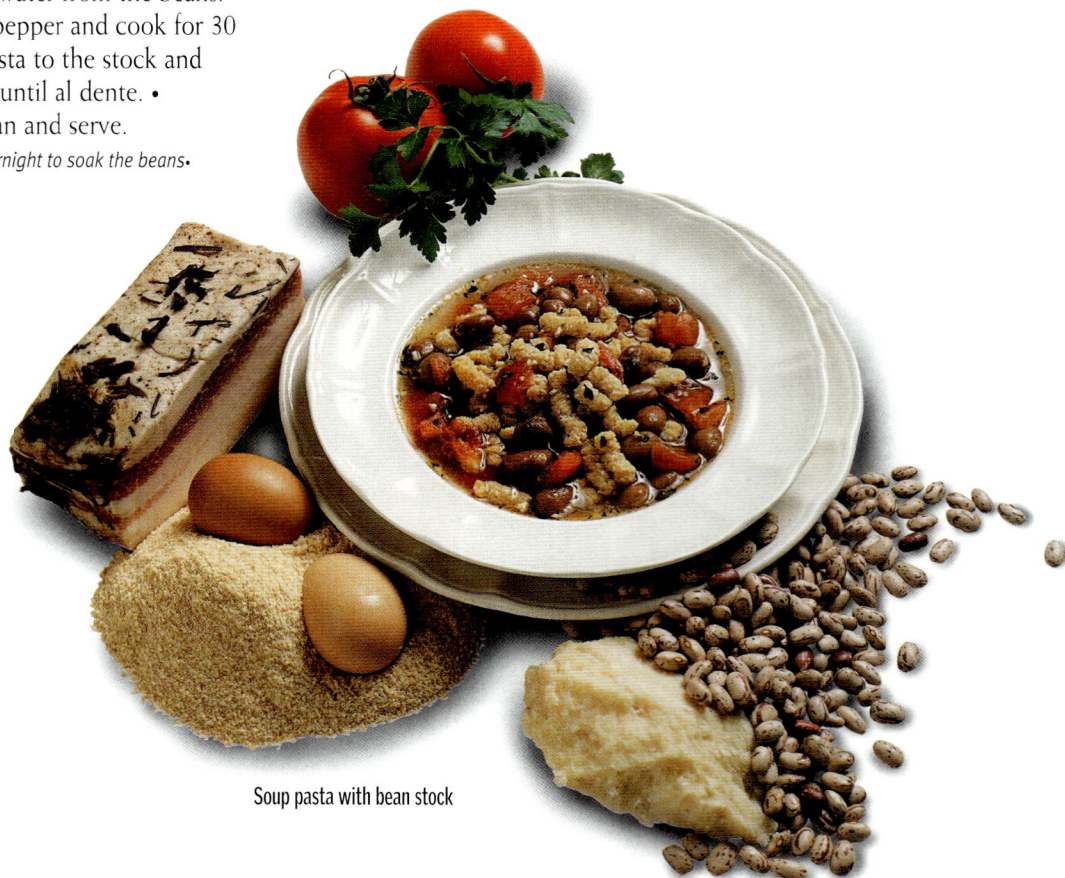

Soup pasta with bean stock

Meatballs in stock

MEATBALLS IN STOCK

Mariconda di carne

- ¹/₄ cup/60 g butter
- 8 oz/250 g veal or beef, sliced
- 7 cups/1.75 liters chicken stock or broth
- salt and freshly ground white pepper
- ²/₃ cup/80 g freshly grated Parmesan cheese
- 1 small egg
- ¹/₈ teaspoon freshly grated nutmeg
- ¹/₂ cup/60 g fine dry bread crumbs (optional)
- ¹/₂ cup/75 g all-purpose/plain flour

The meatballs used in this soup can also be used as filling for cappelletti, just as many of the meat fillings for tortellini, agnolotti, and anolini can be transformed into meatballs.

Melt the butter in a large frying pan and braise the veal for about 15 minutes, or until cooked through, adding about ³/₄ cup (180 ml) of stock to make sure that the meat does not dry out. Season with salt and pepper. Remove from the heat and let cool. • Chop the veal in a food processor until finely ground. Transfer to a large bowl and mix in the egg, nutmeg and about ²/₃ of the Parmesan. Season with salt. If the mixture is too soft, add some bread crumbs. Cover with plastic wrap (cling film) and let rest for 1 hour at room temperature or overnight in the refrigerator. • Form into balls the size of walnuts and coat them lightly in the flour. • Bring the remaining stock to a boil in a large saucepan. Add the meatballs and cook for about 5 minutes, or until the meatballs are cooked through. • Serve in soup bowls, sprinkled with the remaining Parmesan.

Serves 4 • Prep: 45 min + 60 min to rest • Cooking: 30 min • Level: 2

Pizzoccheri with potatoes
and Savoy cabbage

PIZZOCCHERI WITH POTATOES AND SAVOY CABBAGE

Pizzoccheri valtellinesi

Pasta Dough
- 2 cups/300 g buckwheat flour
- 1 cup/150 g all-purpose/plain flour
- 1/8 teaspoon salt
- 3/4 cup/180 ml lukewarm water + more as needed

Sauce
- 7 potatoes, peeled and cut into small chunks
- 1/2 head Savoy cabbage, finely shredded
- 2/3 cup/150 g butter
- 3 cloves garlic, lightly crushed but whole
- 1 sprig fresh sage
- salt and freshly ground black pepper
- 1 cup/125 g freshly grated Parmesan cheese
- 5 oz/150 g Bitto cheese, flaked or Fontina cheese, grated

Bitto is a cheese made of mixed cow and goat milk used commonly in the Valtellina mountains. For this recipe, we advise using a Bitto that has been aged for 3 to 8 months. A well-aged Bitto can be used to sprinkle on the dish.

Pasta Dough: Sift the buckwheat and all-purpose flours and salt onto a surface and make a well in the center. Mix in enough water to make a smooth dough. Knead for 15–20 minutes until smooth and elastic. Shape the dough into a ball, wrap in plastic wrap (cling film), and let rest for 30 minutes. • Roll out the dough on a lightly floured surface to a thickness of 1/4 inch (5 mm). The dough will be very fragile. Cut into 1/2-inch (1-cm) strips, then into 2-inch (5-cm) rectangles. Let stand until ready to cook. • Sauce: Cook the potatoes and cabbage in salted boiling water for 15 minutes. • Melt the butter in a small saucepan with the garlic, sage and a little salt for 1 minute then discard the garlic and sage. • Add the pasta to the potatoes and cabbage and cook for 7–10 minutes until the pasta is al dente and the vegetables are tender. • Drain the pasta and vegetables. • Layer the pasta and vegetables in a serving bowl with the Parmesan, Bitto, and the melted butter. Season with pepper and serve.

Serves 6 • Prep: 90 min + 30 min to rest the dough • Cooking: 25 min • Level: 2

BIGOLI PASTA WITH ANCHOVIES

Bigoli con le sardelle

Bigoli pasta is traditionally made with whole-wheat flour and is shaped slightly thicker than spaghetti.

Pasta Dough: Sift the flour and salt onto a surface and make a well in the center. Break the eggs into the well and mix in with enough water to make a smooth dough. Knead for 15–20 minutes, until smooth and elastic. Shape the dough into a ball and wrap in plastic wrap (cling film) and let rest for 30 minutes. • Make the bigoli using a pasta machine and spread out on a lightly floured board to dry for abut 30 minutes. • Sauce: Sauté the onion in the oil in a medium frying pan over low heat for 2–3 minutes until softened. • Add the garlic, parsley, and anchovies. Use a fork to break up the fish and cook for about five minutes until the anchovies have cooked. Season with salt and remove from the heat. • Cook the pasta in a large pot of salted boiling water for 2–3 minutes, until al dente. • Drain, reserving 2 tablespoons of the cooking water, and spoon the anchovy sauce over the pasta. Add the reserved cooking water. Grind black pepper over the pasta and serve.

Serves 6 • Prep: 1 hr 10 min +60 min to rest and dry the dough • Cooking: 20 min • Level: 1

Pasta Dough
- 2 2/3 cups/400 g whole-wheat/wholemeal flour
- 1/4 teaspoon salt
- 4 large eggs
- 1/4 cup/60 ml cold water

Sauce
- 1 onion, finely chopped
- 5 tablespoons extra-virgin olive oil
- 1 clove garlic, lightly crushed but whole
- 2 tablespoons finely chopped fresh parsley
- 8 oz/300 g fresh anchovies, cleaned, heads removed, and coarsely chopped
- salt
- freshly ground black pepper

Pizzoccheri & Fresh Pasta

Pizzoccheri with Swiss chard
and two cheeses

PIZZOCCHERI WITH SWISS CHARD AND TWO CHEESES

Pizzoccheri con bietola

- 2 cups/300 g all-purpose/plain flour
- 1/8 teaspoon salt
- 1 large egg
- 1/2 cup/125 ml milk
- 1/2 cup/125 ml water
- 1 lb/500 g Swiss chard, tough stems removed, finely shredded
- 1 lb/500 g boiling potatoes, peeled and cut into small chunks

Pizzoccheri are a type of gnocchi or pasta, made from either buckwheat or all-purpose flour.

Sift the flour and salt into a bowl and make a well in the center. Use a balloon whisk to beat in the egg, milk, and water and beat well so that no lumps form. Set aside at room temperature for 30 minutes. • Bring 2 quarts (2 liters) salted water to a boil in a large saucepan. Add the Swiss chard and potatoes and cook for 20–25 minutes, or until tender. • Meanwhile, sauté the onion in the butter in a frying pan over medium heat for 2–3 minutes until softened. Season with salt. • Cover and cook over low heat for 15 minutes. • Working quickly, drop teaspoons of the dough into the pot with the chard and potatoes until the dough is all used up. All the pizzoccheri should be cooked for roughly the same time. • Boil for about 5 minutes from when the last one was added, or until the last ones are soft. • Use a slotted spoon to remove them with the vegetables. Arrange in layers in a large bowl, alternating with the onion and cheeses. Season with pepper and serve immediately.

Serves 4 • Prep: 40 min + 30 min to rest the dough • Cooking: 60 min • Level: 1

- 1 onion, finely chopped
- 1/2 cup/125 g butter
- salt
- 1/2 cup/60 g freshly grated Grana or Parmesan cheese
- 1/4 cup/60 g fresh ricotta
- freshly ground white pepper

PUMPKIN-FILLED TORTELLI

Tortelli di zucca

- 2 lb/1 kg winter squash, unpeeled and cut into large pieces and seeded

Filling
- generous $^3/_4$ cup/100 g amaretti cookies, very finely crushed
- 2 large eggs
- $^3/_4$ cup/90 g freshly grated Parmesan cheese

Mantuan squash (zucca barucca) is shown in the photograph, but any winter squash with firm, sweet, flavorful flesh will do. Mostarda di Cremona is a savory fruit preserve available in Italian delicatessens.

Preheat the oven to 400°F/200°C/gas 6. • Bake the pieces of squash on a large baking sheet for 40–45 minutes, or until tender. • Remove from the oven and let cool. Use a tablespoon to remove the flesh from the peel and puree in a food processor. If the squash is still moist, wrap it in a kitchen cloth and wring out the excess moisture. • Filling: Transfer the squash puree to a large bowl and mix in the amaretti, eggs, Parmesan, Mostarda di Cremona, and nutmeg. Season with salt. If the mixture seems coarse, process until smooth. • Let

rest for at least 1 hour at room temperature or overnight in the refrigerator. • Pasta: Knead the dough for 15–20 minutes, until smooth and elastic. • Roll out the dough on a lightly floured surface to a thickness of $^1/_8$ inch (3 mm). Cut into 2-inch (5-cm) squares. Make into tortelli, following the instructions on page 70. Lay them on a kitchen cloth lightly dusted with flour. • Cook the pasta in small batches in a large pot of salted boiling water for 2–3 minutes. • Use a slotted spoon to transfer to a serving dish and drizzle with the melted butter and a pinch of salt.

Serves 4 • Prep: 60 min + 60 min to rest the filling • Cooking: 60 min • Level: 3«

- scant $^1/_2$ cup/100 g Mostarda di Cremona or fruit chutney, finely chopped
- $^1/_8$ teaspoon freshly grated nutmeg
- salt
- $^1/_3$ cup/80 g butter, melted

Pasta
- Homemade Pasta Dough made with 4 large eggs and $2^2/_3$ cups/400 g all-purpose/plain flour (see page 64)

Pumpkin-filled tortelli

AMARETTI AND SPICE TORTELLI

Tortelli alla cremasca

Pasta Dough
- 2 cups/300 g all-purpose/plain flour
- 1/8 teaspoon salt
- 1 large egg
- about 1/4 cup/60 ml lukewarm water

Filling
- 3 tablespoons fresh bread crumbs
- 2 tablespoons butter, cut up + 2/3 cup/150 g, melted
- 1 1/4 cups/150 g crushed amaretti cookies
- 1 3/4 cups/210 g freshly grated Parmesan cheese
- 1/4 cup/50 g golden raisins/sultanas
- 1/2 cup/50 g finely chopped candied lemon peel
- 1 large egg
- 1 teaspoon ground allspice (cinnamon, cloves and nutmeg in equal quantities)
- salt and freshly ground white pepper
- 1–2 tablespoons vegetable stock or broth (optional)

Pasta Dough: Sift the flour and salt onto a work surface and make a well in the center. Break the egg into the well and mix in enough water to make a smooth dough. Knead for 15–20 minutes, until smooth and elastic. Shape the dough into a ball, wrap in plastic wrap (cling film), and let rest for 30 minutes. • Filling: Toast the bread crumbs in 2 tablespoons of the butter in a medium skillet over medium heat for 5 minutes until crispy. • Transfer to a large bowl with the amaretti cookies, 1 1/4 cups (150 g) of the Parmesan, raisins, candied lemon peel, egg, and spices. Season with salt and pepper. If the mixture is dry and crumbly, add the stock. • Roll out the dough until very thin on a floured surface. Use a fluted pastry wheel to cut into 2-inch (5-cm) squares and drop a teaspoon of filling into the centers. Fold into triangles and seal well. • Cook the pasta in a large pot of salted boiling water for 3–5 minutes until al dente. • Remove with a slotted spoon and transfer to a serving dish. Drizzle with the remaining 2/3 cup (150 g) melted butter and sprinkle with the remaining 1/2 cup (60 g) Parmesan.

Serves 6 • Prep: 60 min + 30 min to rest the dough • Cooking: 20 min • Level: 3

PASTA WITH MASCARPONE CHEESE

Pasta al Mascarpone

Mix the Mascarpone and egg yolks in a large bowl. Place over barely simmering water and cook until the egg mixture registers 160°F/80°C on an instant-read thermometer. Remove from the heat and plunge into a pan of cold water. • Add the Parmesan and season with salt and nutmeg. • Cook the pasta in a large pot of salted boiling water until al dente. • Pour a little of the pasta water into the serving dish first to warm it, then pour off the water. • Drain the pasta and transfer to the serving dish. • Stir the Mascarpone mixture into the pasta, diluting with a few tablespoons of the water to prevent the pasta from sticking together. • Serve hot.

Serves 4 • Prep: 10 min • Cooking: 15 min • Level: 1

- 2/3 cup/150 g fresh Mascarpone cheese
- 2 very fresh large egg yolks
- 1/4 cup/30 g freshly grated Parmesan cheese
- salt
- 1/8 teaspoon freshly grated nutmeg
- 12 oz/300 g dried maltagliati egg pasta or pappardelle egg pasta

Amaretti and spice tortelli

Spinach, potato,
and mortadella tortelli

SPINACH, POTATO, AND MORTADELLA TORTELLI

Casonsei della Valcamonica

Pasta Dough

- 2 cups/300 g all-purpose/plain flour
- 1/8 teaspoon salt
- 3 large eggs

Filling and Topping

- 2 baking/floury potatoes
- 2 tablespoons butter, cut up, + 1/2 cup/125 g, melted
- 1 small onion, finely chopped

<u>Pasta Dough</u>: Sift the flour and salt onto a work surface and make a well in the center. Break the eggs into the well and mix in to make a smooth dough. Knead for 15–20 minutes, until smooth and elastic. Shape the dough into a ball, wrap in plastic wrap (cling film), and let rest for 30 minutes. • <u>Filling</u>: Cook the potatoes in salted boiling water for 15–20 minutes, or until tender. • Drain and peel them. Use a potato masher or fork to mash them until smooth. • Melt 2 tablespoons of the butter in a large frying pan. Add the onion, cover, and cook for 5 minutes over low heat until softened. • Increase the heat and add the spinach. Sauté for 2 minutes and season with salt and pepper. • Transfer the

spinach mixture, mortadella, parsley, 1/2 cup (60 g) of the Parmesan, bread crumbs, and egg to a food processor or blender and process until smooth. • Roll out the dough until very thin on a floured surface. Cut into 4-inch (10-cm) rounds and drop a generous teaspoon of the filling into the centers. Close them into a spike shape (see photo) and seal well. • Cook the pasta in small batches in a large pot of salted boiling water for 4–5 minutes. • Use a slotted spoon to transfer to a serving dish and drizzle with the remaining 1/2 cup (125 g) melted butter. Sprinkle with the remaining 1/2 cup (60 g) Parmesan and serve.

Serves 6 • Prep: 50 min + 30 min to rest the dough • Cooking: 42–50 min • Level: 3

- 2/3 cup/150 g cooked, and finely chopped spinach leaves, squeezed dry
- salt and freshly ground white pepper
- 3/4 cup/90 g diced mortadella
- 1 sprig fresh parsley, finely chopped
- 1 cup/125 g freshly grated Parmesan cheese
- 3 tablespoons fine dry bread crumbs
- 1 large egg

MAKING PLEATED TORTELLI

1. Cut out rounds of pasta dough about 4 inches (10 cm) in diameter. Drop a generous teaspoon of filling into the center of the rounds. Fold one flap of dough over the filling.

2. Continue folding over flaps of dough, alternating from right to left, until you have completely enclosed the filling.

3. The finished pasta should be tapered with a pleated surface, resembling an ear of wheat.

Gnocchi

GNOCCHETTI WITH SAVOY CABBAGE

Gnocchetti di farina bianca

Gnocchetti
- 2 cups/500 ml water
- generous $^1/_3$ cup/100 ml milk
- $^1/_8$ teaspoon salt
- 2 cups/300 g all-purpose/plain flour
- $^1/_4$ cup/60 g butter, cut up
- $^1/_4$ cup/30 g freshly grated Parmesan cheese
- 3 large egg yolks, lightly beaten
- 8 oz/200 g Savoy cabbage, finely shredded
- scant $^1/_2$ cup/100 g butter
- 1 sprig fresh sage leaves, chopped
- $^1/_2$ cup/60 g freshly grated Parmesan cheese

Gnocchetti: Pour the water into a large high-sided, nonstick saucepan and add the milk and salt. Place over low heat and bring to a boil. • Add the flour, remove from the heat, and stir vigorously with a wooden spoon. • Transfer to a large bowl and gradually stir in the butter, Parmesan, and the egg yolks. • Break off small pieces from this dough and form into $^2/_3$-inch (1.5-cm) balls. Put them on a lightly floured surface until required. • Cook the cabbage in a large pot of salted boiling water for 5–7 minutes, or until tender. • Add the gnocchetti in small batches and cook for 3–4 minutes until they rise to the surface, then cook for 1 minute more. • Use a slotted spoon to remove the gnocchetti and cabbage and transfer to a serving dish. • Melt the butter with the sage in a small saucepan and drizzle over the gnocchetti. Sprinkle with Parmesan and serve.

Serves 4–6 • Prep: 30 min • Cooking: 30 min • Level: 2

BAKED SWISS CHARD GNOCCHI

Strangolapreti bergamaschi

Preheat the oven to 400°F/200°C/gas 6. • Cook the Swiss chard in a large pot of salted boiling water over a medium heat for 7–10 minutes, or until tender. • Let cool, then squeeze it dry and finely chop. • Butter a baking dish. • Soak the bread in the milk for 15 minutes, or until softened. • Squeeze out the excess milk and transfer the bread to a food processor or blender. Add the Swiss chard and egg yolks and process until smooth and well mixed. • Mix in the bread crumbs, nutmeg, and salt and pepper. • Break off walnut sized pieces and form into elongated 1$^1/_2$-inch (4-cm) gnocchi. • Cook the gnocchi in small batches in a large pot of salted boiling water for about 5 minutes, until they rise to the surface. • Use a slotted spoon to remove the gnocchi and arrange them in the prepared dish. • Sprinkle with Parmesan. Melt the butter with the sage in a small saucepan and drizzle over the gnocchi. Season with salt. • Bake for 8–10 minutes, or until the cheese is bubbling. • Serve hot.

Serves 6 • Prep: 60 min + 15 min to soak the bread • Cooking: 35 min • Level: 2

- 10 oz/300 g Swiss chard
- 12 oz/400 g day-old bread rolls, crumbled
- 2 cups/500 ml milk
- 2 large egg yolks
- 6 tablespoons fine dry bread crumbs
- $^1/_8$ teaspoon freshly grated nutmeg
- salt and freshly ground black pepper
- $^3/_4$ cup/90 g freshly grated Parmesan cheese
- scant $^1/_2$ cup/100 g butter
- 1 sprig fresh sage leaves, chopped

Squash gnocchi with sausage sauce

Squash gnocchi with sausage sauce

Gnocchi di zucca

Gnocchi

- 2¹/₂ lb/1.25 kg winter squash or pumpkin, cut into large pieces unpeeled but seeded
- 2 large eggs
- ¹/₄ cup/50 g amaretti cookies, crumbled
- 4 tablespoons fresh bread crumbs
- ¹/₄ cup/30 g freshly grated Parmesan cheese
- ¹/₄ teaspoon ground nutmeg
- salt and freshly ground white pepper

Sausage Sauce

- 1 small onion, finely chopped
- ¹/₄ cup/60 g butter
- 4 oz/100 g Italian sausage, crumbled
- 1 clove garlic, lightly crushed but whole
- 1 tablespoon tomato paste/concentrate mixed with 1 tablespoon water
- salt
- ¹/₄ cup/30 g all-purpose/plain flour

Gnocchi: Preheat the oven to 400°F/200°C/gas 6. • Bake the pieces of squash on a large baking sheet for 40–45 minutes, or until tender. • Remove from the oven and let cool. Use a tablespoon to remove the flesh from the peel and puree in a food processor. If the squash is still moist, wrap it in a kitchen cloth and wring out the excess moisture. • Transfer the squash puree to a large bowl and mix in the eggs, amaretti, bread crumbs, and Parmesan. • Season with nutmeg, salt and pepper. • Sausage Sauce: Sauté the onion in the butter in a small saucepan over a medium heat for 5 minutes, until softened. Add the crumbled sausage and garlic and cook over low heat for 10 minutes. • Discard the garlic and add the tomato paste mixture. • Season with salt and remove from the heat. • Form tablespoons of the gnocchi mixture into balls the size of walnuts, pressing them into an oval shape. • Dip in the flour until well coated. • Cook the gnocchi in small batches in a large pot of salted boiling water until they rise to the surface. • Use a slotted spoon to transfer to serving dishes and serve with the sauce.

Serves 4 • Prep: 45 min • Cooking: 75 min • Level: 2

Beef agnolini in stock

Agnolini ripieni di stufato

Pasta Dough: Sift the flour and salt onto a surface and make a well in the center. Break the eggs into the well and mix in with enough water to make a smooth dough. Knead for 15–20 minutes, until smooth and elastic. Shape the dough into a ball, wrap in plastic wrap (cling film), and let rest for 30 minutes. • Filling: Make incisions at regular intervals in the beef and slide a slice of garlic into each cut. • Sear the beef in 2 tablespoons of the butter and the oil in a medium saucepan until browned all over. Add the onion and cook until softened. • Pour in ¹/₄ cup of the wine and season with salt. • Cover and cook over low heat for at least 3 hours, until well cooked and very tender, turning occasionally and adding more wine as the cooking liquid begins to dry. • Sauté the sausage in the remaining 2 tablespoons of butter in a small frying pan for 5–10 minutes, until browned all over. • Chop the meat and sausages in a food processor or a blender until finely ground. Transfer to a large bowl and mix in the Parmesan, eggs, and nutmeg. Season with salt. • Roll out the dough on a lightly floured surface until paper-thin. Cut into 1¹/₂-inch (4-cm) wide strips and then into 1¹/₂-inch (4-cm) squares. Arrange pellets of filling in the center of each square and close as for tortellini (see page 70). • Cook the pasta in small batches in the boiling stock for 4–5 minutes. • Use a slotted spoon to transfer to serving bowls. Sprinkle with Parmesan and serve with the stock.

Serves 8–10 • Prep: 2 hr + 30 min to rest the dough • Cooking: 3 hr 10 min • Level: 3

Pasta Dough

- 3¹/₃ cups/500 g all-purpose/plain flour
- ¹/₄ teaspoon salt
- 4 large eggs
- ¹/₄ cup/60 ml water, + more as needed

Filling

- 1 lb/500 g stew beef, in one piece
- 3 cloves garlic, finely sliced
- ¹/₄ cup/60 g butter
- 2 tablespoons extra-virgin olive oil
- 1 small onion, finely chopped
- 2 cups/500 ml dry white wine
- salt
- 8 oz/200 g fresh Italian salamelle sausage (unspiced pork sausage), coarsely chopped
- 5 tablespoons freshly grated Parmesan cheese
- 2 large eggs
- ¹/₈ teaspoon freshly grated nutmeg
- 1 cup/250 ml + 3 quarts/3 liters beef stock or broth
- 1³/₄ cups/215 g freshly grated Parmesan cheese

NORTHEAST ITALY

The cuisine of Veneto, Friuli-Venetia Giulia, and Trentino-Alto Adige is strongly influenced by its cooler northern climate. Venetians have a long history as fishermen whose catches range from spider crab to baccalà (dried salt cod), thus providing variety for a myriad of exciting dishes. The most traditional local pasta is *bigoli*—whole-wheat, rough-textured large spaghetti—served with poultry or onions and anchovies. The adaptable red radicchio hails from the town of Treviso, where it is frequently added to salads, stewed with pasta, or cooked and served as a vegetable side dish.

Gnocchi with herbs
(see page 59)

Soups, Dumplings & Fresh Pasta

PASTA WITH BEANS

Pasta e fasioi di lamon

- 4 oz/100 g fresh pork rind or ham bone
- 2 cloves garlic, finely chopped
- 1 tablespoon finely chopped fresh parsley
- 1 sprig fresh sage, finely chopped
- 6 tablespoons extra-virgin olive oil
- 2 quarts/2 liters cold water
- 2 cups/200 g dried lamon or borlotti beans, soaked overnight and drained
- 1 onion, finely chopped
- 1 bay leaf
- salt
- 4 oz/100 g dried wheat pasta or egg tagliatelle
- freshly ground black pepper

If using pork rind, blanch it in boiling water for 5 minutes. Drain well and scrape thoroughly to remove any hair. • Sauté the garlic, parsley, and sage in ¼ cup oil in a small frying pan on a low heat for 5 minutes, until the garlic is pale gold. • Bring the water to a boil with the drained beans in a large pot over low heat. Add the onion, bay leaf, pork rind or ham bone, and sautéed herbs. Simmer over low heat for about 2 hours, skimming the grease from the stock as it cooks. Season with salt. • Puree half the soup in a food processor and return the puree to the soup. • Bring to a boil and cook for 20–25 minutes, until thickened. • Add the pasta and cook for 7–10 minutes, until al dente. • Use a slotted spoon to remove the pork rind and cut into strips. • Ladle the soup into bowls and garnish with strips of pork rind. Season with pepper and drizzle with remaining 2 tablespoons of oil.

Serves 4 • Prep: 30 min + overnight to soak the beans • Cooking: 2 hr 45 min • Level: 1

SEMOLINA GNOCCHI IN STOCK

Gnocchi de gries

Bring the milk almost to a boil in a large deep saucepan. Whisk in the salt and the semolina. • Bring to a boil and simmer over low heat for 15–20 minutes, stirring constantly with a wooden spoon. If it becomes gluey and difficult to stir, add the extra milk. • Pour into a large bowl and let cool, stirring occasionally. • Mix in the egg yolks, add the butter, and mix well. • Beat the egg whites in a separate bowl until frothy and add them to the mixture. • Form into ⅔-inch (1.5-cm) gnocchi. • Bring the stock to a boil in a large saucepan. Cook the gnocchi in small batches for 3–4 minutes, or until they rise to the surface. • Use a slotted spoon to transfer to bowls and serve, sprinkled with the Parmesan.

Serves 4–6 • Prep: 30 min • Cooking: 40 min • Level: 2

- 4 cups/1 liter milk, + more as needed (optional)
- ⅛ teaspoon salt
- 1⅔ cups/250 g semolina
- 2 large eggs, separated, + 2 large egg yolks
- 3 tablespoons butter, softened

To serve
- 6 cups/1.5 liters meat stock or broth
- 1 cup/125 g freshly grated Parmesan cheese

GARGANELLI WITH SPECK

Garganelli allo speck

- 1 onion, finely chopped
- 4 tablespoons butter
- 1 cup/120 g speck or smoked bacon, cut into thin strips
- 12 oz/350 g dried garganelli or penne pasta

Speck comes from the Alto Adige region where both German and Italian are spoken. Although "speck" means bacon in German, this pork product is treated with salt and garlic.

Sauté the onion in 2 tablespoons of butter in a large frying pan over medium heat for about 10 minutes. • In a separate frying pan, sauté the speck in the remaining 2 tablespoons of butter over a medium heat for 2–3 minutes (slightly longer if using bacon), until slightly crunchy. • Add the speck to the onion. • Cook the pasta in a large pot of salted boiling water until not quite done. • Drain, reserving 5 tablespoons of the cooking water. Add the pasta and cooking water to the frying pan and cook until al dente. • Serve hot.

Serves 4 • Prep: 15 min • Cooking: 15 min • Level: 1

RYE DUMPLINGS WITH BACON

Canederli neri (schwarze Knödel)

Place the bread in a large bowl and mix in the pancetta, onion, leek, and garlic. • Mix the milk, water, and salt in a small bowl. • Pour the milk over the bread mixture and let rest for 1 hour. • Use your hands to knead in the cornmeal. • Form the mixture into 1½-inch (4-cm) balls and dust them lightly with flour. • Bring the stock to a boil in a large saucepan add the dumplings and cook for 20 minutes over low heat, until cooked through. • Ladle into bowls and serve.

Serves 4 • Prep: 40 min + 60 min to rest • Cooking: 30 min • Level: 2

- 10 oz/300 g rye bread, crusts removed
- 1½ cups/180 g finely chopped smoked pancetta or bacon
- 1 small red onion, finely chopped
- 1 large leek, white part only, finely chopped
- 1 clove garlic, chopped
- 3 tablespoons milk
- 3 tablespoons water
- salt
- ¼ cup/30 g finely ground cornmeal
- ¼ cup/30 g all-purpose/plain flour
- 5 cups/1.25 liters meat stock or broth

Dumplings & Gnocchi

Dumplings with Speck

Canederli allo speck

- 1/2 onion, finely chopped
- 7 tablespoons butter, melted
- 2 large eggs
- 1 cup/250 ml milk, + more as needed
- 5 cups/300 g day-old bread, cut into small cubes
- 1 1/4 cups/150 g diced speck or smoked bacon
- 1 small bunch chives, finely chopped
- 1 teaspoon finely chopped fresh parsley
- 1/4 cup/30 g all purpose/plain flour
- salt

Sauté the onion in 1 tablespoon of butter in a large frying pan over low heat for 20 minutes, until very soft and golden. • Beat the eggs with the milk in a medium bowl. • Add the bread, speck, 1 tablespoon of chives, and parsley. Set aside for 30 minutes. • Add the onion, 2 tablespoons of flour, and salt. • Knead to form a smooth dough, adding more milk if needed. • Form the mixture into 2-inch (5-cm) balls and dip in the remaining 2 tablespoons flour until well coated. • Cook the dumplings in a large pot of salted boiling water or stock for 15–18 minutes, until cooked through. • Drain and drizzle with the remaining 6 table spoons melted butter. Sprinkle with the remaining chives and serve.

Serves 6 • Prep: 60 min + 30 min to rest • Cooking: 40 min • Level: 2

Dumplings, Trentino style

Canederli di magro

Soak the bread in the milk for 10 minutes, or until softened. Drain, squeezing out the excess milk. • Sauté the onion in 2 tablespoons of butter in a large frying pan over low heat for 20 minutes, until very soft and golden. • Season with salt, remove from the heat, and let cool. • Use a wooden spoon to beat the remaining butter in a large bowl until softened. • Add the soaked bread to the butter with the sautéed onion, flour, 1 tablespoon of the parsley, eggs, and nutmeg. • Form the mixture into 1 1/2-inch (4-cm) balls. • Cook the dumplings in a large pot with the boiling stock for about 7 minutes, until cooked through. • Ladle into individual soup bowls and sprinkle with the remaining parsley.

Serves 4 • Prep: 40 min • Cooking: 30 min • Level: 1

- 8 1/2 cups/500 g day-old bread, crusts removed and crumbled
- 1 1/4 cups/310 ml milk
- 1/2 onion, finely chopped
- 1/3 cup/80 g butter
- salt
- 3/4 cup/125 g all-purpose/plain flour
- 1 small bunch fresh parsley, finely chopped
- 5 large eggs
- 1/8 teaspoon freshly grated nutmeg
- 2 3/4 cups/680 ml meat stock or broth, boiling

Dumplings with speck

Cocoa and Ricotta gnocchi

COCOA AND RICOTTA GNOCCHI

Gnocchi con il cacao

Cocoa mixture
- 1 tablespoon cocoa
- 2 tablespoons raisins
- 3/4 cup/90 g freshly grated Parmesan cheese
- 1/2 cup/60 g freshly grated Ricotta Salata cheese
- 3/4 cup/175 g butter, melted
- 1/3 cup/30 g chopped candied lemon peel
- 1/8 teaspoon ground cinnamon
- salt and freshly ground white pepper

Gnocchi
- 3 lb/1.5 kg baking/floury potatoes, diced
- 2 large eggs, beaten
- 2 tablespoons freshly grated Parmesan cheese
- salt and freshly ground white pepper
- 3 1/3 cups/500 g all-purpose/plain flour
- 1/2 cup/60 g Parmesan cheese, to sprinkle

Cocoa mixture: Mix the cocoa, raisins, 3/4 cup (90 g) of Parmesan, Ricotta salata, 1/2 cup (125 g) of butter, candied lemon peel, cinnamon, salt and pepper in a large bowl. • Gnocchi: Cook the potatoes in salted boiling water for 15–20 minutes, or until tender. • Drain and peel them. Use a potato masher or fork to mash them until smooth. Spread the potatoes out on a surface and mix in the eggs, Parmesan, salt and pepper. Add enough flour to form a stiff dough. Break off pieces of dough and form into logs about 3/4-inch (2-cm) wide. Cut into 1-inch (3-cm) lengths. Dust with the remaining flour. Do not leave the gnocchi on the surface too long because they will stick. • Cook the gnocchi in small batches in a large pot of salted boiling water for 3–5 minutes, until they rise to the surface. • Use a slotted spoon to transfer the gnocchi to the bowl of cocoa mixture and toss them together very gently. Transfer to a serving dish, drizzle with the remaining 1/4 cup (60 g) melted butter and sprinkle with the Parmesan. Serve hot.

Serves 6 • Prep: 60 min • Cooking: 35–40 min • Level: 2

GNOCCHI WITH HERBS

Gnocchi con le erbe

Wash and clean the herbs, then boil them in salted water for 5–10 minutes, until they are tender. Drain, squeezing out excess moisture and finely chop. • Cook the potatoes in salted boiling water for 15–20 minutes, or until tender. Drain well. • Use a fork or potato masher to mash them and spread out the potatoes on a clean surface. Let cool to lukewarm. • Sauté the herbs in the oil in a frying pan over medium heat for 2 minutes. • Season the potatoes with salt and pepper and use a fork to work in half the herbs, the egg, and 1 cup (150 g) of the flour. • Break off walnut-sized pieces of dough, shaping them into small logs . Dip in the remaining 4 tablespoons flour until well coated. • Sauté the onion in the butter in a large frying pan over medium heat for 5 minutes. • Pour in the wine and let it evaporate. • Add the garlic and remaining herbs and cook for 10 minutes. • Cook the gnocchi in small batches in a large pot of salted boiling water for 3–5 minutes, until they rise to the surface. • Use a slotted spoon to transfer to serving plates and top with the sauce. Sprinkle with Parmesan.

Serves 4–6 • Prep:60 min • Cooking: 60 min • Level: 2

- 10 oz/300 g mixed herbs (preferably wild, including asparagus, peppermint, spearmint, common fennel, parsley, sage)
- 3 lb/1.5 kg baking/floury potatoes, peeled and cut into small chunks
- 1/4 cup/60 ml extra-virgin olive oil
- salt and freshly ground white pepper
- 1 large egg, lightly beaten
- 1 1/4 cups/200 g all-purpose/plain flour
- 1/2 onion, finely chopped
- 2 tablespoons butter
- 1/4 cup/60 ml dry white wine
- 1 clove garlic, finely chopped
- 6 tablespoons freshly grated Parmesan or Pecorino cheese

Spinach–chocolate parcels

SPINACH–CHOCOLATE RAVIOLI
Cialzons

Pasta Dough
- 2²/₃ cups/400 g all purpose/plain flour
- ¹/₄ teaspoon salt
- 2 large eggs
- 2 tablespoons butter, melted
- 1 tablespoon water, + more if needed

Filling
- ¹/₂ medium onion, finely chopped
- 1 tablespoon butter
- 1 cup/250 g cooked, drained spinach, finely chopped
- 2 tablespoons finely grated semisweet/dark chocolate
- ¹/₄ cup/45 g raisins
- ¹/₄ cup/30 g day-old rye bread crumbs + more if needed
- 2 tablespoons finely chopped candied citron peel
- 1 large egg
- 1 tablespoon finely chopped fresh parsley
- 1 teaspoon sugar
- ¹/₈ teaspoon ground cinnamon
- salt and freshly ground black pepper
- 6 tablespoons butter, melted
- 4 oz/100 g smoked Ricotta Salata cheese, finely grated
- ¹/₈ teaspoon sugar

Pasta Dough: Sift the flour and salt onto a surface and make a well in the center. Break the eggs into the well and mix in with the butter and enough water to make a smooth dough. Knead for 15–20 minutes, until smooth and elastic. Shape the dough into a ball, wrap in plastic wrap (cling film), and let rest for 30 minutes. • Filling: Sauté the onion in the butter in a large frying pan over medium heat for five minutes, until softened. • Add the spinach and sauté for 1 minute. • Remove from the heat and transfer to a large bowl. • Mix in the chocolate, raisins, bread crumbs, citron peel, egg, parsley, sugar, and cinnamon. Season with salt and pepper. • The mixture should hold its shape, if it seems too fluid, add more bread crumbs. • Roll out the dough on a lightly floured surface until paper-thin. Cut out 3-inch (8-cm) rounds. • Drop two teaspoons of filling into the centers of the rounds. Fold in half and seal, forming a crimped finish along the edge. • Cook the pasta in a large pot of salted boiling water for 3–4 minutes, until al dente. • Use a slotted spoon to transfer to a serving bowl and arrange in layers with the melted butter, Ricotta Salata, and sugar.

Serves 4 • Prep: 2 hr + 30 min to rest the dough• Cooking: 15 min • Level: 3

TAGLIATELLE WITH PEAS
Tagliatelle coi bisi

Sauté the onion in ¹/₄ cup (60 g) of the butter in a large frying pan over medium heat for about 10 minutes, or until soft and golden. • Add the pancetta and garlic and cook for 3–4 minutes, until the garlic is pale gold. • Add the peas and season with salt, pepper, and sugar. • Pour in the water and cover and cook for 15 minutes. • Uncover and cook for about 10 minutes, until the sauce has reduced by half. • Cook the pasta in a large pot of salted boiling water until al dente. • Drain and add to the sauce. Dot with the remaining butter and sprinkle with Parmesan and parsley.

Serves 4 • Prep: 20 min • Cooking: 45 min • Level: 1

- 1 onion, finely chopped
- ¹/₃ cup/80 g butter
- ¹/₂ cup/60 g diced pancetta or bacon
- 1 clove garlic, chopped
- 2¹/₂ cups/300 g peas
- salt and freshly ground white pepper
- ¹/₈ teaspoon sugar
- 2 cups/500 ml hot water
- 12 oz/300 g tagliatelle
- ¹/₄ cup/30 g freshly grated Parmesan cheese
- 1 tablespoon finely chopped fresh parsley

POTATO-BEET RAVIOLI
Casonsei

Pasta Dough: Sift the flour and salt onto a surface and make a well in the center. Break the eggs into the well and mix in with enough water to make a smooth dough. Knead for 15–20 minutes, until elastic. Shape into a ball, wrap in plastic wrap, and let rest for 30 minutes. • Potato–Beet Filling: Cook the beets in salted boiling water for 25 minutes, until tender. Let cool. • Cook the potatoes in salted boiling water for 15–20 minutes, or until tender. • Drain and peel them. Transfer to a large bowl and mash until smooth. Let cool to warm. • Peel the beets and coarsely chop. Sauté the beets in the butter in a large frying pan over medium heat for 10 minutes, crushing them with a fork until pureed. • Remove from the heat and let cool to warm. • Mix the beets into the potatoes. Add the egg, Pecorino, and bread crumbs. Season with salt. • Roll out the dough on a lightly floured surface until very thin. Use a pastry cutter to cut out 2¹/₂-inch (6-cm) rounds and drop filling into the centers. Seal in a semi-circular shape. • Cook the pasta in small batches in a large pot of salted boiling water for 2–3 minutes, until al dente. • Drizzle with butter. Sprinkle with Parmesan and poppy seeds.

Serves 6 • Prep: 1 hr + 30 min to rest the dough • Cooking: 60 min • Level: 3

Pasta Dough
- 2²/₃ cups/400 g all-purpose/plain flour
- ¹/₄ teaspoon salt
- 3 large eggs
- ¹/₄ cup/60 ml water or milk, + more as needed

Potato–Beet Filling
- 12 oz/350 g baking/floury potatoes
- 1¹/₄ lb/600 g beets
- ¹/₄ cup/60 g butter
- 1 large egg
- ¹/₂ cup/60 g freshly grated Pecorino cheese
- 2 tablespoons fine dry bread crumbs
- salt
- scant ¹/₃ cup/100 g butter, melted
- 1 cup/125 g freshly grated Parmesan cheese
- 2 tablespoons poppy seeds

SPAGHETTI WITH CHICKEN LIVER SAUCE

Bigoli con ragù di fegatini

- 1 lb/400 g chicken livers, trimmed
- 1/2 cup/125 ml water
- 1/2 cup/125 ml white wine vinegar
- 1/4 cup/60 g butter
- 3 tablespoons extra-virgin olive oil
- 3 leaves fresh sage, finely chopped
- salt and freshly ground white pepper
- 3/4 cup/180 ml chicken stock or broth
- 1 lb/500 g fresh bigoli pasta
- 3/4 cup/90 g freshly grated Parmesan cheese

Soak the chicken livers in the water and vinegar for 15 minutes. Drain. • Heat the butter and oil with the sage in a medium saucepan over low heat. • Add the chicken livers and cook over high heat for 2–3 minutes, until browned all over. Season with salt and pepper. • Remove the chicken livers and coarsely chop. Return the chicken livers to the saucepan and pour in the stock. Cook over high heat for 5 minutes, or until the sauce has reduced by half. • Cook the pasta in a large pot of salted boiling water until al dente. • Drain and add to the sauce. Sprinkle with Parmesan and serve.

Serves 4 • Prep: 10 min + 15 min to soak the liver • Cooking: 25 min • Level: 1

LIVER DUMPLINGS

Canederli di fegato

Soak the bread in the milk for 10 minutes, or until softened. Drain, squeezing out the excess milk. • Sauté the onion in the butter in a large frying pan over medium heat for 10 minutes, or until soft and golden. • Add the liver and cook for 2–3 minutes, until browned all over. (It should be pink inside.) • Add the parsley and marjoram, and season with salt, pepper, and nutmeg. Remove from the heat and let cool. • Transfer the mixture to a large bowl. Mix the soaked bread into the liver mixture with the egg and lemon zest. • Chop the mixture in a food processor or blender until finely ground. • Form into 1 1/2-inch (4-cm) balls. • Bring the stock to a boil in a large saucepan. Add the dumplings and cook for 6–7 minutes, until cooked through. • Spoon into serving bowls with the stock and sprinkle with the chives.

Serves 4 • Prep: 60 min • Cooking: 30 min • Level: 2

- 1 3/4 cups/100 g day-old bread, crumbled
- generous 1/3 cup/100 ml milk
- 1/2 onion, finely chopped
- 2 tablespoons butter
- 8 oz/200 g calf's liver, trimmed and cut in large chunks
- 1 tablespoon finely chopped fresh parsley
- 1 tablespoon finely chopped fresh marjoram
- salt and freshly ground black pepper
- 1/8 teaspoon freshly grated nutmeg
- 1 large egg
- zest of 1/2 lemon

To serve
- 4 cups/1 liter meat stock or broth
- 1 tablespoon finely chopped chives

Spaghetti with chicken liver sauce

Fresh pasta
with radicchio and sausage

TAGLIOLINI WITH RADICCHIO

Tagliolini al radicchio rosso di Treviso

- 1 red onion, finely chopped
- generous $^1/_3$ cup/100 g butter
- 3 oz/100 g smoked pancetta (or bacon), cut into thin slices
- 16 oz/400 g red Treviso radicchio, or chicory, finely shredded
- salt and freshly ground black pepper
- 1 cup/250 ml dry red wine
- 12 oz/350 g dried egg tagliolini or tagliatelle

This simple recipe combines the bitterness of the radicchio with the smoky aroma of the pancetta. If you like, substitute smoked trout, speck, or smoked salmon for the pancetta.

Sauté the onion in the butter in a large frying pan over a medium heat for about 10 minutes, or until soft and golden. • Add the pancetta and cook for 5 minutes, until crisp. • Add the radicchio and season with salt and pepper. Pour in the wine and let it evaporate. • Cook the pasta in a large pot of salted boiling water until al dente. • Drain and add to the radicchio. Serve hot.

Serves 4 • Prep: 20 min • Cooking: 20 min • Level: 1

FRESH PASTA WITH RADICCHIO AND SAUSAGE

Mlinci

Pasta Dough: Sift the flour, cornmeal, and salt onto a work surface and make a well in the center. Break the eggs into the well and mix in to make a smooth dough. Knead for 15–20 minutes, until smooth and elastic. Shape the dough into a ball, wrap in plastic wrap (cling film), and let rest for 30 minutes. • Radicchio–Sausage Sauce: Sauté the garlic in the oil in a large frying pan over low heat for 3 minutes, until pale gold. • Discard the garlic. Add the sausages and sauté for 3 minutes, until browned all over. • Add the onion and cook for 10 minutes, until soft and golden. • Add the radicchio and cook for 3 minutes. • Preheat the oven to 400°F/200°C/gas 6. • Roll out the pasta on a lightly floured surface until very thin. Cut into 3 x 1$^1/_2$-inch (8 x 4-cm) rectangles. • Toast the pasta on a baking sheet for 5 minutes, until golden. • Cook the pasta in a large pot of salted boiling water for 2–3 minutes, until al dente. • Drain and add to the sauce. Serve hot.

Serves 6 • Prep: 60 min + 20 min to rest the dough • Cooking: 30 min • Level: 2

Pasta Dough
- 3$^1/_3$ cups/500 g all-purpose/plain flour
- $^1/_2$ cup/75 g finely ground white cornmeal
- $^1/_4$ teaspoon salt
- 5 large eggs

Radicchio–Sausage Sauce
- 1 clove garlic, lightly crushed but whole
- $^1/_4$ cup/60 ml extra-virgin olive oil
- 2 Italian sausages, peeled and crumbled
- $^1/_2$ onion, finely chopped
- 1 lb/500 g Treviso radicchio or red chicory, shredded

Fresh Pasta

POPPY-SEED LASAGNA

Lasagne da fornel

Pasta Dough

- 1¹/₃ cups/200 g durum wheat flour
- 1¹/₃ cups/200 g all-purpose/plain flour
- ¹/₄ teaspoon salt
- 2 large eggs + 1 large egg yolk
- 1 tablespoon extra-virgin olive oil
- 1 tablespoon water, + more if needed

Filling

- 2 tart apples, such as Granny Smiths
- juice of ¹/₂ lemon
- generous ¹/₄ cup/50 g dried figs, coarsely chopped
- 2 tablespoons raisins, plumped in warm water for 1 hour
- 1 cup/100 g coarsely chopped walnuts
- ²/₃ cup/150 g butter, melted
- ¹/₂ teaspoon ground cinnamon
- ¹/₄ cup/50 g poppy seeds

Pasta Dough: Sift the flours and salt onto a surface and make a well in the center. Mix in the eggs, oil, and enough water to make a smooth dough. Knead for 15–20 minutes, until elastic. Shape into a ball, wrap in plastic wrap, and let rest for 30 minutes. • Filling: Chop one apple into small cubes and cut the remaining apple into thin slices. Place the apple cubes and slices in separate bowls of water and lemon juice. Let stand 15 minutes. Drain well. • Mix the apple cubes, figs, raisins, and walnuts. • Preheat the oven to 325°F/170°C/ gas 3. • Butter a baking dish. • Roll out the dough out on a lightly floured surface until paper-thin. Cut into ³/₄ x 3-inch (2 x 8-cm) rectangles. • Cook the pasta in a large pot of salted boiling water until al dente. • Drain and drizzle with 6 tablespoons of the butter. • Layer the pasta in the dish with the apple mixture. • Drain the apple slices and arrange on the pasta. • Drizzle with the remaining butter and sprinkle with the poppy seeds and cinnamon. • Bake for 25–30 minutes, or until the apple has softened but not burnt. • Cool for 15 minutes before serving.

Serves 4 • Prep: 90 min+30 min to rest dough• Cooking: 40 min • Level: 2

SPATZLE

The tool that is used to make spatzle is similar to a mandoline, with holes in place of the blades, with a funnel-shaped container sliding over it, to hold the batter. If you do not have one of these tools, you can use a potato ricer. As an alternative, you can make a more substantial batter (add more flour, about ¹/₃ cup/ 50 g), and then cut the batter coarsely into 2-inch (5-cm) lengths with a knife on the cutting board. You can then push the spatzle off the cutting board into the cooking water.

Beat the eggs in a large bowl and add the flour, milk, water, and ¹/₈ teaspoon salt until smooth. • Bring a large saucepan of water to a boil and add the salt. • Place the spatzle-maker on the saucepan and let the batter drop into the water. • Cook the drops of batter for 2 minutes, until they rise to the surface. • Drain and drizzle with the melted butter. Sprinkle with ¹/₈ teaspoon salt and Parmesan.

Serves 4 • Prep: 10 min • Cooking: 15 min • Level: 2

- 2 large eggs
- 1¹/₃ cups/200 g all-purpose/plain flour
- generous ¹/₃ cup/100 ml milk
- generous ¹/₃ cup/100 ml water
- 2 teaspoons salt
- ¹/₃ cup/80 g butter, melted
- 1 cup/125 g freshly grated Parmesan cheese

MAKING HOMEMADE PASTA DOUGH

1. Break the eggs into the well of sifted flour on a wooden pastry board.

2. Use your hands to begin mixing the flour from the interior of the well with the eggs.

3. Mix together all the flour and eggs to make a fairly stiff dough.

4. Knead with the palm of your hands, rolling the ball of dough and folding it over onto itself. Knead for 15–20 minutes.

5. The dough has been kneaded sufficiently when it is smooth and has no streaking or layering. Let it rest for 30 minutes before using.

Poppy seed lasagna

Baked Pasta

BAKED RADICCHIO PIE

Pasticcio di radicchio rosso di Treviso

- 1 clove garlic, lightly crushed but whole
- 5 tablespoons butter
- 1/4 cup/60 ml extra-virgin olive oil
- 1 onion, finely chopped
- 10 oz/300 g luganega, or very fresh Italian pork sausage, crumbled
- 3 lb/1.5 kg Treviso radicchio or red chicory, finely shredded
- 2/3 cup/150 ml dry white wine
- salt and freshly ground black pepper
- 8 oz/250 g fresh lasagna pasta
- 4 cups/1 liter Béchamel sauce (made with 6 tablespoons butter, 6 tablespoons all-purpose/plain flour and 1 quart/1 liter milk), page 10
- 3/4 cup/90 g freshly grated Parmesan cheese
- Treviso radicchio, shredded, to serve

Preheat the oven to 400°F/200°C/gas 6. • Butter a large baking dish. • Sauté the garlic in the butter and oil in a large frying pan over a low heat for 2–3 minutes, until pale gold. • Add the onion and sausage and cook over low heat for 10 minutes. • Discard the garlic and increase the heat to medium. Sauté the radicchio for 5 minutes, or until slightly wilted. • Pour in the wine and let it evaporate for 5 minutes. Season with salt and pepper. Cover and cook for 15 minutes. • Blanch the pasta (see page 222) in salted boiling water. • Drain and arrange a layer of pasta in the prepared baking dish. Sprinkle with a quarter of the radicchio, a fifth of the Béchamel, and 2 tablespoons of Parmesan. Continue until you have used up all the ingredients, finishing with a layer of pasta covered with Béchamel and Parmesan. • Bake for 20–25 minutes, or until the cheese is bubbling. • Cool for at least 30 minutes before serving. • Garnish with shredded raw radicchio.

Serves 6 • Prep: 30 min + 30 min to cool • Cooking: 60 min • Level: 2

BAKED CHEESE GNOCCHI

Gnocchi gratinati

Preheat the oven to 400°F/200°C/gas 6. • Butter a baking dish. • Cook the potatoes in salted boiling water for 15–20 minutes, or until tender. • Drain and peel them. Transfer to a large bowl and use a fork or potato masher to mash them until smooth. Let cool. • Mix in the butter, flour, Parmesan, and egg. Season with salt and pepper. • Spread the mixture out on a buttered surface to a thickness of 1/2 inch (1 cm) and let cool completely. • Mix the Emmental, cream, and egg yolk into the Béchamel sauce. Season with salt, pepper, and nutmeg. • Cut the potato mixture into 1 1/4-inch (3-cm) squares. Arrange the gnocchi in the prepared baking dish, alternating with the Béchamel sauce. Sprinkle with Parmesan. • Bake for 15–20 minutes, or until the cheese is bubbling. • Serve hot.

Serves 6 • Prep: 30 min • Cooking: 40 min • Level: 1

- 2 lb/1 kg baking/floury potatoes
- generous 1/3 cup/100 g butter, cut up
- 1 1/3 cups/200 g all-purpose/plain flour
- 3 tablespoons freshly grated Parmesan cheese
- 1 large egg
- salt and freshly ground white pepper
- 1/2 cup/60 g freshly grated Emmental cheese
- 1/4 cup/60 ml heavy/double cream
- 1 large egg yolk
- 2 cups/500 ml Béchamel Sauce (made with 2 tablespoons butter, 2 tablespoons flour, and 2 cups/500 ml milk)
- salt and freshly ground white pepper
- 1/8 teaspoon freshly grated nutmeg
- 5 tablespoons freshly grated Parmesan cheese

EMILIA-ROMAGNA

The homeland of Parmesan cheese and prosciutto, the people of Emilia-Romagna seem wonderfully advantaged with an abundance of internationally renowned produce at their fingertips. Baked spinach tagliatelle is ideal as a hearty primo piatto as well as the warming tortellini baked in pastry. Ferrara is famous for its excellent cured meats and salami. If you're looking for something simpler, try the delicious pinched pasta bows in stock for a winter pick-me-up.

Baked macaroni with ham and mushrooms (see page 87)

TORTELLINI, BOLOGNA STYLE

Tortellini bolognesi

- 4 oz/150 g lean sliced pork
- salt
- 4 oz/100 g mortadella (without pistachios and pepper)
- 4 oz/80 g prosciutto/ Parma ham
- 1 large egg, lightly beaten
- 3 tablespoons freshly grated Parmesan cheese
- freshly ground black pepper
- $1/8$ teaspoon freshly grated nutmeg
- Homemade Pasta Dough (see page 64), made with $2^1/3$ cups/ 350 g all-purpose/plain flour and 3 eggs
- $2^1/2$ quarts/2.5 liters meat stock or broth

Dry-fry the pork in a nonstick frying pan. Begin cooking over high heat, then turn them once to seal. Reduce the heat and cook for 4–5 minutes until cooked through. • Remove from heat, season with salt, and let cool. • Chop the pork with the mortadella and prosciutto in a food processor until finely ground. • Add half the egg (reserve the remaining portion for another use) and Parmesan. Season with salt, pepper, and nutmeg. Transfer to a bowl and refrigerate for 2 hours. • Form into $1/2$-inch (1-cm) balls and set aside. • Roll out the pasta dough on a lightly floured surface. Cut the dough into 1-inch (3.5-cm) squares or into 1-inch (3.5 cm) rounds. Put a ball of filling in the center of each. • Seal the pasta and place them upon a wooden board or a floured cloth. • Bring the stock to a boil in two separate saucepans: $2^3/4$ cups (680 ml) to cook the tortellini and use the remainder to serve them. • Cook the pasta in the boiling stock for 1–2 minutes, until al dente. Drain and transfer to soup bowls with the remaining boiling stock.

Serves 6–8 • Prep: 60 min + 2 hr to chill • Cooking: 20 min • Level: 3

RAVIOLI, ROMAGNA STYLE

Ravioli romagnoli

Other excellent dressings are flakes of white truffle or a simple tomato sauce with grated Parmesan cheese.

Filling: Beat the Ricotta in a large bowl until creamy. • Add the eggs, beating until just blended. • Add the egg yolk, parsley, and $3/4$ cup (90 g) of the Parmesan. Season with nutmeg, salt, and pepper. • Roll out the dough to a thickness of $1/8$ inch (3 mm). • Use a fluted pastry wheel to cut the dough into 3-inch (8-cm) squares. • Drop $1/2$ teaspoon of the Ricotta mixture just off-center of each square, then close each one to form an oblong. Press the three open sides with the tines of a fork to seal and decorate. • Cook the pasta in small batches in salted boiling water for 3–4 minutes, until al dente. • Use a slotted spoon to transfer to a serving dish, drizzle with butter and sprinkle with the remaining Parmesan, continuing to fill the bowl in layers until all the ravioli are cooked.

Serves 6 • Prep: 2 hr • Cooking: 20 min • Level: 3

Filling
- $3^1/4$ cups/810 g Ricotta cheese, strained through a fine mesh
- 2 large eggs + 1 large egg yolk
- 2 tablespoons finely chopped fresh parsley
- $1^1/2$ cups/180 g freshly grated Parmesan cheese
- $1/8$ teaspoon freshly grated nutmeg
- salt and freshly ground white pepper

- One rectangle of Homemade Pasta Dough (see page 64), made with $2^2/3$ cups/ 400 g all-purpose/plain flour and 4 eggs

To serve
- $1/2$ cup/125 g butter, melted

MAKING CAPPELLETTI AND TORTELLINI

1. *To make Cappelletti:* Lay the strips of pasta dough on the pastry board and use a pastry wheel to cut into even squares. Fold over into a triangle, making sure the tips meet.

2. Join the two tips of the base of the triangle to make *cappelletti.*

To make pointed tortellini: Fold the piece opposite the base in half. Join the two corners of the base with the folded piece.

To make rounded tortellini: Use the same procedure to make rounded tortellini. Lay the strips of pasta dough on a pastry board and use a round pastry wheel to cut out rounds. Add the filling.

2. Fold the pasta in half and fold into a crescent shape. Fold in half lengthways and join the two ends to make a ring.

Tortellini, Bologna style

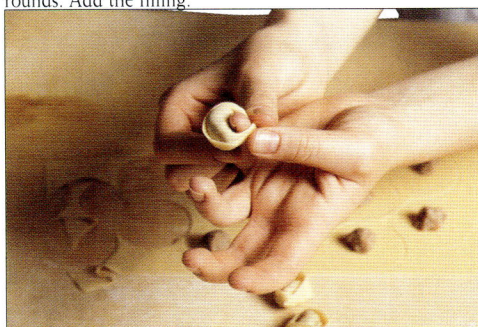

Homemade pasta with beans

HOMEMADE PASTA WITH BEANS
Maltagliati con i fagioli

- 1 lb/500 g fresh shelled beans, such as borlotti beans
- 8 cups/2 liters cold water
- 2 cloves garlic
- 1 bunch fresh sage
- 2 tablespoons extra-virgin olive oil
- salt

Pasta Dough
- 2 cups/300 g all-purpose/plain flour
- 1/4 teaspoon salt
- 3 large eggs

Sauce
- 2 cloves garlic, finely chopped
- 2 tablespoons finely chopped fresh parsley
- 2 tablespoons extra-virgin olive oil
- 6 firm-ripe tomatoes, coarsely chopped
- salt
- freshly ground black pepper

Place the beans in a large saucepan with the water, 2 cloves garlic, sage, and oil. Bring to a boil and simmer over low heat for 1 hour until the beans are tender. • Season with salt and drain, reserving the water. • Pasta Dough: Sift the flour and salt onto a surface and make a well in the center. Break the eggs into the well and mix in to make a smooth dough. Knead for 15–20 minutes, until smooth and elastic. Shape the dough into a ball, wrap in plastic wrap (cling film), and let rest for 30 minutes. • Sauce: Sauté the chopped garlic and parsley in the oil in a Dutch oven (casserole) over medium heat for 2 minutes until the garlic is pale gold. • Stir in the tomatoes and season with salt. • Cook over medium heat for 20 minutes. • Add the beans and a few tablespoons of the cooking water. • Roll out the dough on a lightly floured surface into a thin sheet and cut it into irregularly shaped pieces. • Cook the pasta in a large pot of salted boiling water until al dente. • Drain and serve with the sauce and plenty of black pepper.

Serves 6 • Prep: 75 min + 30 min to rest the dough • Cooking: 90 min • Level: 2

CAPPELLETTI, PARMA STYLE
Cappelletti di Parma o Anolini

Filling: Sauté the beef, onion, carrot, celery, garlic, bay leaf, sage, and rosemary in the butter in a Dutch oven (casserole) over medium heat for 5 minutes, until the meat and vegetables are browned all over. • Pour in the tomato paste mixture. Add the parsley and season with salt and pepper. Cover and cook over very low heat for about 3 hours. • The meat should be tender enough to crumble and the sauce should be very dense. • Pasta Dough: Sift the flour and salt onto a surface and make a well in the center. Break the eggs into the well and mix in to make a smooth dough. Knead for 15–20 minutes, until smooth and elastic. Shape the dough into a ball, wrap in plastic wrap (cling film), and let rest for 30 minutes. • Chop the beef and sauce in a food processor until finely ground. • Sauté the chopped mixture in a nonstick frying pan over medium heat for 1 minute. • Mix in 2 tablespoons of the bread crumbs. Transfer the mixture to a large bowl and let cool to lukewarm. • Mix in the Parmesan, egg, nutmeg, salt and pepper, and the remaining 3 tablespoons of the bread crumbs if the mixture does not hold its shape. • Roll out the dough on a lightly floured surface until paper-thin. Cut into 1 1/2-inch (4-cm) squares and drop pellets of the filling into the centers. • Fold them one by one into cappelletti (see page 70). • Cook the pasta in the boiling stock for 3–5 minutes, until al dente. • Drain and drizzle with butter. Sprinkle with Parmesan and serve.

Serves 6 • Prep: 2 hr 30 min + 30 min to rest the dough • Cooking: 3 hr 30 min • Level: 3

Filling
- 2 lb/1 kg stew beef, cut into pieces
- 1 onion, finely chopped
- 1 carrot, finely chopped
- 1 stalk celery, finely chopped
- 1 clove garlic
- 1/2 bay leaf
- 2 leaves fresh sage
- 1 sprig fresh rosemary
- 2 tablespoons butter, cut up
- 2 tablespoons tomato paste/concentrate dissolved in 2/3 cup/150 ml beef stock or broth
- 1 tablespoon finely chopped fresh parsley
- salt and freshly ground white pepper

Pasta Dough
- 2 cups/300 g all-purpose/plain flour
- 1/4 teaspoon salt
- 3 large eggs
- 5 tablespoons fine dry bread crumbs
- 1/2 cup/60 g freshly grated Parmesan cheese
- 1 large egg
- 1/8 teaspoon freshly grated nutmeg
- salt and freshly ground white pepper
- 8 cups/2 liters beef stock or broth, boiling
- generous 1/3 cup/100 g butter, melted
- 3/4 cup/90 g freshly grated Parmesan cheese

FRESH PASTA WITH SAUSAGE

Giuget

- 1 cup/100 g dried cannellini or borlotti beans, soaked overnight and drained
- 8 cups/2 liters cold water

Pasta Dough
- 1 cup/150 g all-purpose/plain flour
- 1 cup/150 g finely ground cornmeal
- 1/4 teaspoon salt
- 2/3 cup/150 ml water, + more as needed

Sauce
- 1/2 carrot, finely chopped
- 1/2 stalk celery, finely chopped
- 1/2 onion, finely chopped
- 3/4 cup/90 g diced pancetta or bacon
- 2 tablespoons extra-virgin olive oil
- 1 Italian sausage, crumbled
- salt
- 1 tablespoon tomato paste/concentrate
- freshly ground black pepper

Transfer the beans to a large saucepan with the water. Bring to a boil, cover, and simmer over low heat for 1 hour. • Drain, reserving the cooking liquid. • Pasta Dough: Sift the flour, cornmeal, and salt onto a surface and make a well in the center. Mix in enough water to make a smooth dough. Knead for 15–20 minutes, until smooth and elastic. Shape the dough into a ball, wrap in plastic wrap (cling film), and let rest for 30 minutes. • Roll out the dough to a thickness of 1/8 inch (3 mm). Use a fluted pastry wheel to cut into 3/4-inch (2-cm) squares. • Sauce: Sauté the carrot, celery, onion, and pancetta in the oil in a small frying pan over a medium heat for 5 minutes until the pancetta is crispy. • Add the sausage and cook for 2 minutes until browned all over. • Season with salt and cook over low heat for 10 minutes. • Stir in the tomato puree and beans. Simmer over medium heat for 5 minutes. • Season with salt and pepper and pour in the reserved cooking liquid from the beans. • Cook the pasta in a large pot of salted boiling water for about 5 minutes, or until al dente. • Drain them, leaving them wet, and add to the sauce, which should be slightly liquid. Serve hot.

Serves 6 • Prep: 40 min + overnight to soak the beans + 30 min to rest the dough • Cooking: 1 hr 40 min • Level: 2

PASTINA IN STOCK

Malfattini romagnoli

Easy-to-make soup pasta, known in some areas as monfettini or grattini (the latter name refers to the fact that the pasta can be grated as soon as it has dried).

Pasta Dough: Sift the flour, salt, and nutmeg onto a surface and make a well in the center. Break the eggs into the well and mix in with the Parmesan to make a smooth dough. Knead for 15–20 minutes, until elastic. Shape the dough into a ball, wrap in plastic wrap, and let rest for 10 minutes. • Divide the dough into quarters and roll it out to a thickness of about 3/4 inch (2 cm). Let dry on a kitchen cloth for 10 minutes. • Cut the dough into irregularly shaped slices and let dry. Cut the slices finely until the pasta resembles grains of rice. • Spread out on a clean surface and let dry for at least 1 hour in a dry, airy place. They can be kept for 4 days in an airtight container. • Bring the stock to a boil and cook the pastina until al dente. The cooking time depends on how thoroughly the pasta has been dried. Sprinkle with Parmesan and serve.

Serves 6 • Prep: 60 min + 10 min to rest the dough + 60 min to dry the pasta • Cooking: 15 min • Level: 2

Pasta Dough
- 2 2/3 cups/400 g all-purpose/plain flour
- 1/4 teaspoon salt
- 1/8 teaspoon freshly grated nutmeg
- 3 tablespoons freshly grated Parmesan cheese
- 4 large eggs

To serve
- 2 quarts/2 liters meat stock or broth
- 3/4 cup/90 g freshly grated Parmesan cheese

Fresh pasta with sausage

Pinched pasta bows in stock

ROMAGNOL-STUFFED PASTA

Cappelletti di magro romagnoli

Filling

- $3/4$ cup/180 ml creamy soft cheese
- $3/4$ cup/180 g Ricotta cheese
- $3/4$ cup/90 g freshly grated Parmesan cheese
- 2 eggs
- $1/4$ teaspoon freshly grated nutmeg
- $1/8$ teaspoon salt

- One rectangle of Homemade Pasta Dough (see page 64), made with $2^2/3$ cups/ 400 g all-purpose/plain flour and 4 large eggs

To serve

- $1^1/2$ quarts/1.5 liters meat stock

Filling: Mix the cheeses, eggs, nutmeg, and salt in a large bowl. • Roll out the dough on a lightly floured surface to a thickness of $1/4$ inch (5 mm). Cut into 3-inch (8-cm) squares. • Fit a pastry bag with a $1/4$-inch (5-mm) plain tip. Fill the pastry bag with the filling, twist the opening tightly closed, and squeeze the filling into the centers of the pasta squares. Fold them over into triangles and join the tips to make *cappellacci*. • Cook the pasta in the stock for 2–3 minutes, until al dente. • Serve hot.

Serves 6 • Prep: 2 hr 30 min • Cooking: 90 min • Level: 3

PINCHED PASTA BOWS IN STOCK

Strichetti in brodo

Sift the flour, salt, and nutmeg onto a surface and make a well in the center. Break the eggs into the well and mix in to make a smooth dough. Knead for 15–20 minutes, until smooth and elastic. Shape the dough into a ball, wrap in plastic wrap (cling film), and let rest for 10 minutes. • Roll out the dough to a sheet that is not too thin and easily handled. (You can use a pasta machine with the thickness set at the third-to-finest thickness.) • Use a saw-toothed ravioli cutter to cut the sheet of dough into $1/2$ x $3/4$-inch (1 x 2-cm) rectangles. Use your thumb and index finger to pinch the little rectangles in the center. Let the bows dry on a flour-dusted wooden surface. • Meanwhile bring the stock to a boil in a large saucepan. Cook the pasta in the stock for 2–3 minutes, until al dente. • Serve in individual bowls, sprinkled with Parmesan.

Serves 6 • Prep: 60 min + 10 min to rest the pasta • Cooking: 10 min • Level: 2

- $2^2/3$ cups/400 g all-purpose/plain flour
- $1/4$ teaspoon salt
- $1/8$ teaspoon freshly grated nutmeg
- 4 large eggs
- 6 cups/1.5 liters meat stock or broth
- $3/4$ cup/90 g freshly grated Parmesan cheese

Fresh Pasta

GARGANELLI WITH PEAS

Garganelli con i piselli

- 12 oz/350 g Italian sausage, crumbled
- 5 tablespoons butter, cut up
- 1^1/$_3$ cups/310 ml milk
- ^{1}/$_8$ teaspoon freshly grated nutmeg
- ^{1}/$_2$ onion, finely chopped
- 2 tablespoons extra-virgin olive oil
- 2^3/$_4$ cups/350 g fresh or frozen peas
- ^{1}/$_8$ teaspoon sugar
- ^{1}/$_3$–^{3}/$_4$ cup/80 ml–180 ml meat stock or broth
- salt and freshly ground white pepper
- 1 lb/400 g garganelli pasta (see below) or fresh penne pasta
- ^{1}/$_4$ cup/30 g freshly grated Parmesan cheese

Sauté the sausage in 4 tablespoons of butter in a medium saucepan over medium heat for 5 minutes. • Pour in the milk and add the nutmeg. Cook over low heat for 15 minutes until the milk has evaporated. Set aside. • Sauté the onion in the oil in a separate saucepan for 5 minutes until softened. • Add the peas and sugar. • Pour in ^{1}/$_3$ cup (80 ml) of stock if the peas are frozen; pour in ^{3}/$_4$ cup (180 ml) if the peas are fresh. Simmer for 5 minutes. Season with salt and pepper. • Transfer the peas and sausage to a frying pan and sauté over low heat for 1 minute. • Cook the pasta in a large pot of salted boiling water until al dente. • Drain, reserving 1 cup (250 ml) of cooking water. Add the pasta to the sauce, adding some cooking water if the sauce is too dry. • Remove from the heat and dot with the remaining 1 tablespoon of butter. Sprinkle with Parmesan and serve.

Serves 4 • Prep: 15 min • Cooking: 40 min • Level: 1

GARGANELLI

Garganelli are made by wrapping small squares of dough around a rod and running them over a pettine (literally, comb). A rod and pettine can be bought at any good cookware store. However, the end of a wooden spoon and a ridged cutting board can also be used.

Sift the flour onto a surface and make a well in the center. Break the eggs into the well and mix in with the Parmesan and nutmeg to make a smooth dough. Knead for 15–20 minutes, until elastic. Shape the dough into a ball, wrap in plastic wrap, and let rest for 30 minutes. • Run the dough through the pasta machine at the second last thickness setting. Cut into 1^1/$_2$-inch (3.5 cm) squares. • Roll them up, starting from a corner, on the end of the rod. • Turn them on the "pettine" while pressing down slightly. • Slide them off the rod and let dry on a kitchen cloth for about 30 minutes.

Serves 4 • Prep: 60 min + 30 min to rest the dough • Level: 3

- 2^2/$_3$ cups/400 g all-purpose/plain flour
- 4 large eggs
- ^{1}/$_4$ cup/30 g freshly grated Parmesan cheese
- ^{1}/$_8$ teaspoon freshly grated nutmeg
- ^{1}/$_4$ cup/30 g freshly grated Parmesan cheese (optional)

MIXED TAGLIATELLE WITH GORGONZOLA

Paglia e fieno al gorgonzola

- ^{1}/$_4$ cup/60 g butter, cut up
- 8 oz/250 g Gorgonzola Dolce, cut into small cubes
- ^{2}/$_3$ cup/150 ml heavy/double cream (or milk)
- salt and freshly ground white pepper
- 6 oz/180 g fresh egg tagliatelle
- 6 oz/180 g fresh green tagliatelle
- ^{1}/$_4$ cup/30 g freshly grated Parmesan cheese (optional)

Melt the butter in a medium saucepan over low heat and add the Gorgonzola and cream. Season with salt and pepper. Cook over low heat, stirring constantly, until the cheese has melted. • Cook both types of pasta together in a large pot of salted boiling water until al dente. • Transfer 1 tablespoon of the cooking water to each serving bowl to warm it. Discard the water. • Drain the pasta and transfer to the warmed serving bowls. Add the Gorgonzola sauce, mixing carefully with two forks. • Sprinkle with Parmesan, if desired.

Serves 4 • Prep: 10 min • Cooking: 10 min • Level: 1

GARGANELLI WITH CREAMY SAUSAGE SAUCE

Garganelli con la salsiccia

Sauté the onion in 1 tablespoon of butter in a frying pan over low heat for 10 minutes, until the onion is translucent. • Add the sausage, crumbling it with a fork. Sauté over high heat for 3 minutes until browned all over. • Pour in the cream and cook over very low heat for about 20 minutes, or until reduced by half. • Season with nutmeg, salt, and pepper. • Cook the pasta in a large pot of salted boiling water until al dente. • Drain and add to the sauce. • Sprinkle with Parmesan and remove from the heat. Dot with the remaining 1 tablespoon butter, letting it melt into the pasta. Serve hot.

Serves 4 • Prep: 20 min • Cooking: 40 min • Level: 1

- ^{1}/$_2$ onion, finely chopped
- 2 tablespoons butter, cut up
- 10 oz/300 g Italian pork sausage, crumbled
- ^{3}/$_4$ cup/180 ml heavy/double cream
- ^{1}/$_8$ teaspoon freshly grated nutmeg
- salt and freshly ground black pepper
- 12 oz/350 g garganelli pasta (see below) or penne pasta
- ^{1}/$_4$ cup/30 g freshly grated Parmesan cheese

SPINACH GNOCCHI WITH TOMATO SAUCE

Gnocchi verdi

Gnocchi

- 2 lb/1 kg baking/floury potatoes
- 1 cup/150 g all-purpose/plain flour
- 4 oz/100 g spinach leaves, cooked, squeezed dry, and finely chopped
- 3 tablespoons freshly grated Parmesan cheese
- 1 large egg, lightly beaten
- 1/8 teaspoon salt

Tomato Sauce

- 3/4 cup/90 g thinly sliced pancetta or bacon (thin strips)
- 1/4 cup/60 g butter, cut up
- scant 1/2 cup/100 g peeled plum tomatoes, pressed through a fine-mesh strainer (passata)
- 2/3 cup/150 ml heavy/double cream
- salt

Gnocchi: Cook the potatoes in salted boiling water for 15–20 minutes, or until tender. • Drain, peel them, and use a fork or potato masher to mash them. • Transfer to a large bowl and mix in the flour, spinach, Parmesan, egg, and salt. • Dip your hands in flour and knead the mixture until the dough is smooth. • Form the dough into logs 2/3-inch (1.5-cm) in diameter and cut them into 1 1/4-inch (3-cm) sections. • Tomato Sauce: Sauté the pancetta in the butter in a small saucepan over low heat for 5 minutes, until the fat has become translucent. • Stir in the tomatoes and cook over low heat for 10 minutes. • Pour in the cream and season with salt. Remove from the heat. • Cook the gnocchi in small batches in a large pot of salted boiling water for 3–5 minutes, until they rise to the surface. Use a slotted spoon to transfer them to serving plates. Top with the sauce and serve.

Serves 4 • Prep: 40 min • Cooking: 40 min • Level: 2

PASTA SPIRALS WITH SAUSAGE SAUCE

Gramigna con la salsiccia

Sauté the onion in the butter in a large frying pan over low heat for 5 minutes, until softened. • Increase the heat and add the sausage. Sauté over high heat for 10 minutes. • Pour in the wine, tomato sauce, and milk. Season with salt and pepper and cook over low heat for about 20 minutes, or until the sauce has reduced by half. • Cook the pasta in a large pot of salted boiling water until al dente. • Drain and add to the sauce. Sprinkle with Parmesan and serve.

Serves 4 • Prep: 15 min • Cooking: 45 min • Level: 1

- 1 large onion, finely chopped
- 2 tablespoons butter, cut up
- 3 large Italian sausages, crumbled
- 1/4 cup/60 ml dry white wine
- 1/4 cup/60 ml store-bought tomato sauce or 1 tablespoon tomato paste/concentrate
- 1/4 cup/60 ml milk
- salt and freshly ground black pepper
- 12 oz/350 g dried gramigna pasta (short, curved egg pasta)
- 1 cup/125 g freshly grated Parmesan cheese

Pasta spirals
with sausage sauce

Ricotta gnocchi

RICOTTA GNOCCHI

Gnocchi di ricotta

Gnocchi
- 2¹/₂ cups/625 g Ricotta cheese
- 2 cups/300 g all-purpose/plain flour
- 2 large eggs + 3 large egg yolks
- 1¹/₄ cups/150 g freshly grated Parmesan cheese
- salt and freshly ground white pepper

To serve
- 2 cups/500 ml Ligurian Meat Sauce (see page 17)

If the Ricotta is very soft, drain it in a fine mesh strainer. • Mix the Ricotta, flour, eggs and egg yolks, ³/₄ cup (90 g) of Parmesan, and salt and pepper in a large bowl to make a fairly stiff dough. Break off pieces of dough, shape them into ²/₃-inch (1.5 cm) thick logs on a floured board and cut into 1¹/₄ inch (3-cm) sections. • Cook the gnocchi in small batches in a large pot of salted boiling water for 3–5 minutes, until they rise to the surface. • Use a slotted spoon to remove the gnocchi and arrange them in a serving dish. Cover with the meat sauce. Sprinkle with the remaining ¹/₂ cup (60 g) of Parmesan and serve.

Serves 6 • Prep: 40 min • Cooking: 20 min • Level: 2

PASTA WITH PEA AND SAUSAGE SAUCE

Maccheroncini con sugo di piselli e salsiccia

Sauté the onion in the butter in a medium saucepan over medium heat for 3 minutes, until softened. • Stir in the tomato sauce and sausage. • Pour in the cream and cook over low heat for 15 minutes. • Sauté the garlic and sage in the oil in a large frying pan over low heat for 3 minutes, until the garlic is pale gold. • Stir in the peas, sugar, and water. • Cook for 4–8 minutes, until the peas are tender, adding more water if needed. • Season with salt and pepper, add the parsley, and remove from the heat. • Cook the pasta in a large pot of salted boiling water until al dente. • Drain and add to the sauce. • Sprinkle with Parmesan and serve.

Serves 4 • Prep: 30 min • Cooking: 45 min • Level: 1

- ¹/₂ onion, chopped
- 1 tablespoon butter
- 1 tablespoon unseasoned tomato sauce, store-bought or homemade
- 8 oz/200 g Italian sausage, crumbled
- generous ¹/₃ cup/100 ml heavy/double cream
- 1 clove garlic, chopped
- 1 small bunch fresh sage, finely chopped
- 2 tablespoons extra-virgin olive oil
- 2 cups/250 g fresh or frozen peas
- ¹/₈ teaspoon sugar
- 1 cup/250 ml hot water, + more as needed
- salt and freshly ground black pepper
- 1 tablespoon finely chopped fresh parsley
- 12 oz/350 g sedanini or ditalini pasta
- ¹/₄ cup/30 g freshly grated Parmesan cheese

Fresh Pasta

SPINACH ROLL

Rotolo ripieno

- 2 cups/500 g cooked, drained spinach
- 1/2 cup/125 g butter, melted
- 1 1/4 cups/310 g Ricotta cheese
- 1 cup/125 g freshly grated Parmesan cheese
- salt and freshly ground white pepper
- One rectangle of Homemade Pasta Dough (see page 64), made with 2 cups/300 g all-purpose/plain flour and 3 eggs
- 1 small bunch sage

Finely chop the spinach and sauté in 7 tablespoons of butter in a large frying pan over medium heat for 2 minutes. • Remove from the heat and let cool completely. • Drain the Ricotta in a fine mesh strainer and mix it in with 3/4 cup (90 g) of Parmesan. Season with salt and pepper. • Use a large rubber spatula to spread the mixture over the pasta rectangle, leaving a small border at the edges. • Roll up and wrap the dough in a clean kitchen cloth. Tie each end with kitchen string and tie the roll in the center. • Bring a long saucepan (a fish poacher is ideal) filled with salted water to the boil. Lower the pasta roll into it and cook over low heat for 30 minutes. • Remove from the water and remove from the cloth. • Slice the pasta roll 1/2-inch (1-cm) thick and arrange on serving plates. • Melt the remaining tablespoon of butter with the sage in a small saucepan. Discard the sage. Pour over the slices and sprinkle with remaining 1/4 cup (30 g) of Parmesan.

Serves 6 • Prep: 60 min • Cooking: 40 min • Level: 3

PUMPKIN CAPPELLACCI, FERRARA STYLE

Cappellacci di zucca ferraresi

Cappellacci literally means ugly hats.

Preheat the oven to 400°F/200°C/gas 6. • Bake the squash on a large baking sheet for 40–45 minutes, or until tender. • Let cool. Use a tablespoon to remove the flesh from the peel. • Place the squash flesh in a medium saucepan with the butter over high heat. Cook, stirring occasionally, until smooth and pureed. The mixture should be fairly dry. Measure out 2 cups (500 g) and let cool. • Transfer to a large bowl and mix in the Parmesan, eggs, bread crumbs, nutmeg, and salt and pepper. Cover with a kitchen cloth and refrigerate for 30 minutes. • Roll out the dough on a lightly floured surface to a thickness of 1/4 inch (5 mm). Cut into 3-inch (8-cm) squares. • Fit a pastry bag with a 1/4-inch (5-mm) plain tip. Fill the pastry bag with the filling, twist the opening tightly closed, and squeeze the filling into the centers of the pasta squares. Fold them over into triangles and join the tips to make *cappellacci*. • Melt the butter in a saucepan with the sage. Discard the sage. • Cook the pasta in a large pot of salted boiling water for 2–3 minutes, until al dente. • Drain and drizzle with the melted butter and sage. Sprinkle with Parmesan and serve.

Serves 6–8 • Prep: 90 min + 30 min to chill • Cooking: 90 min • Level: 3

- 4 lb/2 kg winter squash or pumpkin, thickly sliced and seeded
- 1/4 cup/60 g butter, cut up
- Pasta Dough made with 4 cups/600 g all-purpose/plain flour and 6 large eggs (see page 64)
- 3/4 cup/90 g freshly grated Parmesan cheese
- 3 large eggs
- 4 tablespoons fine dry bread crumbs
- 1/8 teaspoon freshly grated nutmeg
- salt and freshly ground white pepper
- generous 1/3 cup/100 g butter, melted
- 1 bunch fresh sage
- 6–8 tablespoons freshly grated Parmesan cheese

MAKING A PASTA ROLL

1. Roll out a square of fresh pasta dough on a dry kitchen cloth. Spread the filling evenly over it, leaving a short border around the edges.

2. Using the kitchen cloth as a guide, roll up the dough.

3. Roll it up very tightly so that the pasta roll sticks firmly together.

4. Wrap the kitchen cloth around the pasta roll, tying the ends with cooking string. Tie it around the center as well to help preserve its shape.

5. Cook the pasta roll in a long saucepan (such as a fish kettle or fish poacher) that holds it comfortably one-quarter full with salted water.

6. When it is cooked, use the poaching basket to remove it from the water.

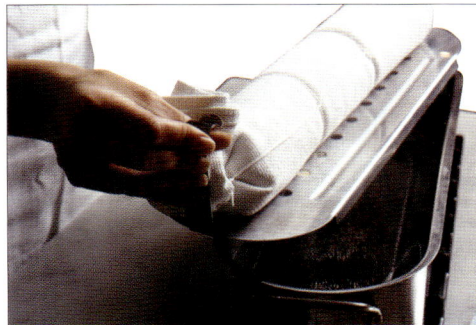

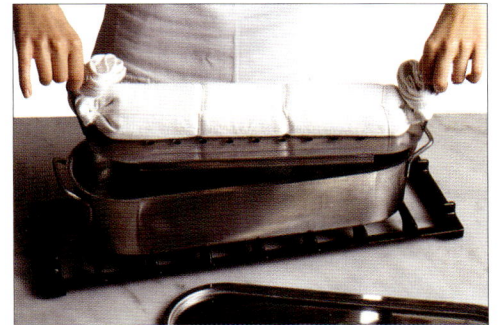

Baked Pasta

BAKED SPINACH TAGLIATELLE

Pasticcio di tagliatelle verdi

- 1 lb/400 g fresh store-bought spinach tagliatelle
- 1/2 cup/60 g prosciutto/Parma ham, finely chopped
- 1/4 cup/60 g butter, cut up
- 2 oz/50 g dried mushrooms, soaked in warm water for 15 minutes
- salt and freshly ground white pepper
- 2³/4 cups/680 ml Béchamel sauce (made with 1/4 cup/60 g butter, 1/4 cup/30 g all-purpose/plain flour, and 2³/4 cups/680 ml milk, page 10)
- 1/4 cup/30 g freshly grated Parmesan cheese

Preheat the oven to 375°F/190°C/gas 5. • Butter a baking dish. • Par-cook the tagliatelle by cooking for half the time suggested on the package. Drain and run under cold water to stop the cooking. • Sauté the prosciutto in the butter in a large frying pan over low heat for about 5 minutes, until crispy. • Drain the mushrooms, straining the water through a coffee filter or paper towel to remove grit. Chop them coarsely • Add to the prosciutto. Cook over medium heat for 6–7 minutes, or until the mushrooms are tender, adding the reserved water. • Season with salt and pepper. • Add the pasta and mix in 2¹/2 cups (625 ml) of Béchamel and 3 tablespoons of Parmesan. • Transfer to the prepared baking dish and spread over the remaining 1/4 cup (60 ml) of Béchamel. Sprinkle with the remaining 1 tablespoon of Parmesan. • Bake for 30–35 minutes, or until golden brown. • Serve hot.

Serves 4 • Prep: 20 min • Cooking: 45 min • Level: 2

TORTELLINI BAKED IN PASTRY

Pasticcio di tortellini

Short-Crust Dough: Sift the flour and salt into a large bowl. Stir in the sugar. • Use a pastry blender to cut in the butter until the mixture resembles coarse crumbs. • Add enough cold water to form a stiff dough. Knead briefly and press the dough into a disk. Wrap in plastic wrap (cling film) and refrigerate for 30 minutes. • Filling: Blanch the tortellini by cooking for half the time suggested on the package. Drain and run under cold water to stop the cooking. • Preheat the oven to 350°F/180°C/gas 4. • Roll out the dough and use it to line a springform pan (see step-by-step below). • Fill with one-third of the tortellini, one-third of the Béchamel, and one-third of the meat sauce. Continue until you have used up all the ingredients. Sprinkle with Parmesan. • Gather the dough scraps, re-roll, and top the pan with a pastry round. • Bake for 45–50 minutes, or until the pastry is golden brown. If it begins to turn dark during baking, cover with aluminum foil. • Serve hot.

Serves 6 • Prep: 30 min + 30 min to chill the dough • Cooking: 60 min • Level: 3

Short-Crust Dough
- 2¹/3 cups/350 g all-purpose/plain flour
- 1 teaspoon salt
- 1 tablespoon sugar
- 3/4 cup/180 g butter, cut up
- 1/4 cup/60 ml cold water, + more if needed

Filling
- 1 lb/500 g fresh store-bought tortellini pasta
- 2 cups/500 ml Béchamel sauce (made with 1/4 cup/60 g butter, 1/4 cup/30 g flour, and 2 cups/500 ml milk, page 10)
- 1²/3 cups/400 g Ligurian Meat Sauce (see page 17)
- 3/4 cup/90 g freshly grated Parmesan cheese

MAKING BAKED PASTA IN PASTRY

1. Use pastry dough to line the pan sides. Let the dough extend 1/2 inch (1 cm) onto the bottom and overlap slightly on top.

2. Place an 8-inch (20-cm) disk of dough on the pan bottom.

3. Prick the dough all over with the tines of a fork.

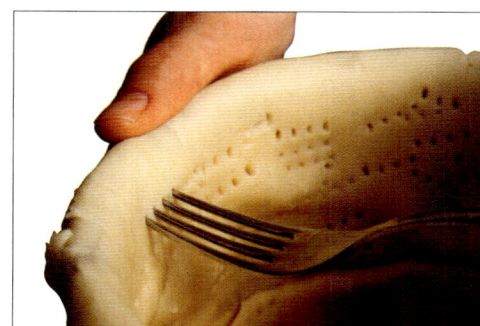

4. Make a layer of tortellini (or any other chosen pasta), meat sauce, and Béchamel sauce inside the pastry.

5. Continue making layers, alternating the ingredients and topping with plenty of Béchamel sauce.

6. Cover with a disk of dough, laying it on top of the Béchamel sauce. Fold back the overlapping dough from the side of the pan to create a decorative border.

Baked Pasta

BAKED RAVIOLI

Ravioli al forno

Pasta Dough
- 2²/₃ cups/400 g all-purpose/plain flour
- ¼ teaspoon salt
- 4 large eggs

Filling
- 2¹/₂ cups/600 g spinach leaves, cooked, squeezed dry, and finely chopped
- ¼ cup/60 g butter, cut up
- salt and freshly ground white pepper
- ¹/₈ teaspoon freshly grated nutmeg
- 1 tablespoon all-purpose/plain flour
- ¼ cup/60 ml milk
- 1 large egg yolk
- ¹/₂ cup/60 g freshly grated Parmesan cheese

To serve
- 6 tablespoons butter, melted
- ³/₄ cup/180 ml unseasoned tomato sauce, store-bought or homemade
- 1 cup/125 g freshly grated Parmesan cheese

Pasta Dough: Sift the flour and salt onto a surface and make a well in the center. Break the eggs into the well and mix in to make a smooth dough. Knead for 15–20 minutes, until smooth and elastic. Shape the dough into a ball, wrap in plastic wrap (cling film), and let rest for 30 minutes. • Filling: Sauté the spinach in the butter in a medium frying pan over medium heat for 2 minutes. Season with salt, pepper, and nutmeg and sprinkle with flour. • Pour in the milk and let it reduce over low heat for 5–8 minutes until the mixture is moist but no liquid remains. • Remove from the heat, let cool, and mix in the egg yolk and Parmesan. • Roll out the dough on a lightly floured surface until paper-thin. Cut into 2¹/₂-inch (6-cm) wide strips and arrange pellets of filling near one edge, about ³/₄ inch (2 cm) apart. Fold each strip of dough lengthwise to cover the filling. Seal, after making sure no air pockets remain, then cut into squares with a saw-toothed ravioli cutter. The ravioli should be smooth on one side and crimped on three sides. • Lay the pasta on a kitchen cloth dusted with flour. • Preheat the oven to 400°F/200°C/gas 6. • Butter a baking dish. • Cook the pasta in small batches in a large pot of salted boiling water for 2–3 minutes, until al dente. • Use a slotted spoon to transfer to the prepared baking dish, filling the dish in layers with the ravioli, melted butter, tomato sauce, and the Parmesan. • Bake for 12–15 minutes, or until the cheese is bubbling. • Serve hot.

Serves 6 • Prep: 60 min + 30 min to rest the dough • Cooking: 45 min • Level: 3

BAKED MACARONI IN PASTRY

Pasticcio di maccheroni

Short-Crust Dough
- 3¹/₃ cups/500 g all-purpose/plain flour
- ¹/₂ teaspoon salt
- ¹/₂ cup/100 g granulated sugar
- 1 cup/250 g butter, cut up
- 2 large egg yolks
- 2 tablespoons brandy
- 1–2 tablespoons cold water (optional)

Sauce
- 5 tablespoons extra-virgin olive oil
- 1 bay leaf
- 1 sprig fresh sage, chopped
- 1 clove garlic
- 3 pigeons or quail, each weighing 4 oz/125 g, cleaned and quartered
- 6 tablespoons dry red wine
- 1 oz/30 g dried porcini mushrooms, soaked in warm water for 15 minutes and coarsely chopped
- scant ¹/₂ cup/100 g peeled plum tomatoes pressed through a fine-mesh strainer (passata)
- generous ¹/₃ cup/ 100 ml meat stock or broth
- ¹/₈ teaspoon freshly grated nutmeg
- salt and freshly ground white pepper
- 1 lb/400 g small dried macaroni
- ³/₄ cup/90 g freshly grated Parmesan cheese
- ¼ cup/60 g butter, cut up
- 1 large egg, lightly beaten

Set out a 9-inch (23-cm) springform pie dish. • Short-Crust Dough: Sift the flour and salt into a large bowl. Stir in the sugar. • Use a pastry blender to cut in the butter until the mixture resembles coarse crumbs. • Mix in the egg yolks and brandy to form a stiff dough, adding the water if needed. • Press the dough into a disk, wrap in plastic wrap (cling film), and refrigerate for 30 minutes. • Sauce: Heat the oil in a medium saucepan with the bay leaf, sage, and garlic over medium heat for 3 minutes, until the garlic is pale gold. Discard the garlic. • Increase the heat and sauté the pigeon for 2 minutes, until browned all over. • Pour in the wine, add the mushrooms, and cook until the wine has evaporated. • Stir in the tomatoes and ¼ cup (60 ml) of stock. Season with nutmeg, salt, and pepper. • Cover and cook over medium heat until the meat is tender, adding the remaining stock if the sauce begins to reduce. • Transfer the pigeon to a cutting board and let cool completely. Remove the large bones and return the meat to the pan. • Blanch the pasta by cooking for half the time indicated on the package in salted boiling water. • Drain and run under cold running water to stop the cooking. • Add to the sauce mixture and mix in the Parmesan and butter. • Roll out two-thirds of the pastry on a lightly floured surface to a thickness of ¼ inch (5 mm). Use the pastry to line the pie dish, letting the excess pastry overlap at the sides. • Fill with the pasta and sauce mixture and level the surface. • Roll out the remaining pastry into a circle to the size of the dish and place it on top. • Brush the top with egg, trimming off the extra pastry and rolling back the edge onto the top. Finish decoratively with finger and thumb. • Prick the dough all over with a fork and garnish the surface with pastry scraps. • Bake for 45–50 minutes, or until the pastry is golden brown. If it begins to turn dark during baking, cover with aluminum foil. • Serve hot.

Serves 6–8 • Prep: 2 hr + 30 min to chill the dough • Cooking: 90 min • Level: 3

Baked macaroni with mortadella

BAKED MACARONI WITH MORTADELLA

Maccheroni alla mortadella

- 7 oz/200 g mortadella, cut into small cubes
- 2 oz/60 g Swiss cheese, such as Gruyère, cut into small cubes
- generous $^3/_4$ cup/ 200 ml heavy/double cream
- $^3/_4$ cup/90 g freshly grated Parmesan cheese
- 12 oz/350 g pasta tubes, such as rigatoni
- salt and freshly ground black pepper

Preheat the oven to 400°F/200°C/gas 6. • Butter a baking dish. • Mix the mortadella and cheese with the cream and $^1/_4$ cup (30 g) of Parmesan in a large bowl. • Cook the pasta in a large pan of salted, boiling water for half the time indicated on the package. Drain and transfer to the bowl. Season with salt and pepper. Mix well and transfer to the prepared dish. • Sprinkle with the remaining $^1/_2$ cup (60 g) of Parmesan. • Bake for 15–20 minutes, or until a golden crust forms on the surface. • Serve hot.

Serves 4 • Prep: 10 min • Cooking: 30 min • Level: 1

POTATO GNOCCHI WITH TOMATO AND PARMESAN

Gnocchi di patate alla Parmigiana

- 2 tablespoons butter, cut up
- 1 lb/500 g firm-ripe tomatoes, peeled and coarsely chopped
- 1 clove garlic, lightly crushed but whole
- $^1/_2$ red onion, thinly sliced
- salt
- Ridged gnocchi made with 2 lb/1 kg potatoes (see page 130)
- $^3/_4$ cup/90 g freshly grated Parmesan cheese

Preheat the oven to 400°F/200°C/gas 6. • Melt the butter in a medium saucepan over medium heat. Add the tomatoes, garlic, onion, and salt. • Cover and cook for about 10 minutes, or until the tomatoes have broken down. Uncover and let reduce for 1 minute. • Remove from the heat and process in a food processor or blender until pureed. • Cook the gnocchi in small batches in a large pot of salted boiling water until they rise to the surface. Use a slotted spoon to transfer them to a baking dish. Cover with half the sauce and sprinkle with half the Parmesan. Make a second layer with the gnocchi, sauce, and Parmesan. • Bake for 12–15 minutes, or until the cheese is bubbling. • Serve hot.

Serves 4–6 • Prep: 30 min • Cooking: 30 min • Level: 1

BAKED MACARONI WITH HAM AND MUSHROOMS

Maccheroni al prosciutto gratinati

Preheat the oven to 400°F/200°C/gas 6. • Butter a large baking dish. • Mix $^1/_4$ cup (30 g) Parmesan into the Béchamel. • Sauté the mushrooms in 2 tablespoons of the butter in a frying pan over high heat for 2–3 minutes, until lightly golden. • Add the ham and cook for 3 minutes, until crispy. • Cook the pasta in a large pot of salted boiling water until just al dente. • Drain and arrange half the pasta in the prepared baking dish. Top with half the mushrooms and ham. Cover with half of the Béchamel. Make a second layer with the pasta, mushrooms and ham, and Béchamel. Sprinkle with the remaining $^1/_4$ cup (30 g) of Parmesan and dot with the remaining 2 tablespoons of butter. • Bake for 12–15 minutes, or until the cheese is bubbling and the surface is golden brown. • Serve hot.

Serves 6 • Prep: 30 min • Cooking: 60 min • Level: 2

- $^1/_2$ cup/60 g freshly grated Parmesan cheese
- 2 cups/500 ml Béchamel sauce (made with 3 tablespoons butter, 3 tablespoons flour, and 2 cups/500 ml milk, page 10)
- 5 oz/150 g white mushrooms, thinly sliced
- $^1/_4$ cup/60 g butter, cut into flakes
- $^3/_4$ cup/90 g diced ham
- 1 lb/500 g dried pasta tubes, such as rigatoni
- 5 oz/150 g prosciutto/ Parma ham, cut into thin strips

Baked Pasta

LASAGNA, FERRARA STYLE

Lasagne alla ferrarese

Pasta Dough
- 2 cups/300 g all-purpose/plain flour
- ¹/₄ teaspoon salt
- 3 large eggs

Meat Sauce
- 5 oz/150 g prosciutto/Parma ham, chopped
- 1 onion, chopped
- 1 stalk celery, chopped
- 1 carrot, finely chopped
- 8 oz/250 g ground beef
- generous ¹/₃ cup/100 ml dry white wine
- ²/₃ cup/150 g chopped tomatoes
- ¹/₂ cup/125 ml meat stock or broth + more as needed
- salt and freshly ground black pepper
- 2 cups/500 ml Béchamel sauce (made with 3 tablespoons butter, 3 tablespoons flour, and 2 cups/500 ml milk, page 10)
- ³/₄ cup/90 g freshly grated Parmesan cheese

Pasta Dough: Sift the flour and salt onto a surface and make a well in the center. Break the eggs into the well and mix in to make a dough. Knead for 15–20 minutes, until elastic. Shape the dough into a ball, wrap in plastic wrap, and let rest for 30 minutes. • Roll out the dough on a lightly floured surface until paper-thin. Cut into 6 x 8-inch (15 x 20-cm) rectangles. • Blanch the pasta and lay the pieces out on a damp cloth (see page 222). • Meat Sauce: Sauté the prosciutto, onion, celery, and carrot in the butter in a large frying pan over medium heat for 2 minutes until browned. • Add the beef and cook for 2–3 minutes until browned all over. • Pour in the wine and let it evaporate. • Stir in the tomatoes and ¹/₂ cup (125 ml) of stock. Season with salt, cover, and cook over low heat for about 2 hours, adding more stock if needed. Season with salt and pepper. • Preheat the oven to 400°F/200°C/gas 6. • Butter a baking dish. • Arrange four layers of pasta in the prepared dish, alternating with meat sauce, Béchamel, and Parmesan. • Bake for 20–25 minutes, or until bubbling. • Serve warm.

Serves 6 • Prep: 60 min + 30 min to rest the dough • Cooking: 3hr • Level: 2

LASAGNA, BOLOGNA STYLE

Lasagne alla bolognese

- Homemade Pasta Dough, made with 2 cups/300 g all-purpose/plain flour and 3 large eggs (see page 64)
- 2 cups/500 ml Ligurian Meat Sauce (see page 17)
- 4 cups/1 liter Béchamel sauce (made with ¹/₃ cup/80 g butter, ¹/₂ cup/80 g flour, and 1 quart/1 liter milk, page 10)
- ²/₃ cup/80 g freshly grated Parmesan cheese

Preheat the oven to 400°F/200°C/gas 6. • Butter a baking dish. • Roll out the dough on a lightly floured surface until paper-thin. Cut the sheet of dough into 6 x 8-inch (15 x 20-cm) rectangles. • Blanch the dough and lay it out on a damp cloth (see page 222). • Arrange four layers of the pasta in the prepared dish, alternating with the meat sauce, Béchamel, and Parmesan. • Bake for 20–25 minutes, or until the cheese is bubbling. • Let stand for 30 minutes.

Serves 6 • Prep: 20 min • Cooking: 20–25 min • Level: 2

BAKED CANNELLONI

Cannelloni ripieni di carne

Pasta Dough: Sift the flour and salt onto a surface and make a well in the center. Break the eggs into the well and mix in to make a smooth dough. Knead for 15–20 minutes, until smooth and elastic. Shape the dough into a ball, wrap in plastic wrap (cling film), and let rest for 30 minutes. • Roll out the dough and cut into 4 x 7-inch (10 x 18-cm) rectangles. • Blanch the pasta in salted boiling water with the oil. Drain and lay on a damp cloth (see page 222). • Filling: Sauté the onion in the butter in a small frying pan over low heat for 5 minutes until translucent. • Increase the heat and add the veal, ham, and chicken and cook for 5 minutes, until browned all over. • Pour in the wine and let it evaporate. • Pour in the stock and season with salt and pepper. Use a wooden spoon to scrape off any residue that begins to stick to the bottom of the pan. • Add the 3 tablespoons of Béchamel and cook for 15 minutes, stirring often. • Remove from the heat and let cool to lukewarm. • Preheat the oven to 400°F/200°C/gas 6. • Butter a baking dish. • Transfer the filling to a food processor or blender and chop the meat finely. • Mix in the egg, Parmesan, and nutmeg. • Drop a small amount of filling on the pasta rectangles and roll them up. • Lay the cannelloni in a single layer in the prepared baking dish. Cover with the Béchamel, meat sauce, and dot with the butter. • Bake for 15–20 minutes, or until the sauces are bubbling. • Let rest for 10 minutes before serving.

Serves 6 • Prep: 2 hr + 30 min to rest the dough • Cooking: 60 min • Level: 3

Pasta Dough
- 2²/₃ cups/400 g all-purpose/plain flour
- ¹/₄ teaspoon salt
- 4 large eggs
- 2 tablespoons extra-virgin olive oil

Filling
- ¹/₂ onion, finely chopped
- 6 tablespoons butter, cut up
- 8 oz/300 g lean ground/minced veal or beef
- ³/₄ cup/90 g finely chopped ham
- 4 oz/90 g ground/minced chicken breast
- 6 tablespoons dry white wine
- 6 tablespoons meat stock or broth
- salt and freshly ground white pepper
- 3 tablespoons Béchamel sauce (see page 10)
- 1 large egg
- ¹/₄ cup/30 g freshly grated Parmesan cheese
- ¹/₈ teaspoon freshly grated nutmeg

Sauces
- 2²/₃ cups/650 ml Béchamel sauce (see page 10)
- 1¹/₄ cups/310 ml Ligurian meat sauce (see page 17)
- ¹/₄ cup/60 g butter, cut into flakes

TUSCANY

P ici (unevenly rolled and dried spaghetti) is the local pasta from south of Siena, best served with a garlic sauce. In the winter months, Tuscans indulge in hearty soups made with pasta and legumes. Potato tortelli are a favorite filled pasta from the Mugello in northern Tuscany. It is traditional in Florence to make lasagna between St. Lawrence's Day (August 10) and the Feast of the Assumption of the Virgin Mary (August 15). Try the lasagna with a bell pepper or poultry sauce.

Mushroom–sausage sauce
(see page 95)

Soups

TUSCAN GARBANZO BEAN SOUP

Pasta e ceci

- $1^2/_3$ cups/160 g dried garbanzo beans/chickpeas, soaked overnight and drained
- 8 cups/2 liters cold water
- 4 cloves garlic, lightly crushed but whole
- 2 sprigs fresh rosemary
- salt
- 6 tablespoons extra-virgin olive oil
- $^1/_4$ cup/60 g tomato concentrate/paste
- 1 cup/250 ml beef stock or broth, boiling (optional)
- 8 oz/250 g small dried soup pasta
- freshly ground black pepper

Put the beans in a large pot and pour in the water. Add 2 cloves of garlic and 1 sprig of rosemary. Partially cover and simmer for 1 hour, or until the beans are very tender. Season with salt and remove from the heat. • Drain, reserving the water and discarding the garlic and rosemary. • Puree three-quarters of the garbanzo beans in a food processor, leaving the remainder whole. • Sauté the remaining 2 cloves garlic and sprig of rosemary in 3 tablespoons of oil in a large saucepan over low heat for 2 minutes, until the garlic is pale gold. • Discard the garlic. Stir in the tomato paste and cook over medium heat for 2 minutes. • Add the pureed and whole garbanzo beans and the reserved cooking liquid and bring to a boil. If the soup is very thick, dilute with a little hot stock. • Add the pasta and cook until al dente. Season with salt and pepper. Drizzle with the remaining 3 tablespoons of oil, discard the rosemary, and serve.

Serves 4 • Prep: 20 min + overnight to soak beans • Cooking: 75 min • Level: 1

PASTA AND POTATO SOUP

Minestra di patate

Put the potatoes, beans, tomato, leek, celery, sage, thyme, and parsley in a large saucepan with the oil and salt. Pour in the water and bring to a boil over low heat. Simmer for 45 minutes. • Run the soup through a food mill or process in a food processor or blender. If it seems too dense, dilute with boiling water. • Return the soup to the saucepan, bring to a boil, add the pasta and cook until al dente. • Season with pepper and the Parmesan.

Serves 4–6 • Prep: 20 min • Cooking: 75 min • Level: 1

- $1^1/_4$ lb/600 g waxy potatoes, peeled and cut into chunks
- 1 cup/100 g fresh beans, such as cannellini
- 1 firm-ripe tomato, peeled and coarsely chopped
- white of 1 leek, finely chopped
- 1 stalk celery, finely chopped
- 2 leaves fresh sage, chopped
- 1 sprig thyme, chopped
- 1 small bunch fresh parsley, finely chopped
- 3 tablespoons extra-virgin olive oil
- $^1/_8$ teaspoon salt
- 8 cups/2 liters water + extra boiling water as needed
- 8 oz/200 g dried ridged ditali
- freshly ground black pepper
- 5 tablespoons freshly grated Parmesan cheese

Soup pastas

Pastine (soup pasta) are available in an array of shapes and sizes—ditalini (tubes, pictured right), stelline (stars), and farfalline (bows). These tiny pasta types appeared in the Mediterranean during the Middle Ages in the area under Arab rule, from Sicily to Andalucia in Spain. In Tuscany, ditalini feature in winter bean soups, but it is also common to serve soup pasta in a clear, flavorful stock or broth.

Sauces

HOMEMADE SPAGHETTI WITH GARLIC

Pici all'aglione

Pasta Dough

- 3⅓ cups/500 g all-purpose/plain flour
- ¼ teaspoon salt
- 1 large egg lightly beaten
- 1 tablespoon water, + more if needed

Garlic Sauce

- 8–10 cloves garlic, lightly crushed but whole
- 5 tablespoons extra-virgin olive oil
- 2 lb/1 kg tomatoes, peeled, seeded, and finely chopped
- ⅛ teaspoon crumbled dried chile pepper
- salt

The ingredients of this pici dough are not exactly traditional, but this is a version that is widely used. This garlic sauce is the most traditional sauce for all types of pici.

Pasta Dough: Sift the flour and salt onto a surface and make a well in the center. Mix in half an egg (reserve the remaining portion for another use) and enough water to make a fairly sticky dough. Knead for 15–20 minutes, until smooth. • Roll out the dough out on a lightly floured surface to a thickness of ½ inch (1 cm). Cover with a damp cloth and set aside to rest for 30 minutes. • Tear off strips of dough, pulling the strips until the diameter of the strips is the size of large spaghetti. Wrap them into nests and let dry on a floured cloth for about 30 minutes until just before cooking. • Garlic Sauce: Sauté the garlic in the oil in a large saucepan over low heat for 2 minutes, until pale gold. • Add the tomatoes and chile and season with salt. • Cook over low heat for 40 minutes, or until the garlic has almost dissolved. Season with salt. • Cook the pasta in a large pot of salted boiling water for 4–5 minutes, depending on the diameter, or until al dente. • Drain and add to the sauce. Serve immediately.

Serves 4–6 • Prep: 1 hr + 30 min to rest the dough • Cooking: 60 min • Level: 3

Homemade spaghetti with garlic

TAGLIOLINI WITH MULLET

Tagliolini con sugo di triglia

- 2 cloves garlic, finely chopped
- 1 tablespoon finely chopped fresh parsley
- $^1/_4$ cup/60 ml extra-virgin olive oil
- generous $^1/_3$ cup/100 ml dry white wine
- 1 lb/500 g mullets, cleaned, filleted, and cut into small chunks
- 12 cherry tomatoes, thinly sliced
- salt
- $^1/_8$ teaspoon crumbled dried chile pepper
- 12 oz/300 g fresh store-bought egg tagliolini pasta

Ask your fish salesperson to clean and fillet the fish.

Sauté the garlic and parsley in the oil in a large frying pan over low heat for 2 minutes, until the garlic is pale gold. • Pour in the wine and add the fish and tomatoes. • Season with salt and chile pepper. Cook for 10 minutes. • Cook the pasta in a large pot of salted boiling water until al dente. • Drain, reserving a little cooking water. Add to the water to thin the sauce if needed. Serve hot.

Serves 4 • Prep: 30 min • Cooking: 20 min • Level: 1

PASTA WITH MUSHROOM–SAUSAGE SAUCE

Sugo di funghi e salsiccia

This sauce is also excellent when served with polenta.

Sauté the onion in the oil in a large frying pan over medium heat for 3 minutes until softened. • Add the sausages and sauté over high heat for 2 minutes until browned all over. • Drain the mushrooms, straining the water through a coffee filter or paper towel to remove grit. Chop them coarsely • Add the garlic and the chopped mushrooms and their liquid. Pour in the wine and let it evaporate. • Stir in the fresh mushrooms, thyme, and salt and pepper. Cover and cook for 30 minutes, adding the stock if the sauce begins to thicken too much. Remove the thyme. • Cook the pasta in a large pot of salted boiling water until al dente. • Drain and add to the sauce. Sprinkle with the parsley and serve.

Serves 4 • Prep: 45 min + 15 min to soak mushrooms •
Cooking: 45 min • Level: 1

- 1 small red onion, finely chopped
- $^1/_4$ cup/60 ml extra-virgin olive oil
- 2 Italian sausages, weighing about 5 oz/150 g, cut into small chunks
- 2 cloves garlic, finely chopped
- 1 oz/30 g dried porcini mushrooms, soaked for 15 minutes in warm water, drained, and finely chopped
- $^1/_2$ cup/125 ml dry red wine
- 1 lb/500 g mushrooms, rinsed and finely chopped
- 1 sprig fresh thyme
- salt and freshly ground black pepper
- $^1/_4$ cup/60 ml meat stock or broth (optional)
- 12 oz/350 g pasta, such as dried egg tagliatelle or short pasta made of semolina
- 1 tablespoon finely chopped fresh parsley

Tagliolini with mullet

Long pasta with basil-walnut sauce

PAPPARDELLE WITH DUCK SAUCE

Pappardelle al sugo di anatra

- 1 red onion, chopped
- 1 bay leaf
- 1 bunch sage, chopped
- 1/2 carrot, chopped
- 1 tablespoon finely chopped fresh parsley
- 2 celery leaves, finely chopped (optional)
- 4 oz/90 g ham, chopped
- 5 tablespoons extra-virgin olive oil
- 1 duck (about 3 lb/ 1.5 kg), cleaned and cut in quarters
- 2/3 cup/150 ml red wine
- 1 lb/500 g firm-ripe tomatoes, chopped
- salt and freshly ground black pepper
- 3/4 cup/180 ml meat stock or broth
- 1 lb/500 g fresh storebought pappardelle
- 1 cup/125 g freshly grated Parmesan cheese

Sauté the onion, bay leaf, sage, carrot, parsley, celery leaves (if using), and ham in the oil in a Dutch oven (casserole) over low heat for 15 minutes. • Add the duck and cook over high heat for 10 minutes. • Pour in the wine and cook for 15 minutes more. • Stir in the tomatoes and season with salt and pepper. • Pour in the stock, cover, and cook for 1 hour. • Bone the duck and cut the meat into small chunks. Return the meat to the sauce and simmer for about 15 minutes. • Cook the pasta in a large pot of salted boiling water until al dente. • Drain and add to the sauce. Sprinkle with Parmesan and serve.

Serves 6–8 • Prep: 30 min • Cooking: 2 hr • Level: 3

TUSCAN GNOCCHI

Topini

Topini are excellent when served with a meat sauce, pesto, or tomato sauce. For a simple dish, drizzle with sage-flavored butter.

Cook the potatoes in salted boiling water for 15–20 minutes, or until tender. • Peel and use a potato masher or fork to mash them. • Spread out the mashed potatoes on a clean surface, season with salt, and let cool to lukewarm. • Mix in the flour, egg, Parmesan, and salt and pepper. Knead until the dough is smooth. • Perform a test cooking by breaking off a small ball of dough, dusting it with flour, and cooking it in boiling water. If it falls apart during cooking, add more flour to the dough. • Form into logs 2/3 inch (1.5 cm) in diameter and cut into 1 1/4-inch (3-cm) pieces. Dust them with flour. • Cook the gnocchi in small batches in a large pot of salted boiling water for 3–5 minutes until they rise to the surface. Use a slotted spoon to transfer them to serving plates. Season with salt and pepper and serve.

Serves 4 • Prep: 40 min • Cooking: 40 min • Level: 2

- 2 lb/1 kg baking/floury potatoes
- 1 1/3 cups/200 g all-purpose/plain flour
- 1 large egg
- 2 tablespoons freshly grated Parmesan cheese
- salt and freshly ground white pepper

LONG PASTA WITH BASIL—WALNUT SAUCE

Pastasciutta alla fornaia

- Leaves from 2 large bunches fresh basil, torn
- 2/3 cup/100 g walnuts
- 1 cup/125 g freshly grated Pecorino cheese
- salt and freshly ground black pepper
- 6 tablespoons extra-virgin olive oil
- 12 oz/350 g dried bavette, linguine, or spaghetti

This sauce is sometimes also called pesto toscano, while in other areas of Tuscany, alla fornaia refers to a fake ragù, that is, a meat sauce without the meat.

Crush the basil with the walnuts in a pestle and mortar or chop them finely in a food processor. • Transfer to a serving bowl and add 3 tablespoons of Pecorino. Season with salt and pepper. • Pour in the oil and mix until creamy. • Cook the pasta in a large pot of salted boiling water until al dente. Drain and transfer to the serving bowl. • Sprinkle with the remaining Pecorino and serve.

Serves 4 • Prep: 15 min • Cooking: 15 min • Level: 1

Bavette with waterfowl sauce

BAVETTE WITH WATERFOWL SAUCE

Bavette alla folaga

- 2 waterfowl, such as duck, weighing about 2 lb/1 kg in total
- ¹/₄ cup/60 ml white wine vinegar
- 2¹/₄ cups/560 ml dry red wine
- 1 large red onion, finely chopped
- 1 carrot, finely chopped
- 1 stalk celery with leaves, finely chopped
- 2 tablespoons butter
- 2 tablespoons extra-virgin olive oil
- ¹/₄ cup/30 g finely chopped fresh parsley
- 1 tablespoon finely chopped fresh rosemary
- 1 tablespoon finely chopped fresh sage

Cut the fowl into quarters and wash carefully. Dry and wash again with vinegar. • Place in a large bowl with 1 cup (250 ml) of the wine, onion, carrot, and celery. • Let marinate in the refrigerator for 12 hours. • Remove the pieces of fowl from the marinade and dry them. Drain the vegetables and set them aside. • Heat the butter and oil in a Dutch oven (casserole) over high heat. Add the vegetables and sauté for 5 minutes. • Add the fowl, parsley, rosemary, sage, and juniper berries and cook, turning the fowl constantly, for 10 minutes. • Pour in the remaining wine and tomato sauce. Season with salt and pepper. Cover and cook over low heat for about 90 minutes, or until the meat is tender, adding stock if the sauce begins to thicken too much. • Remove the fowl and bone it, breaking it up with your fingers. Return the fowl to the pan and cook until the sauce has reduced by half, about 5 minutes. • Cook the pasta in a large pot of salted boiling water until al dente. • Drain and add to the sauce.

Serves 4 • Prep: 40 min + 12 hr to marinate • Cooking: 2 hr • Level: 2

- ¹/₄ teaspoon finely chopped juniper berries
- 1 cup/250 ml unseasoned tomato sauce, store-bought or homemade
- salt and freshly ground black pepper
- ¹/₄ cup/60 ml meat stock or broth (optional)
- 12 oz/350 g dried pasta (such as bavette, linguine, or trenette)

POTATO TORTELLI, MUGELLO STYLE

Tortelli di patate mugellani

Pasta Dough

- 1¹/₃ cups/200 g all-purpose/plain flour
- ¹/₄ teaspoon salt
- 2 large eggs
- 2 tablespoons lukewarm water, + more as needed

Filling

- 1 lb/500 g baking/floury potatoes
- ¹/₂ cup/60 g freshly grated Parmesan cheese
- ¹/₄ cup/60 g butter, cut up
- 1 clove garlic, finely chopped
- 2 teaspoons finely chopped fresh parsley
- ¹/₈ teaspoon freshly grated nutmeg
- salt and freshly ground white pepper

Tomato Sauce

- 2 sprigs rosemary
- 2 cloves garlic, lightly crushed but whole
- 1 dried chile pepper
- ¹/₄ cup/60 ml extra-virgin olive oil
- 1¹/₂ lb/700 g tomatoes, peeled, seeded, and coarsely chopped
- salt

The Mugello is the verdant region north of Florence famous for its lake and woodland scenery.

Pasta Dough: Sift the flour and salt onto a surface and make a well in the center. Break the eggs into the well and mix in with enough water to make a smooth dough. Knead for 15–20 minutes, until elastic. Shape into a ball, wrap in plastic wrap, and let rest for 30 minutes. • Filling: Cook the potatoes in salted boiling water for 15–20 minutes, or until tender. • Drain and peel them. Transfer to a large bowl and use a fork or potato masher to mash until smooth. Let cool completely. • Mix in the Parmesan, butter, garlic, parsley, nutmeg, salt, and pepper. • Roll out the dough until very thin. Cut into 4-inch (10-cm) wide strips and arrange pellets of filling near one edge, about ³/₄ inch (2 cm) apart. Fold each strip of dough lengthwise to cover the filling. Seal, after making sure no air pockets remain, then cut into squares with a saw-toothed ravioli cutter. The tortelli should be smooth on one side and crimped on three sides. Lay the pasta on a kitchen cloth dusted with flour. • Tomato Sauce: Sauté the rosemary, garlic, and chile in the oil in a frying pan over low heat for 2 minutes until aromatic. Discard the garlic and rosemary. • Stir in the tomatoes and season with salt. • Cook the pasta in small batches in a large pot of salted boiling water for 2–3 minutes, until al dente. • Use a slotted spoon to transfer them to serving bowls. Top with the sauce and serve.

Serves 4 • Prep: 60 min + 30 min to rest the dough • Cooking: 60 min • Level: 3

RABBIT SAUCE

Sugo di coniglio

This sauce is delicious served with an egg pasta, such as pappardelle.

Sauté the rabbit meat with the carrot, celery, onion, sage, rosemary, parsley, and garlic in the oil in a large frying pan over high heat for 10 minutes, stirring constantly. • Pour in the Vin Santo and season with salt and pepper. • Lower the heat, cover, and cook for 10–15 minutes, or until the garlic dissolves and the meat is tender.

Serves 6 • Prep: 30 min • Cooking: 30 min • Level: 1

- 12 oz/300 g rabbit meat, cut into small chunks
- 1 carrot, coarsely chopped
- 1 stalk celery, coarsely chopped
- 1 onion, coarsely chopped
- Leaves from 1 bunch fresh sage, finely chopped
- 1 sprig fresh rosemary, finely chopped
- 1 tablespoon finely chopped fresh parsley
- 1 clove garlic, lightly crushed but whole
- ¹/₄ cup/60 ml extra-virgin olive oil
- ¹/₂ cup/125 ml dry Vin Santo (a Tuscan sweet dessert wine) or dry Sherry
- salt and freshly ground white pepper

Rabbit sauce

Sauces

BAVETTE WITH COCKLES

Bavette con le telline

- 2 lb/1 kg cockles or clams
- 2 cloves garlic, finely chopped
- 1 tablespoon finely chopped fresh parsley
- 6 tablespoons extra-virgin olive oil
- generous $1/3$ cup/100 ml dry white wine
- $1/4$ cup/60 ml unseasoned tomato sauce, store-bought or homemade
- salt
- 12 oz/350 g dried bavette pasta or linguine

Soak the cockles in a large bowl of warm salted water for 1 hour. • Transfer the cockles to a large saucepan of boiling water (enough to cover them) and cook over high heat for 3–5 minutes until they open up. Discard any that do not open. Strain the liquid and set aside. • Sauté the garlic and parsley in the oil in a large frying pan over high heat for 1–2 minutes until pale gold. • Pour in the wine and let it evaporate. • Mix the tomato sauce and reserved cooking liquid. Add to the sauce and lower the heat. • Add the cockles and cook for 2–3 minutes. Season with salt. • Cook the pasta in a large pot of salted boiling water until al dente • Drain, reserving 2 tablespoons of the cooking water. Add to the sauce, adding the cooking water to thin the sauce if needed. • Serve hot.

Serves 4 • Prep: 15 min + 60 min to soak the cockles • Cooking: 20 min • Level: 1

HOMEMADE SPAGHETTI WITH ANCHOVIES

Pici con le briciole

Preheat the oven to 300°F/150°C/gas 4. • Crumble the slices of bread on a baking sheet and toast them lightly for 2–3 minutes. • Heat the oil in a large frying pan over medium heat. Add the anchovies and let them dissolve for about 5 minutes, taking care not to let them burn. • Add the bread crumbs and mix for a few minutes. Season with pepper. • Cook the pasta in a large pot of salted boiling water for 4–5 minutes, or until al dente • Drain, reserving 2 tablespoons of the cooking water. Transfer the pasta to the sauce, adding the cooking water if the mixture looks too dry.

Serves 4 • Prep: 15 min • Cooking: 15 min • Level: 1

- 3 slices day-old firm-textured bread (preferably saltless)
- generous $1/3$ cup/100 ml extra-virgin olive oil
- 3 anchovies packed in salt, rinsed, and filleted
- freshly ground black pepper
- 12 oz/350 g fresh Homemade spaghetti (see page 104)

BAVETTE WITH SEAFOOD SAUCE

Bavette sul pesce

- 1 lb/400 g squid or cuttlefish, cleaned
- 2 cloves garlic, finely chopped
- $1/2$ cup/125 ml extra-virgin olive oil
- 4 jumbo shrimp or king prawns, shelled, leaving the head on
- 4 crayfish, shelled, leaving the head on
- 4 shrimp/prawns, shelled, leaving the head and claws on
- 12 oz/350 g dried bavette or linguine
- generous $1/3$ cup/100 ml dry white wine
- salt
- 4 cups/1 liter fish stock or broth, boiling

This is an unusual way of preparing pasta since it is almost treated like the rice for a risotto.

Cut the squid bodies into small chunks and slice the tentacles in half. • Sauté the garlic in the oil in a large frying pan over high heat for 1–2 minutes until pale gold. • Add the squid, jumbo shrimp, crayfish, and shrimp and cook over medium heat for 4 minutes. • Cook the pasta for one-third of the time indicated on the package in a large pot of salted boiling water. • Drain and add to the sauce. • Pour in the wine, season with salt, and cook for about 5 minutes, gradually adding the boiling fish stock and mixing occasionally until the pasta is al dente. Season with salt and serve.

Serves 4 • Prep: 30 min • Cooking: 30 min • Level: 2

SPAGHETTI WITH FRESH ANCHOVIES

Spaghetti alle acciughe

Sauté the garlic, parsley, and chile in the oil in a medium saucepan over medium heat for 3 minutes until the garlic is pale gold. • Pour in the wine and add the anchovies. • Simmer over medium heat for 5 minutes. • Stir in the tomatoes and season with salt. Cook for about 20 minutes, or until the oil separates from the tomatoes. • Cook the pasta in a large pot of salted boiling water until al dente • Drain and transfer to a large bowl. Spoon the anchovy sauce over the pasta, toss well, and serve.

Serves 4 • Prep: 40 min • Cooking: 35 min • Level: 1

- 2 cloves garlic, finely chopped
- 2 tablespoons finely chopped fresh parsley
- 1 fresh red chile pepper, finely chopped
- 5 tablespoons extra-virgin olive oil
- generous $1/3$ cup/100 ml dry white wine
- 1 lb/400 g fresh anchovies, filleted, heads removed, and chopped into small chunks
- 12 oz/300 g firm-ripe tomatoes, peeled, seeded, and coarsely chopped
- salt
- 12 oz/350 g dried spaghetti

Tuscan meat ragù

TUSCAN MEAT RAGÙ

Ragù di carne toscano

- 2 carrots, chopped
- 2 stalks celery, chopped
- 2 red onions, chopped
- $^2/_3$ cup/150 ml extra-virgin olive oil
- 2 cloves garlic, chopped
- 2 tablespoons finely chopped fresh parsley
- 12 oz/300 g lean ground/minced beef
- generous $^2/_3$ cup/ 200 ml dry red wine
- 2 lb/1 kg peeled plum tomatoes, pressed through a fine mesh strainer (passata)
- 1 bay leaf
- 1 sprig fresh rosemary, finely chopped
- small piece lemon zest
- salt and freshly ground black pepper
- water (optional)

This is an adaptable sauce that can be served with pasta tubes or in a baked dish, layered with Béchamel.

Chop together the carrots, celery, and onions to make a very finely chopped mixture. • Heat the oil in a Dutch oven (casserole) and add the vegetables. Cook over medium-low heat for 20 minutes. • Add the garlic and parsley and cook for 10 minutes more. The sautéed mixture should be nicely browned but not burnt. • Increase the heat, add the beef, and cook for 2–3 minutes until brown all over. • Pour in the wine and add the tomatoes, bay leaf, rosemary, and lemon. Season with salt and pepper. • Cover and cook over very low heat for 3 hours, adding water if the mixture starts to dry. Remove the bay leaf and lemon zest before serving.

Serves 6–8 • Prep: 30 min • Cooking: 3 hr 30 min • Level: 1

SPAGHETTI WITH MANTIS SHRIMP

Spaghetti alle cicale

Mantis shrimp are found in warm and temperate waters throughout the world but are rarely found on menus outside of the Mediterranean and Asia. Substitute regular shrimp or lobster and make a stock from their shells.

Wash the shrimp and remove the eyes. Cut them open with shears on the underside (belly). Use a teaspoon to remove the flesh from the shell, put in a large bowl, and set aside. • Fill a large saucepan with cold water, season with salt, and add the shrimp shells. Boil for 20 minutes, then strain the stock. • Sauté the garlic in 2 tablespoons of butter in a large frying pan over high heat for 1–2 minutes until pale gold. • Add the shrimp flesh and simmer for 5 minutes. • Pour in the wine, season with salt, and remove from the heat. • Cook the pasta in the strained stock until al dente. • Drain, reserving 2 tablespoons of the stock. Add the pasta and the reserved stock to the frying pan. • Dot with the remaining 4 tablespoons of butter, letting it melt into the pasta. Sprinkle with parsley and serve.

Serves 4 • Prep: 30 min • Cooking: 45 min • Level: 1

- 2 lb/1 kg mantis shrimp, such as cicale (canocchie) or substitute regular shrimp or lobster
- salt
- 2 cloves garlic, finely chopped
- 6 tablespoons butter, cut up
- $^1/_4$ cup/60 ml dry white wine
- 12 oz/350 g dried spaghetti
- 1 tablespoon finely chopped fresh parsley

PENNE WITH CRABMEAT

Penne al favollo

Stock
- 3 quarts/3 liters cold water
- 1 red onion, sliced
- 1 stalk celery, sliced
- 1 firm-ripe tomato
- 3–4 stalks parsley
- 1 clove garlic
- $^1/_4$ teaspoon salt
- 2 lb/1 kg large crabs, cleaned

- 2 cloves garlic, chopped
- 2 tablespoons finely chopped fresh parsley

Stock: Bring the water to a boil in a large saucepan with the onion, celery, tomato, stalks of parsley, garlic, and salt. Simmer for 15 minutes. • Add the crabs and cook for 20 minutes. Drain, reserving the stock. • Cool the crabs to lukewarm, then remove the flesh from the shells, leaving the claws whole. • Sauté the garlic, 1 tablespoon parsley, chile, and sage in the oil in a large saucepan for 2 minutes, until the garlic is pale gold. • Stir in

the tomatoes, the crab claws, and salt and pepper, and simmer for 15 minutes. • Add the crabmeat and pour in 2 cups (500 ml) of the reserved stock. Cook for 30 minutes. • Cook the pasta in a large pot of salted boiling water until al dente. Drain and transfer to the sauce to finish cooking. • Sprinkle with the parsley, dot with the remaining butter, letting it melt into the pasta, and serve.

Serves 4 • Prep: 30 min • Cooking: 90 min • Level: 2

- 1 dried chile pepper, finely chopped
- 1 bunch fresh sage, finely chopped
- 5 tablespoons extra-virgin olive oil
- $1^1/_2$ lb/700 g firm-ripe tomatoes, peeled, seeded, and coarsely chopped
- salt and freshly ground black pepper
- 12 oz/350 g dried penne
- 1 tablespoon butter

Fresh Pasta & Sauces

PASTA SHEETS
WITH MUSHROOMS AND TOMATOES
Tacconi alla lucchese

Pasta Dough
- 2²/₃ cups/400 g all purpose/plain flour
- ¹/₄ teaspoon salt
- 3 large eggs
- 1 tablespoon extra-virgin olive oil
- 6 tablespoons water + more if needed

Sauce
- 2 cloves garlic, finely chopped
- 6 tablespoons extra-virgin olive oil
- 1 lb/500 g fresh porcini mushrooms (or cultivated white mushrooms), finely chopped
- 1 tablespoon dried porcini mushrooms, soaked in warm water for 15 minutes and drained
- ³/₄ cup/180 ml dry white wine
- 4 firm-ripe tomatoes, peeled, seeded, and coarsely chopped
- salt and freshly ground black pepper
- 1 tablespoon finely chopped fresh parsley
- ¹/₄ cup/30 g freshly grated Parmesan cheese (optional)

Pasta Dough: Sift the flour and salt onto a work surface and make a well in the center. Break the eggs into the well and mix in with the oil and enough water to make a smooth dough. Knead for 15–20 minutes, until smooth and elastic. Shape the dough into a ball, wrap in plastic wrap (cling film), and let rest for 30 minutes. • Roll out the dough on a lightly floured surface until paper-thin. Cut into 2-inch (5-cm) squares and let dry for 5 minutes. • Sauce: Sauté the garlic in the oil in a frying pan for 2 minutes until pale gold. • Add the mushrooms and cook for 8 minutes until tender. • Drain the dried mushrooms, straining the water through a coffee filter or paper towel to remove grit. Chop them coarsely and add to the pan. • Pour in the wine and cook over high heat until evaporated. • Add the tomatoes and season with salt and pepper. • Cook over medium heat for 15–20 minutes, or until the sauce thickens. • Cook the pasta in a large pot of salted boiling water until al dente. • Drain, reserving 2 tablespoons of cooking water, and add to the sauce. Add the reserved cooking water, if needed. • Sprinkle with parsley and Parmesan and serve.

Serves 4 • Prep: 2 hr + 30 min to rest the dough • Cooking: 30 min • Level: 2

PENNE WITH
CREAMY MEAT SAUCE
Penne strascicate

Cook the pasta in a large pot of salted boiling water until not quite al dente. • Drain and set aside. • Melt 2 tablespoons of butter in a large frying pan and add the meat sauce. Cook until it begins to bubble. • Add the pasta and finish cooking until al dente, mixing in the cream. • Sprinkle with Parmesan and remove from the heat. • Dot with the remaining 2 tablespoons of butter, letting it melt into the pasta, and serve.

Serves 4 • Prep: 10 min • Cooking: 10 min • Level: 1

- 12 oz/350 g dried penne
- ¹/₄ cup/60 g butter, cut up
- 1¹/₄ cups/310 ml meat sauce (such as Tuscan meat ragù, page 103)
- generous ¹/₃ cup/100 ml heavy/double cream
- ¹/₄ cup/30 g freshly grated Parmesan cheese

HOMEMADE SPAGHETTI
Pici

Sift 3 cups (450 g) of the flour and salt onto a pastry board or surface and make a well in the center. • Add the water and knead for 15–20 minutes, until smooth and elastic. Cover with plastic wrap (cling film) and let rest for at least 30 minutes. • Break off pieces of dough the size of an almond. Use your hands to form the *pici* or roll out the dough on the surface with your fingers extended so that you obtain cylinders just a little thicker than spaghetti. This operation is known as *appiciare* in Italian. • Spread out the pici on a canvas when they are ready. Do not dry them. • Cook the pasta in a large pot of salted boiling water for 4–5 minutes, until al dente. Drain and serve as desired.

Serves 5—6 • Prep: 60 min + 30 min to rest the dough • Cooking: 4–5 min • Level: 2

- 3¹/₃ cups/500 g all-purpose/plain flour
- ¹/₈ teaspoon salt
- 1 cup/250 ml water, + more as needed

Fresh Pasta

PAPPARDELLE WITH BELL PEPPERS

Lasagne ai peperoni e pancetta

- 1 onion, finely chopped
- 1 stalk celery, finely chopped
- 1 carrot, finely chopped
- 1/4 cup/60 ml extra-virgin olive oil
- 1 1/4 cups/100 g finely chopped pancetta
- 1 lb/500 g yellow bell peppers/capsicums, seeded and cut into thin strips
- salt and freshly ground black pepper
- 12 oz/300 g fresh egg pappardelle, cut into 1 x 4-inch/3 x 10-cm strips
- 2 tablespoons butter, cut up
- 1 cup/125 g freshly grated Parmesan cheese
- 1 small bunch parsley, finely chopped

Sauté the onion, celery, and carrot in the oil in a medium saucepan over low heat for 15 minutes, or until aromatic. • Add the pancetta and sauté until crisp, about 5 minutes. • Add the bell peppers and continue cooking, covered, over medium heat for 10 minutes, or until softened. Season with salt and pepper. • Cook the pasta in a large pot of salted boiling water until al dente. • Drain and transfer to serving plates. Top with the bell pepper sauce. Melt the butter over the top and sprinkle with Parmesan and parsley.

Serves 4 • Prep: 20 min • Cooking: 20 min • Level: 1

LASAGNA WITH BELL PEPPERS

Lasagne ai peperoni

- 1 onion, finely chopped
- 1/4 cup/60 ml extra-virgin olive oil
- 1 lb/500 g bell peppers/capsicums, mixed colors, seeded and cut into thin strips
- salt and freshly ground black pepper
- 12 oz/300 g fresh egg tagliatelle, cut into 1 x 4-inch/3 x 10-cm strips
- 2 tablespoons butter, cut up
- 1 cup/125 g freshly grated Parmesan cheese

Sauté the onion in the oil in a medium saucepan over low heat for 15 minutes, or until aromatic. • Add the bell peppers and continue cooking, covered, over medium heat for 10 minutes, or until softened. Season with salt and pepper. • Cook the pasta in a large pot of salted boiling water until al dente. • Drain and transfer to serving plates. Top with the bell pepper sauce. Melt the butter over the top and sprinkle with Parmesan.

Serves 4 • Prep: 20 min • Cooking: 25 min • Level: 1

TORTELLI, VERSILIAN STYLE

Tordelli

Tordelli and tortelli are typically made in Versilia, the part of Tuscany adjoining the river Versilia. This pasta is usually served with a meat sauce.

<u>Filling</u>: Melt the butter in a frying pan over medium heat, add the slices of meat, and sauté for 2–3 minutes until browned all over. Pour in the stock and season with salt. Cook over medium heat for about 5 minutes until the sauce has thickened. Remove from the heat and let cool completely. • Soak the bread in the milk for a few seconds until softened. Drain well and squeeze out any excess. • Process the cooked meat and cooking liquid, mortadella, soaked bread, garlic, and parsley in a food processor or blender until finely chopped. • Transfer to a large bowl and mix in the Swiss chard, Parmesan, and eggs. Season with salt and pepper and refrigerate for 12 hours. • <u>Pasta Dough</u>: Sift the flour and salt onto a surface and make a well in the center. Break the eggs into the well and mix in with enough water to make a smooth dough. Knead for 15–20 minutes, until smooth and elastic. Shape the dough into a ball, wrap in plastic wrap, and let rest for 30 minutes. • Roll out the dough on a lightly floured surface until very thin. Cut into 4-inch (10-cm) wide strips and arrange small heaps of filling near one edge, about 3/4 inch (2 cm) apart. Fold each strip of dough lengthwise to cover the filling. Seal, after making sure no air pockets remain, then cut into squares with a saw-toothed ravioli cutter. The tortelli should be smooth on one side and crimped on three sides. • Lay the pasta on a kitchen cloth dusted with flour. • Cook the pasta in small batches in salted boiling water for 2–3 minutes, until al dente. • Use a slotted spoon to remove them and arrange them in layers in a serving dish, alternating with the meat ragù. Serve hot.

Serves 6 • Prep: 60 min + 12 hr to chill + 30 min to rest the dough • Cooking: 40 min • Level: 3

Filling
- 6 tablespoons butter
- 8 oz/250 g thinly sliced beef
- 2/3 cup/150 ml meat stock or broth
- salt and freshly ground black pepper
- 2 slices firm-textured bread (saltless if possible), crusts removed
- 1 cup/250 ml milk
- 5 oz/150 g mortadella, chopped
- 2 cloves garlic
- 5 sprigs fresh parsley
- generous 3/4 cup/200 g finely chopped cooked Swiss chard or spinach, squeezed dry
- 1/2 cup/60 g freshly grated Parmesan cheese
- 3 large eggs

Pasta Dough
- 4 cups/600 g all-purpose/plain flour
- 1/4 teaspoon salt
- 3 large eggs
- 8–10 tablespoons lukewarm water
- 1 quantity Tuscan Meat Ragù (see page 103)

SPINACH AND RICOTTA DUMPLINGS

Gnudi

- ¹/₄ cup/60 g butter
- generous ²/₃ cup/200 ml store-bought unseasoned tomato sauce
- 2 cups/500 g sheep's milk Ricotta, strained through a fine mesh
- scant 1¹/₂ cups/350 g finely chopped cooked spinach, drained
- 2 large eggs
- 1 cup/125 g + 2 tablespoons freshly grated Parmesan cheese
- 6 tablespoons all-purpose/plain flour
- salt and freshly ground black pepper
- grated zest of ¹/₂ lemon

These dumplings can be made in advance, arranged in a serving dish, and refrigerated without sauce. Heat them in the oven or in a microwave oven, and then season with sauce and serve.

Melt the butter in a small saucepan and add the tomato sauce. Simmer over low heat for 5 minutes. • Remove from heat and set aside. • Mix the Ricotta and spinach in a large bowl. • Add the eggs, 1 cup (125 g) Parmesan, and ¹/₂ cup (75 g) flour. Season with salt and pepper and add the lemon zest. • Dip your hands in the remaining 2 tablespoons flour and form 2-inch (5-cm) balls. • Cook the dumplings in a large pot of salted boiling water for 8–10 minutes, until they rise to the surface. • Remove with a slotted spoon and transfer to individual serving dishes. • Cover with the tomato sauce and sprinkle with the remaining 2 tablespoons Parmesan cheese. • Serve hot or warm.

Serves 4 • Prep: 30 min • Cooking: 20 min • Level: 2

CHESTNUT GNOCCHI

Gnocchi di castagne

If using fresh chestnuts, cook them in salted boiling water with a bay leaf for 35–45 minutes, or until softened. • Drain and transfer to a large bowl. Use a fork or potato masher to mash the chestnuts until pureed. • Mix in the Pecorino and eggs. Season with salt and pepper, and add 2–3 tablespoons of flour to make a smooth dough. • Test the consistency by breaking off a small ball of dough, dusting it with flour, and cooking it in boiling water. If it falls apart during cooking, add more flour. • Form the dough into balls the size of hazelnuts. Roll in the flour and lay them out on a plate dusted with flour. • Cook the gnocchi in small batches in a large pot of salted boiling water for about 5 minutes until they rise to the surface. • Use a slotted spoon to transfer to serving dishes. Drizzle with the melted butter, and sprinkle with the sage and Parmesan. • Serve hot.

Serves 4 • Prep: 30 min • Cooking: 70 min • Level: 2

- 1¹/₂ lb/650 g raw peeled chestnuts or drained canned chestnuts
- ¹/₂ cup/60 g freshly grated Pecorino cheese
- 2 large eggs
- ¹/₂ cup/75 g semolina flour + more as needed
- salt and freshly ground white pepper
- 6 tablespoons butter, melted
- 1 sprig fresh sage, finely chopped
- ¹/₄ cup/30 g freshly grated Parmesan cheese

Spinach and Ricotta dumplings

Chestnut tortelli

CHESTNUT TORTELLI

Tortelli di castagne

Pasta Dough
- 2 1/3 cups/350 g all-purpose/plain flour
- 1 cup/150 g chestnut flour
- 1/8 teaspoon salt
- 3 large eggs
- 8–10 tablespoons warm water

Pasta Dough: Sift the all-purpose and chestnut flours and salt onto a surface and make a well in the center. Break the eggs into the well and mix in with enough water to make a smooth dough. Knead for 15–20 minutes, until smooth and elastic. Shape the dough into a ball, wrap in plastic wrap (cling film), and let rest for 30 minutes. • Filling: Slice the chestnuts in half and blanch in boiling water for 10 minutes. • Drain and strip them of their internal and external peels. Transfer to a large saucepan and add enough water to cover them completely. Season with salt and add the bay leaf. • Bring to a boil and cook for

35–45 minutes, or until tender. Drain. • Mash the chestnuts and add the Ricotta, eggs, and 3/4 cup (90 g) Parmesan. Season with salt and pepper. • Roll out the pasta dough on a lightly floured work surface until paper-thin. Cut into 1 1/2–2-inch (4–5-cm) rounds and drop a small amount of filling into the center. Seal in a semi-circular shape. • Cook the pasta in a large pot of salted boiling water for 3–5 minutes until they rise to the surface. • Drain well and transfer to serving plates. Drizzle with the butter and sprinkle with the remaining 3/4 cup (90 g) Parmesan.

Serves 6–8 • Prep: 2 hr • Cooking: 45 min • Level: 3

Filling
- 1 1/2 lb/650 g chestnuts
- salt
- 1 bay leaf
- generous 3/4 cup/200 g Ricotta cheese
- 2 large eggs
- 1 1/2 cups/180 g freshly grated Parmesan cheese
- 1/2 cup/125 g butter, melted
- salt and freshly ground black pepper

UMBRIA

S outh of Tuscany and north of Rome, this landlocked central region is one of the main wine-producing regions in Italy. It is also home to the highly sought-after earthy black Norcian truffles and great-tasting porcini mushrooms. The area's capital, Perugia, plays host to Italy's most productive chocolate manufacturer—Perugina, which produces the famous silver-wrapped Baci. The traditional pasta from this region is *stringozzi*, stringy thin spaghetti. Try the sweet Christmas pasta as a dessert or a snack during the holiday season.

Fresh pasta with walnut pesto
(see page 124)

Soups

SPELT SOUP

Minestra di farro

- 1 raw salted ham bone (with some ham still on the bone)
- 2 quarts/2 liters water
- 1 onion, cut into quarters
- 1 carrot, coarsely chopped
- 1 stalk celery, coarsely chopped
- 1 firm-ripe tomato, cut in half
- 4 sprigs fresh parsley
- $1/8$ teaspoon whole black peppercorns
- salt
- 2 cups/200 g crushed spelt (farro)
- $3/4$ cup/90 g freshly grated Pecorino cheese

Farro is a softer, quicker-cooking form of spelt, an nutritious ancient grain with a nut-like flavor.

If the bone comes from a very salty cooked ham, soak it overnight in cold water, then drain. • Blanch in boiling water for 3 minutes. • Place the ham bone in a large saucepan and pour in the water. Add the onion, carrot, celery, tomato, parsley, and peppercorns. Bring to a boil over low heat and simmer for about 45 minutes, or until all the vegetables are very tender. • Use a slotted spoon to remove the vegetables and process them in a food processor or blender until pureed. • Remove the meat from the bone and return the meat to the saucepan. Add the pureed vegetables. Season with salt and bring to a boil. • Add the spelt and cook for about 30 minutes, stirring occasionally, until the spelt is tender. • Sprinkle with Pecorino and serve.

Serves 4 • Prep: 40 min + 12 hr to soak the bone (if needed) • Cooking: 75 min • Level: 1

GARBANZO BEAN AND MALTAGLIATI SOUP

Pasta e ceci

Maltagliata translates as "badly cut." It is a homemade pasta, often made from scraps, cut into diamond or irregular shapes. If you like, buy sheets of fresh lasagna and cut them into diamond shapes.

Process the lard, garlic, rosemary, and sage in a food processor or blender until minced. • Cook the minced mixture with the oil in a Dutch oven (casserole) over medium heat for 5 minutes. • Stir in the garbanzo beans and pour in the water. Bring to a boil and stir in the tomatoes. Season with salt and pepper. • Cover and cook over medium heat for 20 minutes, adding more water if the soup reduces to less than half its original volume. • Add the pasta and cook until al dente. • Serve in individual bowls, drizzled with oil and a grinding of black pepper.

Serves 4 • Prep: 20 min • Cooking: 30 min • Level: 2

- 6 tablespoons lard or butter, chopped
- 2 cloves garlic, finely chopped
- Leaves from 2 sprigs fresh rosemary, finely chopped
- Leaves from 1 sprig fresh sage, finely chopped
- $1/4$ cup/60 ml extra-virgin olive oil + extra to drizzle
- 3 cups/500 g cooked garbanzo beans/chickpeas
- 2 cups/500 ml water + more as needed
- generous $3/4$ cup/200 g peeled and chopped tomatoes
- salt and freshly ground black pepper
- 4 oz/150 g fresh egg maltagliati pasta

PASTA DIAMONDS

Testaroli

- $1^2/3$ cups/250 g all-purpose/plain flour
- $1/8$ teaspoon salt
- $2^1/3$ cups/580 ml water
- 2 tablespoons extra-virgin olive oil

Mix the flour, salt, water, and 2 tablespoons of oil to make a fairly fluid batter, or pastella. If there are lumps, let the pastella rest for 1 hour, stirring occasionally with a wooden spoon. • Heat a 10-inch (25-cm) frying pan and grease it lightly with the oil. • Pour out a thin layer of pastella. Cover and cook over medium heat for 7–10 minutes. Little depressions will form on the surface. • Repeat until you have used up all the batter, greasing the pan each time. • Cut into 1 x 4-inch (3 x 10-cm) diamond shapes and keep them in an airtight container, or in the refrigerator, for 3 days. • Blanch them briefly in salted, boiling water. • Serve with Pecorino, if liked.

Serves 4 • Prep: 25 min + 1 hr to rest the pastella (if needed) • Cooking: 40 min • Level: 2

CHRISTMAS SOUP

Minestra di natale

Cook the Belgian endive in a large saucepan of salted boiling water until tender. • Drain, squeezing it dry, and chop finely. • Transfer to a large bowl and mix in the eggs, Parmesan, and nutmeg. • Pour the boiling stock over the egg mixture, and mix well. • Arrange the bread in individual serving bowls and ladle the soup over the top. Serve hot.

Serves 4 • Prep: 20 min • Cooking: 20 min • Level: 1

- 14 oz/400 g Belgian endive or Swiss chard, rinsed and finely shredded
- 4 eggs, lightly beaten
- 4 tablespoons freshly grated Parmesan cheese
- $1/8$ teaspoon freshly grated nutmeg
- $1^1/4$ quarts/1.25 liters meat stock or broth, boiling
- 4 slices firm-textured bread, toasted

Sauces

SPAGHETTINI
WITH MINT, GARLIC, AND OLIVES

Spaghettini aromatici

- 2 cloves garlic, lightly crushed but whole
- 6 tablespoons extra-virgin olive oil
- 3 anchovies, cleaned and finely chopped
- 4 leaves fresh mint, finely chopped
- Leaves from 3 small bunches fresh parsley, finely chopped
- 1 lb/500 g dried spaghettini
- 1 tablespoon capers in brine, rinsed
- 12 black olives, pitted and coarsely chopped

Sauté the garlic in the oil in a large frying pan over low heat for 2–3 minutes, until the garlic is pale gold. • Add the anchovies and cook until they have dissolved completely, 5–10 minutes. • Remove from the heat and add the mint and parsley. Cook the pasta in a large pot of salted boiling water until al dente. • Drain and add to the sauce. • Sprinkle with the capers and olives and serve.

Serves 6 • Prep: 20 min • Cooking: 20 min • Level: 2

HOMEMADE SPAGHETTI
WITH SPICY TOMATO SAUCE

Stringozzi alla spoletina

Pasta Dough: Sift the flour and salt onto a work surface and make a well in the center. Mix in enough water to make a smooth dough. Knead for 15–20 minutes, until smooth and elastic. Shape the dough into a ball, wrap in plastic wrap (cling film), and let rest for 30 minutes. • Roll out the dough on a lightly floured surface until about $^1/_8$ inch (3 mm) thick. Cover with a cloth and let dry for 30 minutes. • Sauce: Sauté the garlic, parsley, and chile in the oil in a large frying pan over medium heat for 2 minutes, until the garlic is pale gold. • Stir in the tomatoes and cook over high heat until the tomatoes have broken down, 5 minutes. • Season with salt and remove from the heat. • Use a knife to cut the pasta into $^1/_8$ inch (3 mm) strips. • Cook the pasta in a large pot of salted boiling water for 5 minutes, or until al dente. • Drain and add to the sauce. Cook over high heat, stirring until the sauce sticks to the pasta. Serve hot.

Serves 4 • Prep: 2 hr + 30 min to rest the dough + 30 min to dry the pasta • Cooking: 25 min • Level: 2

Pasta Dough
- 2$^1/_3$ cups/350 g whole-wheat flour
- $^1/_4$ teaspoon salt
- lukewarm water

Sauce
- 2 cloves garlic, finely chopped,
- 1 fresh red chile pepper, finely chopped
- 1 tablespoon finely chopped fresh parsley
- 6 tablespoons extra-virgin olive oil
- 1 lb/500 g firm-ripe tomatoes, peeled and coarsely chopped
- salt

Homemade spaghetti
with spicy tomato sauce

Homemade spaghetti
with garlic and oil

HOMEMADE SPAGHETTI WITH GARLIC AND OIL

Ciriole ternane

Pasta Dough
- 2¹/₃ cups/350 g all-purpose/plain flour
- ¹/₄ teaspoon salt
- lukewarm water
- ¹/₄ cup/60 ml extra-virgin olive oil
- 2 cloves garlic, finely chopped
- 1 tablespoon finely chopped fresh parsley

Sift the flour and salt onto a work surface and make a well in the center. Add enough water to make a stiff dough. Knead for 15–20 minutes. Set aside for 30 minutes. Break off pieces of dough and roll them into 8-inch (20-cm) long spaghetti. Use flour to prevent sticking. Leave the spaghetti to dry on the board covered with a cloth for at least 1 hour. • Cook the pasta in a large pot of salted boiling water for about 10 minutes, or until al dente. • Drain and transfer to serving plates. • Heat the oil with the garlic in a small saucepan over low heat for 3 minutes, until the garlic is pale gold. • Drizzle the oil over the pasta and sprinkle with parsley.

Serves 4 • Prep: 40 min + 30 min to rest the dough + 60 min to dry the pasta • Cooking: 15 min • Level: 2

TAGLIATELLE WITH ROASTED TOMATO SAUCE

Tagliatelle al pomodoro crudo

Preheat the oven to 400°F/200°C/gas 6. • Cut the tomatoes in half and remove the seeds. Place the tomato shells upside-down on a baking sheet. • Bake for 20–25 minutes, or until the tomatoes have lost their excess water and the skins are burnt. • Let cool completely. • Slip off the skins and mash the flesh in a large bowl. • Stir in the garlic, oil, parsley, and salt. • Cook the pasta in a large pot of salted boiling water until al dente. • Drain and add to the sauce. Serve hot.

Serves 6 • Prep: 20 min • Cooking: 20–25 min • Level: 2

- 2 lb/1 kg firm-ripe tomatoes
- 2 cloves garlic, finely chopped
- 6 tablespoons extra-virgin olive oil
- 1 tablespoon finely chopped fresh parsley
- salt
- 1 lb/500 g fresh store-bought egg tagliatelle

SPAGHETTI WITH PANCETTA

Spaghetti col rancetto

- 1³/₄ cups/190 g pancetta, cut into small cubes
- 2 tablespoons extra-virgin olive oil
- 1 red onion (or white, if you like), finely chopped
- 8 oz/200 g tomatoes, peeled, seeded, and coarsely chopped
- Leaves from 1 small bunch marjoram, finely chopped
- salt and freshly ground black pepper
- 12 oz/350 g dried spaghetti
- ¹/₂ cup/60 g freshly grated Pecorino cheese

An Umbrian variation on the famous pasta all'amatriciana, this recipe takes its name from the pancetta, which was used even if it was slightly old (rancid).

Sauté the pancetta in the oil in a saucepan over low heat for 5 minutes, until translucent. • Remove the pancetta and set aside. • Sauté the onion in the same saucepan for 3 minutes, until softened. • Add the tomatoes and cook over high heat for about 5 minutes, until they soften and begin to thicken. Add the pancetta. • Cook for 5 minutes, add the marjoram, and remove from the heat. Season with salt and pepper. • Cook the pasta in a large pot of salted boiling water until al dente. • Drain well. Serve with the sauce and sprinkle with Pecorino.

Serves 4 • Prep: 20 min • Cooking: 20 min • Level: 1

UMBRIAN RAGU SAUCE

Ragu umbro

- 1 carrot, finely chopped
- 2 stalks celery, finely chopped
- 1 medium onion, finely chopped
- 1 tablespoon butter
- 12 oz/350 g ground/minced pork
- 4 oz/125 g ground/minced beef
- 1 cup/125 g diced ham
- ²/₃ cup/150 ml dry white wine
- 4 large plum tomatoes, seeded and coarsely chopped
- salt and freshly ground black pepper to taste
- ¹/₄ teaspoon freshly ground nutmeg
- 1 small black truffle, cut into shavings (optional)

Cook the carrot, celery, and onion in the butter over medium heat in a large frying pan over medium heat for 5 minutes, or until softened. • Add the pork and beef and cook for 5 minutes, or until browned. • Add the ham and cook for 1 minute. • Increase the heat to high, pour in the wine, and let it evaporate, about 5 minutes. • Stir in the tomatoes. Season with salt, pepper, and nutmeg. • Cover and simmer over low heat for about 35 minutes, or until the sauce has reduced by half. Add the truffle. Cover the pan and let the truffle add flavor to the ragu for 2–3 minutes. • Serve with short pasta types.

Serves 6 • Prep: 30 min • Cooking: 55 min • Level: 1

PORK-STUFFED TORTELLINI IN STOCK

Tortellini in brodo

Pasta Dough: Sift the flour and salt onto a work surface and make a well in the center. Break the eggs into the well and mix in to make a smooth dough. Knead for 15–20 minutes, until smooth and elastic. Shape the dough into a ball, wrap in plastic wrap (cling film), and let rest for 30 minutes. • Filling: Heat the butter with the sage in a small saucepan over medium heat. Add the pork and sauté over medium heat, turning frequently, until browned all over. • Add the chicken liver and sauté for 2–3 minutes, until cooked but still slightly pink on the inside. • Add the mortadella and cook for 3 minutes. • Remove from the heat and discard the sage. Let cool completely. • Transfer to a food processor and process until finely chopped. Transfer to a large bowl and mix in the egg, Parmesan, salt and pepper, and nutmeg. • Roll out the dough on a lightly floured surface until very thin. Cut into 1¹/₂-inch (4-cm) squares and drop a nugget of the filling the size of walnuts into the centers. • Fold them into tortellini (see step by step, page 70). • Cook the pasta in the boiling stock for 3–5 minutes, until al dente. • Spoon into serving bowls and sprinkle with Parmesan.

Serves 6 • Prep: 2 hr + 30 min to rest the dough • Cooking: 40 min • Level: 3

Pasta Dough
- 2 cups/300 g all-purpose/plain flour
- ¹/₄ teaspoon salt
- 3 large eggs

Filling
- 2 tablespoons butter
- 5 leaves fresh sage
- 12 oz/300 g pork loin, cut into small chunks
- 1 chicken liver, trimmed and cut into quarters
- 1¹/₄ cups/150 g diced mortadella
- 1 large egg
- ¹/₄ cup/30 g freshly grated Parmesan cheese
- salt and freshly ground black pepper
- ¹/₈ teaspoon freshly grated nutmeg

To serve
- 8 cups/2 liters beef stock or broth, boiling
- ³/₄ cup/90 g freshly grated Parmesan cheese

Sauces

Gnocchi with duck sauce and Pecorino

TAGLIATELLE WITH LAMB SAUCE

Tagliatelle al ragù di agnello

- 3 cloves garlic, finely chopped
- 1 sprig fresh rosemary
- 6 tablespoons extra-virgin olive oil
- 1 lb/500 g fatty or lean lamb, cut into small chunks
- generous $^1/_3$ cup/100 ml dry white wine
- 1 lb/500 g firm-ripe tomatoes, peeled, seeded, and coarsely chopped
- salt and freshly ground black pepper
- 12 oz/300 g fresh store-bought egg tagliatelle

Sauté the garlic and rosemary in the oil in a medium saucepan over medium heat for 2 minutes until the garlic is pale gold. • Add the lamb and sauté for 2–3 minutes, until browned all over. • Increase the heat and pour in the wine. • Stir in the tomatoes and season with salt and pepper. Cover and cook for about 30 minutes, or until the lamb is tender. • Cook the pasta in a large pot of salted boiling water until al dente. • Drain and add to the sauce. Cook for 1 minute or until the sauce sticks to the pasta, and serve.

Serves 4 • Prep: 45 min • Cooking: 60 min • Level: 1

GNOCCHI WITH DUCK SAUCE AND PECORINO

Gnocchi al sugo d'oca

Heat the oil in a Dutch oven (casserole) over low heat. Add the onion, celery, and carrot and sauté for about 15 minutes, adding some water if the vegetables begin to burn. • Add the pieces of meat and cook fro 2–3 minutes, until browned all over. • Increase the heat and pour in the wine and tomatoes. Cover and cook over low heat for about 45 minutes, or until the meat is tender. Remove the meat, bone it, and remove the skin. Break it up with your fingers. Return the meat to the pan and cook for 1 minute. • Cook the gnocchi in small batches in a large pot of salted boiling water for 3–5 minutes, until they rise to the surface. • Use a slotted spoon to drain the gnocchi and arrange in a bowl with the sauce. Sprinkle with the Pecorino. Serve hot.

Serves 6 • Prep: 60 min • Cooking: 60 min • Level: 2

- 5 tablespoons extra-virgin olive oil
- 1 red or white onion, finely chopped
- 1 stalk celery, finely chopped
- $^1/_2$ carrot, finely chopped
- water (optional)
- $1^1/_2$ lb/750 g goose or duck, excess fat removed and cut into large chunks
- 1 cup/250 ml dry white wine
- 2 cups/500 g peeled and chopped tomatoes
- 1 recipe Potato gnocchi (see page 130)
- $1^1/_4$ cups/150 g freshly grated Pecorino cheese

BLACK TRUFFLE SAUCE

Sugo alla Norcina

- 2 cloves garlic, lightly crushed but whole
- $^1/_4$ cup/60 ml extra-virgin olive oil
- 2 Italian sausages, casing removed and crumbled
- $^2/_3$ cup/150 ml dry white wine
- salt
- $1^1/_2$ oz/40 g black truffle, coarsely grated

This sauce is excellent with all sorts of long pasta, both dried, such as spaghetti or bucatini, and fresh, such as tagliatelle or maccheroni alla chitarra {see page 157}.

Sauté the garlic in the oil in a saucepan over medium heat for 2 minutes, until pale gold. • Add the sausage and brown it for 2 minutes. • Pour in the wine, season with salt, and add the truffle. Cook for 5–10 minutes until the wine has evaporated. Discard the garlic. • Remove from the heat and serve with your chosen pasta.

Serves 4–6 • Prep: 15 min • Cooking: 15 min • Level: 1

TAGLIOLINI WITH BLACK TRUFFLES

Tagliolini al tartufo nero di Norcia

Clean the truffles carefully with a vegetable brush and grate them finely. • Sauté the garlic in the oil in a small saucepan over medium heat for 2 minutes, until pale gold. • Add the truffles, mix well, and remove from the heat. Discard the garlic. • Cook the pasta in a large pot of salted boiling water until al dente. • Drain, reserving a few tablespoons of the cooking water, and transfer to a serving dish. Add the sauce and, if needed, the reserved cooking water. Serve immediately.

Serves 4 • Prep: 20 min • Cooking: 15 min • Level: 1

- 5 oz/150 g black truffles, preferably from Norcia
- 1 clove garlic, lightly crushed but whole
- $^1/_2$ cup/125 ml extra-virgin olive oil
- 12 oz/300 g fresh store-bought egg tagliolini

Black truffle sauce

Sauces

PASTA WITH BELL PEPPERS

Frascarelli ai peperoni

Pasta Dough
- 2 large eggs
- $^1/_3$–$^1/_2$ cup/80–125 ml water
- 2$^2/_3$ cups/400 g all-purpose/plain flour
- $^1/_4$ teaspoon salt

The unusual name of this type of pasta comes from the tool used to prepare it: a branch or a leafy frond. This recipe is also common in northern Lazio, and it can be served almost dry, with a sauce, or in a homemade meat stock.

Pasta Dough: Beat the eggs and water in a large bowl. • Sift a small amount of flour and salt over a clean work surface. • Dip a leafy branch, or a small bundle of broomcorn, into the eggs and brush it over the flour. • Use your other hand to move the flour around so that it forms a number of small clumps. Gather the clumps and work through a fairly coarse sieve. • Arrange on a wooden cutting board and sift the remaining flour onto the work surface. Repeat the process until you have used up all the ingredients. If you want to store the frascarelli, make sure they are quite dry before putting them away for storage. • Sauce: Sauté the onion in the oil in a saucepan over low heat for 3–4 minutes until softened. • Add the bell peppers and tomatoes. Season with salt. • Cook, covered, over low heat until the bell peppers are tender, adding water if needed, 5–10 minutes. • Remove from heat and run through a strainer. • Season with salt and pepper. • Stir in the Mascarpone and mix well to make a smooth sauce. • Cook the pasta in a large pot of salted boiling water for 2–3 minutes, or until al dente. • Drain and transfer to the sauce. Sprinkle with Pecorino Romano and serve.

Serves 4 • Prep: 90 min • Cooking: 30 min • Level: 2

Sauce
- 1 onion, thinly sliced
- $^1/_4$ cup/60 ml extra-virgin olive oil
- 1 red bell pepper/capsicum, seeded, and cut into thin strips
- 1 yellow bell pepper/capsicum, seeded, and cut into thin strips
- 4 ripe tomatoes, coarsely chopped
- salt and freshly ground white pepper
- 2 tablespoons Mascarpone cheese
- $^3/_4$ cup/90 g freshly grated Pecorino Romano cheese

TAGLIATELLE WITH MEAT SAUCE

Tajarin al sugo di arrosto

- 12 oz/350 g dried spaghetti
- 2 cloves garlic, lightly crushed but whole
- 1 sprig rosemary
- 6 tablespoons butter
- 5 tablespoons extra-virgin olive oil
- 1 lb/500 g lean veal, tied with kitchen string
- salt and freshly ground

Sauté the garlic and rosemary in 5 tablespoons butter and oil in a thick-bottomed saucepan over medium heat until the garlic is lightly browned and aromatic. • Add the veal and brown it all over. Season with salt and pepper. Lower the heat, cover and cook for about 40 minutes, adding stock every time the meat begins to dry. This will create an abundance of cooking juices. • Remove the meat (which you can then serve separately), run the juices through a fine-mesh strainer, crushing the garlic cloves, and collect them in a medium frying pan. • Cook the pasta in a large pot of salted boiling water until al dente. Drain and add to the frying pan, adding a little cooking water if needed. Dot with the remaining 1 tablespoon butter, letting it melt into the pasta. Sprinkle with the grated truffle, if using, and the Parmesan. • Serve hot.

Serves 4 • Prep: 20 min • Cooking: 1 hr • Level: 1

- white pepper
- 2 cups/500 ml meat stock or broth
- 1$^1/_2$ oz/40 g white truffle, grated (optional)
- 1 cup/125 g freshly grated Parmesan cheese

Sauces

PAPPARDELLE WITH GAME SAUCE

Pappardelle alla lepre

- 1 hare or rabbit (about 3 lb/1.5 kg in weight) cut into 6 chunks, complete with liver, heart, and spleen
- 1 carrot, coarsely chopped
- 1 stalk celery, coarsely chopped
- 1 onion, coarsely chopped
- 3 cloves garlic, lightly crushed but whole
- generous $1/3$ cup/100 ml white wine vinegar
- 4 cups/1 liter dry white wine + more as needed
- 5 tablespoons extra-virgin olive oil

- 1 bunch fresh sage
- 1 sprig fresh rosemary
- 2 cups/500 ml beef stock or broth
- 3 tablespoons capers in vinegar
- salt and freshly ground black pepper
- 1 cup/100 g black olives, pitted
- 1 lb/500 g fresh store-bought egg pappardelle

Place the hare (without the giblets) in a ceramic bowl with the carrot, celery, onion, 2 cloves garlic, and $1/4$ cup (60 ml) of the vinegar. Pour in enough wine to cover and let marinate, covered, for 12 hours. • Remove the hare and pat it dry on paper towels. • Chop the vegetables finely and reserve the marinade liquid. • Sauté the vegetables in the oil in a Dutch oven (casserole) over low heat for 10 minutes, or until lightly golden. • Add the sage, rosemary, and hare and cook over high heat for 15 minutes, or until browned all over. • Pour in $1/4$ cup (60 ml) of the reserved marinade liquid from the marinade. Add $1/2$ cup (125 ml) stock, the giblets, 2 tablespoons of the capers, and salt and pepper. Cook, partially covered, for about 1 hour, adding more stock if the mixture starts to evaporate. • Remove the larger pieces of hare, place on a cutting board, and bone them. Transfer the boned meat to a food processor or blender, reserving one piece for garnish. Add the drippings, giblets, the remaining clove of garlic, and the remaining 1 tablespoon of capers. Process until finely chopped. • Return the processed mixture to a saucepan still containing the small pieces of hare. Pour in the remaining vinegar, tasting to ensure that it does not become too acidic. Adjust the consistency with some stock if it is too thick. • Stir in the olives and cook for 5 minutes more. • Cook the pasta in a large pot of salted boiling water until al dente. • Drain and add to the sauce. Garnish with the reserved piece of meat.

Serves 6 • Prep: 60 min + 12 hr to marinate • Cooking: 1 hr 45 min • Level: 2

CHESTNUT TAGLIATELLE

Tagliatelle more

Chestnuts
- 2 cups/500 ml milk
- 15 dried chestnuts
- $1/8$ teaspoon salt

Pasta Dough
- 8 oz/250 g chestnut flour
- $3/4$ cup/125 g all-purpose flour (or semolina flour)
- $1/8$ teaspoon salt
- $3/4$ cup/180 ml lukewarm water, + more as needed

Sauce
- 4 tablespoons heavy/double cream
- generous $3/4$ cup/200 g Ricotta cheese
- $1/8$ teaspoon freshly grated nutmeg
- 4 tablespoons freshly grated Parmesan cheese
- salt

Chestnuts: Bring the milk and salt to a boil in a large saucepan. • Cook the chestnuts for 1 hour, or until tender. • Use a fork or potato masher to mash the chestnuts in a large bowl until pureed, adding a little of the cooking liquid to form a puree. • Pasta Dough: Sift both flours and salt onto a work surface and make a well in the center. Add the eggs and enough water to make a smooth dough. Shape the dough into a ball, wrap in plastic wrap, and let rest for 30 minutes. • Roll out the dough into a sheet that is not too thin. Cut into $3/4$-inch (2-cm) wide strips. • Sauce: Heat the cream in a frying pan over low heat. Mix in the Ricotta, nutmeg, and salt. • Cook the pasta in a large pot of salted boiling water until al dente. • Drain and add to the sauce along with the Parmesan and almost all the chestnut puree. • Garnish with the remaining chestnut puree and serve.

Serves 4 • Prep: 90 min + 30 min to rest the dough • Cooking: 1 hr 15 min • Level: 2

Sauces & Fresh Pasta

Homemade spaghetti with mushrooms

HOMEMADE SPAGHETTI WITH MUSHROOMS

Ciriole ai funghi

Pasta Dough
- 2¹/₃ cups/350 g all-purpose/plain flour
- ¹/₄ teaspoon salt
- lukewarm water

Sauce
- 1 lb/500 g mixed fresh mushrooms or porcini mushrooms
- ¹/₄ cup/60 ml extra-virgin olive oil
- salt
- 2 cloves garlic, finely chopped
- 1 fresh red chile pepper, finely chopped
- 2 tablespoons finely chopped fresh parsley

Pasta Dough: Sift the flour and salt onto a surface and make a well in the center. Add enough water to make a stiff dough. Knead for about 10 minutes. Set aside for 5 minutes. Break off pieces of dough and roll them into 8-inch (20-cm) long spaghetti. Use flour to prevent sticking. Leave the spaghetti to dry on the board covered with a cloth for at least 1 hour. • Sauce: Wash the dirt from the mushrooms, rinse carefully, and pat them dry. Separate the stems from the caps and coarsely chop the stems. Thinly slice the caps. • Sauté the mushroom stems in 3 tablespoons oil in a frying pan over high heat for 2 minutes. • Add the sliced caps and cook for about 10 minutes, or until tender. Season with salt. • Sauté the garlic, chile, and 1 tablespoon parsley in 1 tablespoon of the oil in a medium saucepan over medium heat for 2 minutes, until the garlic is pale gold. • Add the mushrooms. Cook for 5 minutes more. Stir in the remaining 1 tablespoon of parsley and remove from the heat. • Cook the pasta in a large pot of salted boiling water until al dente. • Drain and add to the sauce.

Serves 4 • Prep: 30 min • Cooking: 30 min • Level: 1

FRESH PASTA WITH WALNUT PESTO

Pasta fresca al pesto di noci

Pasta Dough: Sift the all-purpose and semolina flours and salt onto a surface and make a well in the center. Add enough water to make a smooth dough. Knead for 15–20 minutes, until smooth and elastic. Shape the dough into a ball, wrap in plastic wrap (cling film), and let rest for 30 minutes. • Roll out the dough on a lightly floured surface to a thickness of ¹/₈ inch (3 mm) and cut into 1-inch (3-cm) squares. Let dry on a floured kitchen towel for about 30 minutes. • Walnut Sauce: Blanch the walnuts in boiling water for 1 minute. Drain and transfer to a large cotton kitchen towel. Fold the towel over the nuts and rub them to remove the thin inner skins. • Process the nuts with the sugar, liqueur, chocolate, bread crumbs, lemon zest, and cinnamon until smooth. • Cook the pasta in a large pot of salted boiling water until al dente. • Drain, transfer to a serving dish, and cover with the sauce. • Serve cool.

Serves 6 • Prep: 2 hr • Cooking: 20 min + 30 min to rest the dough • Level: 2

Pasta Dough
- 1¹/₃ cups/200 g all-purpose/plain flour
- 1¹/₃ cups/200 g semolina flour
- ¹/₄ teaspoon salt
- ²/₃ cup/150 ml lukewarm water + more as needed

Walnut Sauce
- ³/₄ cup/100 g walnuts
- ¹/₂ cup/100 g granulated sugar
- ¹/₄ cup/60 ml Alchermes liqueur or dark rum
- 1¹/₂ oz/45 g semisweet/plain chocolate, coarsely chopped
- 1 tablespoon fine dry bread crumbs
- grated zest of ¹/₂ lemon
- ¹/₄ teaspoon ground cinnamon

SPAGHETTI WITH WILD ASPARAGUS

Spaghetti agli asparagi

- 1¹/₂ lb/700 g wild or cultivated asparagus
- ¹/₄ cup/60 ml extra-virgin olive oil
- 2 cloves garlic, finely chopped
- 1 lb/500 g firm-ripe tomatoes, peeled and seeded
- salt
- 12 oz/350 g dried spaghetti
- ¹/₄ cup/30 g freshly grated aged Pecorino cheese

Remove the woody part of the asparagus, peel the rest of the stalk, and cut into short sections. Split off the tips. • Sauté the asparagus stalks in the oil in a frying pan over medium heat for 5 minutes. • Add the garlic and tomatoes and season with salt. Cover and cook over low heat for 15 minutes. • Add the asparagus tips, and cook for 15 minutes more, or until the asparagus is tender. • Cook the pasta in a large pot of salted boiling water until al dente. • Drain and add to the asparagus sauce. Sprinkle with Pecorino and serve.

Serves 4 • Prep: 30 min • Cooking: 45 min • Level: 1

SWEET MACARONI

Maccheroni dolci con le noci

This sweet pasta dish is a traditional dish served during the Christmas vigil.

Cook the pasta in a large pot of salted boiling water until al dente. • Drain and transfer to a large bowl. • Mix in the sugar, walnuts, cocoa, bread crumbs, cinnamon, and lemon zest. • Serve hot.

Serves 6 • Prep: 10 min • Cooking: 12 min • Level: 1

- 12 oz/300 g fresh store-bought macaroni pasta
- ¹/₃ cup/70 g granulated sugar
- 2 cups/200 g finely chopped walnuts
- ¹/₃ cup/50 g unsweetened cocoa powder
- ³/₄ cup/90 g fine dry bread crumbs
- ¹/₄ teaspoon ground cinnamon
- grated zest of 1 lemon

Spaghetti with wild asparagus

MARCHES

The Marchigiani have a simple healthy cuisine based on fresh ingredients from the sea and from the farm. Halfway down the Adriatic coastline, expect to indulge in Dublin Bay shrimp and juicy mussels at Ancona, the region's harbor capital. Farther inland, the region's favorite baked pasta dish, *vincisgrassi*, is prepared in homes and restaurants the way that *nonna* (grandmother) makes it. Truffles and porcini mushrooms are used sparingly in the pasta recipes from this region but when used, they add a rustic flavor to many dishes.

Spaghetti with black truffles and anchovies (see page 132)

THIN SPAGHETTI WITH SEAFOOD

Tagliolini di Campofilone al calamari

- 2 cloves garlic, finely chopped
- 5 tablespoons extra-virgin olive oil
- 8 oz/200 g small squids cut into thin rings and with tentacles split in half
- 6 large Dublin Bay prawns or jumbo shrimp (weighing 5 oz/150 g in total), cut in half lengthwise with kitchen shears
- ¹/₄ cup/60 ml dry white wine
- salt
- 1 lb/400 g store-bought tagliolini di Campofilone (a very fine long pasta), or dried capellini, spaghettini, or angel hair pasta
- 1 small bunch parsley, finely chopped

Sauté the garlic in the oil in a large frying pan over low heat for 3 minutes, until aromatic. • Add the squid and eight half-prawns and cook over low heat for 15 minutes. • Pour in the wine and cook for 2–3 minutes until evaporated. • Season with salt and remove from the heat. • Cook the pasta in a large pot of salted boiling water until not quite al dente. • Blanch the remaining half-prawns in pot with the pasta water for 3–4 minutes, until cooked. • Remove the prawns with a slotted spoon and set aside. Drain the pasta, reserving 4 tablespoons of the cooking water, and add to the frying pan with the sauce. Add cooking water to adjust the consistency, if needed. • Transfer to a serving plate and garnish with the blanched half-prawns and sprinkle with parsley.

Serves 4 • Prep: 20 min • Cooking: 30 min • Level: 1

THIN SPAGHETTI WITH ANCHOVIES AND MUSSELS

Spaghetti del marinaio

Soak the mussels in a large bowl of warm salted water for 1 hour. Pull off the beards. • Transfer the mussels to a large saucepan of salted boiling water and cook until they open up. Discard any that do not open. Strain the liquid and set aside. • Leave eight mussels in their shells. Shell the rest and chop the flesh coarsely. • Sauté the onion, garlic, and parsley in the oil in a large frying pan with a pinch of salt over low heat for 20 minutes. • Add the salted anchovies and capers and cook over low heat for 5–10 minutes until the anchovies have dissolved. • Add the fresh anchovies and chopped mussel flesh. • Add the strained cooking liquid from the mussels and cook for 10 minutes. Pour in the wine and cook for 5 minutes, or until evaporated. Season with salt and chile pepper. • Cook the spaghetti in a large pot of salted boiling water until al dente. • Drain and add to the pan. • Transfer to serving dishes and garnish with the reserved mussels in shell.

Serves 4 • Prep: 45 min + 60 min to soak the mussels • Cooking: 45 min • Level: 1

- 1 lb/400 g mussels, rinsed and ready for cooking
- 1 onion, finely chopped
- 1 clove garlic, finely chopped
- 2 teaspoons fresh parsley, finely chopped
- ¹/₄ cup/60 ml extra-virgin olive oil
- 2 anchovies packed in salt, rinsed, and boned
- 1 tablespoon capers, packed in salt, rinsed
- 8 oz/250 g fresh anchovies, boned and filetted
- ²/₃ cup/150 ml dry white wine
- ¹/₈ teaspoon crumbled dried chile pepper
- salt
- 12 oz/350 g spaghetti

Thin spaghetti
with anchovies and mussels

Gnocchi

RIDGED GNOCCHI WITH DUCK SAUCE
Gnocchi col sugo di papera

Ridged Gnocchi
- 2 lb/1 kg baking/floury potatoes
- 1²/₃ cups/250 g all-purpose/plain flour
- ¹/₈ teaspoon salt
- 1 large egg, lightly beaten
- 3 tablespoons freshly grated Parmesan cheese

Duck Sauce
- 6 tablespoons extra-virgin olive oil
- 1 red or white onion, finely chopped
- 1 stalk celery, finely chopped
- 1 carrot, finely chopped

Ridged Gnocchi: Cook the potatoes in salted boiling water for 15–20 minutes, or until tender. Drain and peel them. Use a potato masher or fork to mash them and spread them on a work surface to cool. • Add the flour, salt, egg, and Parmesan. Knead the mixture into a ball. Pull off pieces of dough and form into ¹/₂-inch (1-cm) logs. Cut the logs into 1-inch (3-cm) lengths and slide them onto a floured surface (a ridged board, if you have one, see below, or press them against a fork), making sure they are not too close together. • Duck Sauce: Heat the oil in a Dutch oven (casserole) and sauté the onion, celery, carrot, and parsley over low heat for 15 minutes. • Add the garlic and cook for 3 minutes, until pale gold. • Increase the heat

and add the duck, browning it all over for 2 minutes. • Pour in the wine and season with salt and pepper. • Stir in the tomatoes, tomato paste (dissolved in 2 tablespoons of warm water), and bay leaf. Cover and cook over low heat for about 1 hour, stirring occasionally, or until the duck is tender. • Remove the duck, bone it, discard the skin, and chop coarsely. Return the duck to the pan and cook for 15 minutes more. • Cook the gnocchi in small batches in a large pot of salted boiling water until they rise to the surface. • Use a slotted spoon to drain the gnocchi and add to the sauce. Sprinkle with Parmesan and serve.

Serves 4–6 • Prep: 60 min • Cooking: 90 min • Level: 2

- 1 sprig fresh parsley, finely chopped
- 1 clove garlic, finely chopped
- 1 small duck, cut into eight pieces, excess fat removed
- ¹/₄ cup/60 ml dry white wine
- salt and freshly ground black pepper
- 1²/₃ cups/400 g peeled plum tomatoes, pressed through a fine mesh strainer (passata)
- 1 tablespoon tomato paste/concentrate
- 1 bay leaf
- ¹/₂ cup/60 g freshly grated Parmesan cheese

MAKING POTATO GNOCCHI

1. Peel the boiled potatoes while they are still hot and use a potato masher or fork to mash them until smooth or run them through a potato ricer.

2. Mix in the flour and salt and knead the ingredients together until the dough is smooth.

3. Break off little bits of dough and roll them out into cylinders about as thick as your finger. Cut them into short lengths.

To make a different shape: Dust with a little more flour as you shape them. You can roll the short sections on a flour-dusted ridged wooden board.

To make without a ridged board: Pass them against the back of a grater or press against the tines of a fork.

To cook: Boil the gnocchi in small batches in plenty of salted water for 3–5 minutes, until they rise to the surface. Remove the gnocchi with a slotted spoon.

BAKED HAM AND MUSHROOM LASAGNA

Vincisgrassi

Pasta Dough
- 2 cups/300 g all-purpose/plain flour
- $^1/_4$ teaspoon salt
- 2 large eggs
- 3 tablespoons Marsala wine
- 1 tablespoon extra-virgin olive oil

Meat Sauce
- 1 onion, finely chopped
- $^1/_2$ cup/125 g butter
- 1 oz/30 g dried mushrooms, soaked in warm water for 15 minutes and finely chopped
- 2 oz/60 g fatty and lean cooked ham, cut into thin strips
- generous $^1/_3$ cup/100 ml chicken stock or broth
- thighs and breasts of 1 chicken, boned and cut into small strips

Pasta Dough: Sift the flour and salt onto a surface and make a well in the center. Break the eggs into the well and mix in with the wine and oil to make a smooth dough. Knead for 15–20 minutes, until smooth and elastic. Shape the dough into a ball, wrap in plastic wrap (cling film), and let rest for 30 minutes. • Roll out the dough into exceedingly thin rectangles, about $1^1/_2$ x 8 inches (4 x 20 cm). • Blanch the pasta in small batches in a large pot of salted boiling water with a little oil for 1 minute . Remove and place in cold water with oil and salt. Squeeze them dry and lay them out on damp cloths (see page 222). • Meat Sauce: Sauté the onion in $^1/_4$ cup (60 g) of the butter in a small saucepan over low heat for about 10 minutes, or until softened. • Add the mushrooms and sauté them for 2 minutes. • Add the ham and a little stock. • Stir in the chicken and cook until browned all over. • Add the chicken livers and the calf's liver, if using. Increase the heat and

pour in the Marsala. Add enough hot water or stock to cover and season with salt and pepper. • Stir in the truffle and cook over low heat for about 20 minutes. • Butter a baking dish. • Béchamel Sauce: Melt the butter in a saucepan over medium heat and add the flour to make a thick paste. • Gradually add the milk and season with salt, pepper, and nutmeg. Bring to a boil over low heat, stirring constantly, and boil for 10 minutes, until thickened. • Arrange a rectangle of pasta in the prepared baking dish. Top with the Béchamel sauce and cover with the meat sauce. Sprinkle with the Parmesan. Continue to layer the pasta with the Béchamel and meat sauces until all the ingredients are used up, finishing with a layer of pasta. Dot with the remaining $^1/_4$ cup (60 g) butter and let rest at room temperature for at least 2 hours. • Preheat the oven to 350°F/180°C/gas 5. • Bake for 25–35 minutes, or until the pasta is slightly crunchy on top. • Serve warm.

Serves 6 • Prep: 90 min + 30 min to rest dough + 2 hr to rest lasagna • Cooking: 90 min • Level: 3

- 8 oz/300 g chicken livers, trimmed and diced
- 5 oz/150 g calf's liver, blanched (optional)
- generous $^1/_3$ cup/100 ml Marsala wine
- salt and freshly ground black pepper
- 1 black truffle, finely chopped (2 tablespoons canned/tinned or truffle paste is fine)

Béchamel Sauce
- $^1/_4$ cup/60 g butter
- $^1/_4$ cup/30 g all-purpose/plain flour
- $2^1/_3$ cups/580 ml milk
- salt and freshly ground white pepper
- freshly grated nutmeg
- 3 tablespoons freshly grated Parmesan cheese

SPAGHETTI WITH BLACK TRUFFLES AND ANCHOVIES

Spaghetti al tartufo

- 6 tablespoons extra-virgin olive oil
- 1 clove garlic, finely chopped
- 2 anchovies packed in salt, rinsed, boned, and finely chopped
- 2 teaspoons store-bought unseasoned tomato sauce

Heat the oil with the garlic in a small saucepan over medium heat. Let sauté briefly, making sure that the garlic does not turn brown. • Lower the heat, add the anchovies, and cook for 5–10 minutes until dissolved. • Add the tomato sauce and season with salt and pepper. • Cook for 4–5

minutes, until aromatic. • Cook the pasta in a large pot of salted boiling water until al dente. • Drain and transfer to serving dishes. Sprinkle with the truffles and top with the anchovy sauce. • Garnish with the parsley.

Serves 4 • Prep: 10 min • Cooking: 15 min • Level: 1

- salt and freshly ground white pepper
- 12 oz/350 g dried spaghetti
- 1 oz/30 g black truffles, finely grated
- Leaves from 1 small bunch parsley, finely chopped

BAKED MACARONI WITH BLACK TRUFFLES AND CHICKEN

Maccheroni alla pesarese

- 1 onion, thinly sliced
- scant $^1/_2$ cup/100 g butter
- 1 tablespoon tomato paste/concentrate mixed with $^1/_4$ cup/ 60 ml meat stock (or broth)
- salt and freshly ground black pepper
- 5 oz/150 g boneless, skinless chicken breast
- 5 oz/150 g veal, in a single piece

Sauté the onion in 2 tablespoons butter in a saucepan over low heat for 30 minutes, or until softened. • Add the tomato paste mixture and season with salt and pepper. Cook until the liquid has evaporated. • Sauté the chicken and veal in 4 tablespoons butter in a frying pan over high heat for 2 minutes until brown. Lower the heat and cook for 15 minutes. • Remove from the heat and let cool. • Preheat the oven to 400°F/200°C/gas 6. Butter a baking dish. • Process the chicken, veal, and ham with $^1/_2$ cup (125 ml) of cream and the truffles in a food processor until smooth. • Cook the pasta in a large pot of salted boiling water for half the time indicated on the package. Drain and run under cold water to cool. • Using a pastry bag, fill the pasta with the meat mixture. • Transfer half the filled pasta to the prepared dish and top with the onion sauce and dot with 3 tablespoons butter. Sprinkle with $^1/_4$ cup (30 g) of Swiss cheese. • Transfer the remaining filled macaroni on top and cover with the remaining $^1/_4$ cup (60 ml) cream. Top with the remaining 3 tablespoons butter and Swiss cheese. • Bake for 15–20 minutes, or until the pasta is slightly crispy. • Serve piping hot.

Serves 4 • Prep: 30 min • Cooking: 60 min • Level: 2

- 8 oz/200 g cooked ham, thickly sliced
- $^3/_4$ cup/180 ml heavy/double cream
- $^1/_2$ oz/20 g black truffles
- 10 oz/300 g large dried smooth or ridged tube pasta
- $^3/_4$ cup/90 g grated Swiss cheese

Baked macaroni with black truffles and chicken

LAZIO

The center of the region of Lazio and home to the Eternal City, Rome has a cuisine that is abundant and classical. *Carbonara* is the quintessential pasta dish—sautéed pancetta and pasta tossed with seasoned eggs. *Bucatini*, thick spaghetti with a hollowed-out center, can be found on every menu, served with a spicy tomato sauce. This simple but tasty spaghetti with garlic and olive oil is ideal for a light lunch. Or try serving fresh egg fettuccine with butter and cream or a rich meat ragù for a dinnertime *primo*.

Fettuccine, Roman style (see page 141)

Soups & Sauces

PASTA AND PEAS IN STOCK

Pasta e piselli in brodo

- ¹/₄ cup/60 g lard or butter, cut up
- 1 onion, finely chopped
- 2 cloves garlic, lightly crushed but whole
- 5 leaves fresh basil
- 1³/₄ cups/215 g fresh or frozen peas, thawed if frozen
- 2 oz/50 g prosciutto/ Parma ham, finely shredded
- 1 tablespoon tomato paste/concentrate
- 6 cups/1.5 liters meat stock or broth
- salt and freshly ground white pepper
- 4 oz/125 g quadrucci or any small soup pasta (fresh or dried)
- ¹/₄ cup/30 g freshly grated Pecorino cheese

Quadrucci are small square soup pastas. They can be made by cutting a long pasta such as tagliatelle into small squares.

Chop together the lard, onion, garlic, and basil. • Sauté the chopped mixture with the peas and prosciutto in a large saucepan over medium heat. • Mix the tomato paste with ³/₄ cup (180 ml) stock and add to the saucepan. • Cook, covered, over low heat, adding more stock if needed. Season with salt and pepper. • When the peas are tender, add the remaining stock. • Bring to a boil, add the pasta, and cook until al dente. • Sprinkle with Pecorino and serve.

Serves 4 • Prep: 30 min • Cooking: 45 min • Level: 1

TAGLIATELLE WITH CREAM AND HAM

Tagliatelle panna e prosciutto

- 3 oz/100 g ham, cut into thin strips
- 4 tablespoons butter
- generous ³/₄ cup/200 g heavy/double cream
- salt and freshly ground white pepper
- ¹/₈ teaspoon freshly grated nutmeg
- 14 oz/400 g fresh egg tagliatelle
- ¹/₂ cup/60 g freshly grated Parmesan cheese

Sauté the ham in the butter in a large frying pan over medium heat for 5 minutes without letting it burn. • Pour in the cream and cook until thickened. • Season with salt, pepper, and nutmeg. (The ham will already have flavored the sauce.) • Cook the pasta in a large pot of salted boiling water until al dente. • Drain and add to the pan with the sauce. Simmer and, if needed, add a small amount of cooking water to the pasta. • Sprinkle with the Parmesan and serve hot.

Serves 4 • Prep: 15 min • Cooking: 15 min • Level: 1

FISH AND BROCCOLI SOUP

Pasta e broccoli con brodo di razza

Bring plenty of water to a boil in a fish poacher with the celery, onion, the whole garlic clove, and 1 tablespoon of the parsley. Season with salt and add the ray. Cook for about 20 minutes, or until the flesh breaks away from the bones. Drain the fish and fillet it. Return the bones to the fish poacher and boil for about 30 minutes to make a good stock. The filleted fish, seasoned with oil and lemon, should be served as a main course accompanied by steamed vegetables. Strain the stock and set it aside. • Sauté the remaining chopped garlic, 2 tablespoons parsley, chile, and anchovy in the oil in a large saucepan for 5–10 minutes, or until the garlic is pale gold and the anchovy has dissolved. • Stir in the tomatoes and let them simmer for 5 minutes • Increase the heat and pour in the wine. • Divide the broccoli into florets and stems. Peel the stems and chop finely. • Add the broccoli florets and stems to the sautéed mixture and add enough of the fish stock to cover. Season with salt and simmer for 20 minutes. • Pour in more stock (about 5 cups/ 1.25 liters) and bring to a boil. Season with salt and add the pasta. Cook for the time indicated on the package. • Serve hot in individual serving bowls.

Serves 4–6 • Prep: 30 min • Cooking: 90 min • Level: 2

- 8 cups/2 liters water
- 1 stalk celery, cut into short lengths
- ¹/₂ onion, thinly sliced
- 1 clove garlic, lightly crushed but whole + 2 cloves garlic, finely chopped
- 3 tablespoons finely chopped fresh parsley
- salt
- 1 ray or skate, weighing about 2 lb/1 kg, cleaned
- 1 fresh red chile pepper, finely chopped
- 1 anchovy packed in salt, rinsed of salt and filleted
- 5 tablespoons extra-virgin olive oil
- 12 oz/300 g firm-ripe tomatoes, peeled, seeded, and finely chopped
- generous ¹/₃ cup/100 ml dry white wine
- 1 lb/500 g broccoli
- 8 oz/300 g short dried soup pasta (small pennette)

FRASCARELLI IN STOCK

Frascarelli in brodo

Pasta Dough
- 1 large egg
- ²/₃–³/₄ cup/150–180 ml water
- 2 cups/300 g all-purpose/plain flour
- ¹/₄ teaspoon salt

For these frascarelli, *served in stock, it is best to make the pasta dough with less egg than is used in the Umbrian recipe. The procedure remains the same but the proportions are slightly different. The stock in which the frascarelli are cooked is already sufficiently rich that two eggs are not required.*

<u>Pasta Dough</u>: Beat the egg and water in a large bowl. • Sift a small amount of flour and salt over a clean surface. • Dip a leafy branch, or a small bundle of broomcorn, into the eggs and brush it over the flour. • Use your other hand to move the flour around so that it forms a number of small clumps. Gather the clumps and work through a fairly coarse sieve. • Spread out on a wooden cutting board and sift the remaining flour onto the surface. Repeat the process until you have used up all the ingredients. If you want to store the frascarelli, make sure it is quite dry before putting it away for storage. • <u>Stock</u>: Chop the lard, garlic, onion, celery, carrot, and parsley to make a very fine mixture. • Sauté the chopped mixture in the oil in a large saucepan over medium heat for 7–10 minutes until very soft. • Add the bay leaf and sauté for 3 minutes over high heat. • Add the tomatoes with their liquid and the chicken stock. • Remove the bay leaf and season with salt and pepper. • Simmer for 30 minutes over low heat. • Increase the heat, add the frascarelli and cook for 2–3 minutes. Serve piping hot.

Serves 4 • Prep: 90 min • Cooking: 45 min • Level: 2

Stock
- 4 oz/100 g lard or butter, cut up
- 2 cloves garlic, finely chopped
- ¹/₂ onion, finely chopped
- 1 stalk celery, finely chopped
- 1 small carrot, finely chopped
- 3 sprigs fresh parsley, finely chopped
- 2 tablespoons extra-virgin olive oil
- 1 bay leaf
- 8 oz/200 g peeled and chopped tomatoes
- 3 cups/750 ml chicken stock or broth
- salt and freshly ground white pepper

Frascarelli in stock

PASTA AND FRESH BEAN SOUP

Minestra di pasta e fagioli freschi

- 1 lb/400 g fresh cannellini or cranberry beans, shelled
- 2 cloves garlic
- 1 sprig fresh sage
- 4 firm-ripe tomatoes
- 2 tablespoons extra-virgin olive oil
- 8 cups/2 liters water + more as needed
- salt
- 1 cup/100 g diced prosciutto (Parma ham) or pancetta or bacon
- 1 onion, finely chopped
- 1 stalk celery, finely chopped
- $^1/_4$ cup/60 ml extra-virgin olive oil
- 1 cup/250 ml unseasoned store-bought tomato sauce
- 2 medium potatoes, peeled and finely chopped
- 8 oz/200 g fresh store-bought tagliatelle egg pasta
- freshly ground black pepper

Put the beans with the garlic, sage, tomatoes, and oil in a large saucepan or Dutch oven (casserole) over low heat. Pour in the water and bring to a boil. • Simmer for about 1 hour, or until the beans have softened. • Season with salt and remove from the heat. • Sauté the prosciutto, onion, and celery in 2 tablespoons of the oil in a large saucepan over medium heat for about 15 minutes, or until the pancetta is crispy. • Stir in the tomato sauce and cook for 5 minutes. • Add the beans and their cooking water and potatoes. Bring to a boil and cook for 20 minutes. • Add the pasta and cook until al dente. • Drizzle with the remaining 2 tablespoons of oil and add a grinding of black pepper.

Serves 4 • Prep: 25 min •Cooking: 4 hr • Level: 1

GARBANZO BEAN SOUP

Minestra di pasta e ceci

Put the beans in a large saucepan and add the water. Bring to a boil over low heat. Skim off the froth. Cook over low heat for about 3 hours, or until the beans are very soft. • Season with salt and remove from the heat (there should still be plenty of cooking water). • Heat the oil and lard in a medium saucepan. Sauté the garlic and rosemary for 2 minutes until the garlic is pale gold. • Stir in the tomato sauce and simmer for 3 minutes. • Add the garbanzo beans and about 6 cups (1.5 liters) of the cooking water. Bring to a boil and add the pasta. Cook for the time indicated on the package. Discard the rosemary. • Serve in bowls with a drizzle of extra-virgin olive oil.

Serves 4–6 • Prep: 30 min + overnight to soak the beans • Cooking: 4 hr • Level: 1

- 3 cups/300 g dried garbanzo beans/chickpeas, soaked overnight and drained
- 4 quarts/4 liters water + more as needed
- salt
- $^1/_4$ cup/60 ml extra-virgin olive oil + extra to drizzle
- 1 tablespoon finely chopped lard or butter
- 2 cloves garlic, finely chopped
- 1 sprig fresh rosemary
- 3 tablespoons unseasoned store-bought tomato sauce
- 8 oz/200 g short pasta or dried egg fettuccine, broken into short lengths

Pasta and bean soup

Fresh pasta squares with fava beans

Fresh pasta squares with fava beans

Quadrucci con le fave

Pasta Dough
- 1¹/₃ cups/200 g all purpose/plain flour
- ¹/₄ teaspoon salt
- 2 large eggs

Soup
- 2 oz/50 g prosciutto/Parma ham
- 1 tablespoon finely chopped mint
- ¹/₂ red onion, finely chopped
- salt
- ¹/₄ cup/60 ml extra-virgin olive oil
- 4 firm-ripe tomatoes, peeled and coarsely chopped
- 2¹/₂ cups/250 g fresh fava/broad beans
- generous ³/₄ cup/200 ml meat stock + more as needed, boiling
- freshly ground black pepper

Pasta Dough: Sift the flour and salt onto a surface and make a well in the center. Break the eggs into the well and mix in to make a smooth dough. Knead for 15–20 minutes, until smooth and elastic. Shape the dough into a ball, wrap in plastic wrap (cling film), and let rest for 30 minutes. • Roll out the dough on a floured surface. Cut into 1-inch (3-cm) squares and arrange on a kitchen cloth to dry. • Soup: Finely chop the prosciutto with the mint, onion, and a pinch of salt. • Sauté the chopped mixture in the oil in a saucepan over medium heat for 3 minutes until aromatic. • Add the tomatoes and fava beans and sauté for 3 minutes. • Pour in the hot stock. Cook, covered, for about 1 hour over low heat, adding more stock if the mixture becomes too dry. • Season with salt and pepper. • Cook the pasta in a large pan of salted boiling water for 2–3 minutes until al dente. • Drain and add to the pan with the fava beans. • Serve piping hot.

Serves 4 • Prep: 1 hr • Cooking: 75 min • Level: 1

Walnut pesto

Nociata

- 1¹/₃ cups/200 g walnuts
- 2 tablespoons brown sugar
- ¹/₈ teaspoon ground cinnamon
- grated zest of ¹/₂ lemon
- 12 oz/350 g dried short pasta, such as penne

Blanch the walnuts in boiling water for 1 minute. Drain and transfer to a large cotton kitchen towel. Fold the towel over the nuts and rub them to remove the thin inner skins. • Transfer the nuts to a cutting board and chop finely. • Mix the nuts with the brown sugar, cinnamon, and the lemon zest. • Cook the pasta in a large pot of salted boiling water until al dente. • Drain and add to the pesto. • Serve hot

Serves 4 • Prep: 30 min • Cooking: 20 min • Level: 1

Fettuccine, Roman style

Fettuccine alla romana

- 1 red onion, finely chopped
- 1 small carrot, finely chopped
- 1 small stalk celery, finely chopped
- ¹/₄ cup/60 ml extra-virgin olive oil
- 8 oz/200 g lean ground/minced beef
- generous ¹/₃ cup/100 ml dry red wine
- 4 oz/100 g chicken livers, trimmed and diced
- 1¹/₄ cups/310 g peeled

Sauté the onion, carrot, and celery in the oil in a large saucepan over medium heat for 5 minutes, or until the onion is lightly browned. • Stir in the ground beef and cook for 3 minutes until browned all over. • Increase the heat and pour in the wine. • Add the chicken livers and cook over low heat for 15 minutes. • Add the tomatoes,

mushrooms, and bay leaf and season with salt and pepper. Cook over low heat for about 1 hour. • Cook the pasta in a large pot of salted boiling water until al dente. • Drain and add to the sauce. Sprinkle with the Parmesan, dot with the butter, letting it melt into the pasta, and serve.

Serves 4 • Prep: 30 min • Cooking: 90 min • Level: 1

plum tomatoes, pressed through a fine mesh strainer (passata)
- ¹/₂ oz/15 g dried porcini mushrooms, soaked in warm water for 15 minutes and finely chopped
- 1 bay leaf
- salt and freshly ground black pepper
- 12 oz/350 g fresh store-bought egg fettuccine
- 1 cup/125 g freshly grated Parmesan cheese
- ¹/₄ cup/60 g butter, cut up

BUCATINI WITH PANCETTA AND PECORINO

Bucatini all'amatriciana bianca

- 1¼ cups/150 g diced pancetta or bacon
- ¼ cup/60 ml extra-virgin olive oil
- 1 onion, finely chopped
- ¼ cup/60 ml dry white wine
- salt and freshly ground black pepper
- 12 oz/350 g dried bucatini
- 2 tablespoons finely chopped fresh parsley
- ¼ cup/30 g freshly grated Pecorino Romano cheese

Sauté the pancetta in the oil in a small frying pan over low heat for 5 minutes. • Remove from the pan and set aside. • Add the onion to the same oil and sauté for 10–15 minutes, or until soft. Return the pancetta to the pan, increase the heat, and pour in the wine. Season with salt and pepper. • Cook the pasta in a large pot of salted boiling water until al dente. • Drain and add to the sauce. Sprinkle with parsley and Pecorino and serve.

Serves 4 • Prep: 10 min • Cooking: 25 min • Level: 1

SPAGHETTI WITH CLAMS AND MUSSELS

Spaghetti vongole e cozze

Soak the clams and mussels in separate large bowls of warm salted water for 1 hour. • Pull off the beards from the mussels. • Drain the clams and mussels and transfer to a large saucepan, add ¼ cup (60 ml) of the wine, and cook over high heat for 3–5 minutes, until they open up. Discard any that do not open. • Strain the cooking liquid and set aside. • Sauté the garlic and chile in the remaining oil in a large frying pan over medium heat for 2 minutes, until the garlic is pale gold. • Add the clams and mussels with their shells and cook for 2 minutes. • Pour in the remaining wine and let it evaporate. • Cook the pasta in a large pot of salted boiling water until al dente. • Drain and add to the sauce, adding a little of the strained cooking liquid from the clams. • Stir in the butter and sprinkle with the parsley.

Serves 4 • Prep: 30 min + 60 min to soak the seafood • Cooking: 25 min • Level: 2

- 1 lb/500 g clams, in shell
- 1½ lb/700 g mussels, in shell
- ⅔ cup/150 ml dry white wine
- 4 cloves garlic, finely chopped
- ⅛ teaspoon dried chile pepper
- 6 tablespoons extra-virgin olive oil
- 12 oz/350 g dried spaghetti
- 1 tablespoon butter, cut up
- 1 tablespoon finely chopped fresh parsley

Bucatini with pancetta and Pecorino

Spaghetti with Pecorino

Spaghetti with Pecorino

Spaghetti cacio e pepe

- 1¹/₄ cups/150 g freshly grated Pecorino Romano cheese
- salt and freshly ground black pepper
- ¹/₂ cup/125 ml water
- 1 lb/500 g dried spaghetti

Mix the Pecorino and ¹/₈ teaspoon of pepper in a large bowl. Dilute with the water. • Cook the pasta in a large pot of salted boiling water until al dente. • Drain, reserving a little cooking water, and add the pasta to the bowl with the Pecorino. Add a little of the cooking water and a grinding of black pepper. Do not add too much water or the cheese will melt into strings instead of making a creamy sauce.

Serves 6 • Prep: 5 min • Cooking: 10 min • Level: 1

Fettuccine with cream and butter

Fettuccine al doppio burro

Cook the pasta in a large pot of salted boiling water until al dente. Drain reserving ¹/₄ cup (60 ml) of the cooking liquid. • Heat 2 tablespoons of the butter in a large frying pan. As soon as it begins to melt, add the fettuccine with the cooking water. • Stir in 1 tablespoon of the cream, 1 tablespoon of the butter, and 1 tablespoon of the Parmesan. • Continue adding until you have used up all the ingredients. Cook for 1 minute, removing the pasta very carefully with a pair of forks. Serve immediately.

Serves 4 • Prep: 5 min • Cooking: 15 min • Level: 1

- 12 oz/350 g fresh store-bought egg fettuccine
- generous ¹/₃ cup/100 g butter
- ³/₄ cup/180 ml heavy/double cream
- ¹/₂ cup/60 g freshly grated Parmesan cheese

Sauces

HOMEMADE PASTA
WITH MIXED VEGETABLE SAUCE
Lombrichelli

Pasta Dough
- 2¹/₃ cups/350 g all-purpose/plain flour
- ¹/₄ teaspoon salt
- lukewarm water

Sauce
- 1 large red onion, finely chopped
- 1 carrot, finely chopped
- 1 stalk celery, finely chopped
- 6 tablespoons extra-virgin oil or lard
- salt
- 2 cloves garlic, finely chopped
- 1 tablespoon finely chopped fresh parsley
- 1 fresh red chile pepper, finely chopped
- 3 cups/750 g peeled and chopped tomatoes
- 2 tablespoons freshly grated Pecorino Romano cheese

Homemade pasta like these lombrichelli *reflect their Etruscan origins. They are made throughout central Italy. The names differ from place to place and are often imaginative. The recommended sauce is a typical country sauce, a poor version of the meat sauce used for special occasions.*

Pasta Dough: Sift the flour and salt onto a surface and make a well in the center. Mix in enough water to make a smooth dough. Knead for 15–20 minutes, until smooth and elastic. Shape the dough into a ball, wrap in plastic wrap (cling film), and let rest for 30 minutes. • Break off pieces of dough and roll into 6 x ¹/₈-inch (15-cm x 3-mm) lengths. Let dry on a flour-dusted cloth overnight to prevent them from sticking together. • Sauce: Put the onion, carrot, and celery in the oil in a large frying pan over medium heat. Season with salt. Cover and cook for about 30 minutes, or until the vegetables are very soft. • Add the garlic, parsley, and chile and cook over high heat for 1 minute. • Stir in the tomatoes and cook over medium heat for 30 minutes. Season with salt and remove from the heat. • Cook the pasta in a large pot of salted boiling water for about 10 minutes, or until al dente. • Drain and add to the sauce. Sprinkle with Pecorino and serve.

Serves 4 • Prep: 40 min + 12 hr to dry the pasta • Cooking: 75 min • Level: 2

PENNE WITH
SPICY TOMATO SAUCE
Penne all'arrabbiata

Arrabbiata, *meaning "angry," is a recipe that is very common in central Italy in various forms. Chile pepper and tomato are classic elements.*

Sauté the pancetta in the oil in a frying pan over medium heat for 5 minutes until crispy. • Remove from the heat and transfer the pancetta to a plate, keeping it warm. • In the same oil, sauté the chile pepper and garlic for 2 minutes until the garlic is pale gold. • Stir in the tomatoes and season with salt. Add the parsley and let simmer for about 10 minutes, or until the tomatoes have broken down. • Add the pancetta and cook for 3 minutes. • Cook the pasta in a large pot of salted boiling water until al dente. Drain and add to the sauce. Sprinkle with the Pecorino and serve.

Serves 4 • Prep: 30 min • Cooking: 45 min • Level: 1

- 4 oz/100 g pancetta or bacon, cut into small strips
- 6 tablespoons extra-virgin olive oil
- 2 fresh spicy red chile peppers
- 3 cloves garlic, finely chopped
- 10 oz/300 g tomatoes, peeled, seeded, and coarsely chopped
- salt
- 1 tablespoon finely chopped fresh parsley
- 12 oz/350 g dried penne
- ¹/₄ cup/30 g freshly grated Pecorino cheese

SPAGHETTI CARBONARA
Carbonara

Sauté the onion in the oil in a small saucepan over medium heat for 2–3 minutes until lightly browned. • Add the pancetta and sauté for about 5 minutes, or until crispy. Remove from the heat and set aside. • Beat the egg yolks and cream in a large bowl. Season with salt and pepper and sprinkle with the Parmesan. • Cook the pasta in a large pot of salted boiling water until al dente. • Drain and add to the pancetta. Return to high heat, add the egg mixture, and toss the pasta briefly so that the eggs cook lightly but are still creamy. • Serve hot.

Serves 4 • Prep: 15 min • Cooking: 20 min • Level: 2

- ¹/₂ onion, finely chopped
- 2 tablespoons extra-virgin olive oil
- 1 cup/120 g diced smoked pancetta or bacon
- 4 large egg yolks
- ¹/₄ cup/60 ml heavy/double cream (optional)
- salt and freshly ground black pepper
- 2 tablespoons freshly grated Parmesan cheese
- 12 oz/350 g dried spaghetti

Sauces & Gnocchi

HOMEMADE PASTA SPIRALS

Ciufulitti di rieti

- 2¹/₃ cups/350 g all-purpose/plain flour + extra for rolling
- boiling water

Serve this typical Roman pasta with a lamb and bell pepper sauce (see page 152).

Sift the flour into a large bowl and add enough water to form a stiff dough. • Turn out onto a surface and knead for about 10 minutes. Set aside for 5 minutes. • Break off pieces of dough and roll them into 4-inch (10-cm) long spaghetti. Use plenty of flour to prevent sticking. Roll each piece of pasta on a floury stick (about the size of a thick knitting needle) and slip onto the floured board. • Cook the pasta in a large pot of salted boiling water for about 5 minutes, or until al dente. • Drain and serve as desired.

Serves 4 • Prep: 30 min • Cooking: 5 min • Level: 2

RICOTTA-FILLED RAVIOLI

Ravioli di ricotta

<u>Pasta Dough</u>: Sift the flour and salt onto a work surface and make a well in the center. Break the eggs into the well and mix in with enough water to make a smooth dough. Knead for 15–20 minutes, until smooth and elastic. Shape the dough into a ball, wrap in plastic wrap (cling film), and let rest for 30 minutes. • <u>Filling</u>: Mix the Ricotta, Pecorino, eggs, salt and pepper, and nutmeg in a large bowl. • Roll out the dough until thin. Cut into 4 x 16-inch (10 x 40-cm) strips and arrange small heaps of filling near one edge, about ³/₄ inch (2 cm) apart. Fold each strip of dough lengthwise to cover the filling. Seal, after making sure no air pockets remain, then cut into squares with a saw-toothed ravioli cutter. The ravioli should be smooth on one side and crimped on three sides. • Lay the pasta on a kitchen cloth dusted with flour. • Cook the pasta in small batches in a large pot of salted boiling water for 2 minutes. • Transfer to a serving dish with a slotted spoon and drizzle with melted butter. Sprinkle with Parmesan and serve.

Serves 6 • Prep: 2 hr • Cooking: 10 min • Level: 3

Pasta Dough
- 2²/₃ cups/400 g all-purpose/plain flour
- ¹/₄ teaspoon salt
- 3 large eggs
- 3 tablespoons water + more as needed

Filling
- 1¹/₃ cups/330 g Ricotta cheese
- 5 tablespoons freshly grated partially aged Pecorino cheese
- 2 large eggs
- salt and freshly ground white pepper
- ¹/₈ teaspoon freshly grated nutmeg

To serve
- 6 tablespoons butter, melted
- ³/₄ cup/90 g freshly grated Parmesan cheese

Homemade pasta spirals

Fried gnocchi

FRIED GNOCCHI

Gnocchi di latte

- ²/₃ cup/100 g potato starch
- ¹/₈ teaspoon ground nutmeg
- ¹/₈ teaspoon ground cinnamon
- ¹/₈ teaspoon salt
- 2 cups/500 ml milk
- 1 large egg + 5 large egg yolks, lightly beaten
- 1 tablespoon sugar
- ¹/₂ cup/125 g butter, cut up
- 1 cup/150 g all-purpose/plain flour
- 1 cup/125 g fine dry bread crumbs
- 5 tablespoons freshly grated Parmesan cheese

Sift the potato starch, nutmeg, cinnamon, and salt into a medium bowl. Mix in the milk to form a smooth paste. • Use a balloon whisk to beat the egg yolks and sugar in a large bowl until frothy. • Beat in the flour paste until well blended. • Pour the mixture into a heavy-bottomed saucepan with 2 tablespoons of the butter and place over low heat. Bring to a boil, stirring constantly. Cook for 3 minutes. • Butter a surface and pour the mixture on top. Use a spatula to smooth it out to a thickness of ¹/₂ inch (1 cm) and let cool completely. • Cut into 1¹/₂-inch (4-cm) diamond shapes. Dip in the flour, followed by the beaten egg, and then in the bread crumbs. • Melt the remaining 6 tablespoons butter in a large frying pan over medium heat. Fry the gnocchi for about 5–7 minutes, or until golden brown and crispy. • Drain and pat dry on paper towels. Sprinkle with Parmesan and serve hot.

Serves 4 • Prep: 20 min • Cooking: 20 min • Level: 2

SEMOLINA GNOCCHI

Gnocchi di semolino

Preheat the oven to 400°F/200°C/gas 6. • Butter a baking dish. • Bring the milk to a boil with ¹/₄ cup (60 g) of the butter and the salt, pepper, and nutmeg. Sprinkle in the semolina and beat vigorously with a whisk to prevent clumps from forming. • Cook for 20 minutes, stirring constantly. Remove from the heat, let cool, and add 2 tablespoons of the Parmesan and the egg yolks. • Pour the semolina onto a surface greased with oil. Use your hands and a spatula to smooth it out and let cool completely. • Use a smooth pastry cutter to cut the dough into 2¹/₂-inch (6-cm) rounds. • Arrange the leftover dough scraps in the bottom of the prepared baking dish. Top with the rounds, overlapping them slightly. • Sprinkle with the remaining butter and Parmesan. • Bake for 12–15 minutes, or until golden brown. • Serve hot.

Serves 6 • Prep: 40 min • Cooking: 45 min • Level: 2

- 4 cups/1 liter milk
- generous ¹/₃ cup/100 g butter
- salt and freshly ground white pepper
- ¹/₈ teaspoon freshly grated nutmeg
- 1²/₃ cups/250 g semolina flour
- 1 cup/125 g freshly grated Parmesan cheese
- 3 large egg yolks, beaten with 1 tablespoon milk

SPAGHETTI WITH TUNA
Spaghetti al tonno

- 2 cloves garlic, finely chopped
- $1/4$ cup/60 ml extra-virgin olive oil
- 7 oz/150 g tuna, packed in oil, crumbled
- generous $1/3$ cup/100 ml dry white wine
- 1 lb/400 g cherry tomatoes, halved
- salt and freshly ground white pepper to taste
- 12 oz/350 g dried spaghetti
- 1 tablespoon finely chopped parsley

Sauté the garlic in the oil in a large frying pan over medium heat for 2 minutes, until pale gold. • Add the tuna and sauté briefly. • Pour in the wine and cook until evaporated. • Add the tomatoes. Season with salt and pepper and cook for 15 minutes, crushing the tomatoes with a wooden spoon against the sides of the skillet. • Cook the pasta in a large pot of salted boiling water until al dente. • Drain and transfer to serving bowls. • Top with the hot sauce. • Sprinkle with parsley and serve immediately.

Serves 4 • Prep: 10 min • Cooking: 30 min • Level: 1

PASTA WITH GARLIC AND OIL
Pasta aglio e olio

- 2 cloves garlic, finely chopped
- $1/2$ cup/125 ml extra-virgin olive oil
- 2 anchovies packed in salt or 4 anchovy fillets packed in oil, rinsed and finely chopped (optional)
- 2 oz/50 g day-old bread, crumbled
- 1 tablespoons finely chopped fresh parsley
- $1/8$ teaspoon red pepper flakes
- 12 oz/350 g dried long pasta (such as bucatini, spaghetti or vermicelli)

Sauté the garlic in the oil in a small frying pan over medium heat for 1 minute. • Add the anchovies, if using, and let them dissolve. • Add the bread, parsley, and red pepper flakes and sauté over high heat for 5 minutes. • Cook the pasta in a large pot of salted boiling water until al dente. • Drain and add to the sauce. • Serve hot.

Serves 4 • Prep: 15 min • Cooking: 15 min • Level: 1

BEEF STEW WITH CLOVES
Garofolato

This beef stew is flavored with clove (known in the Roman dialect, or romanesco, as the garofolo). The sauce is a favorite with fettuccine. Serve the meat as a main course to follow the pasta dressed with the sauce.

Sprinkle the salt, pepper, 1 tablespoon of the parsley, and half the garlic on a cutting board. Roll the lard in this mixture. Lard the meat by cutting holes in the direction of the grain with a long, thin knife and inserting strips of lard. • Tie up the meat with kitchen string so it keeps its shape. • Heat the oil in a large saucepan with the lard over medium heat. Add the remaining garlic, parsley, onion, and celery and sauté for 2 minutes until the garlic is pale gold. • Add the beef and sear all over. Season with salt, pepper, nutmeg, and the crushed cloves. • When the vegetables begin to brown, pour in the wine. Cook for 30 minutes more, adding water if the mixture becomes too thick. • Stir in the tomatoes and enough water or stock to cover the meat. • Cook over very low heat for about 2 hours, or until the sauce has thickened. • Serve the sauce with a long pasta.

Serves 6 • Prep: 45 min • Cooking: 3 hr • Level: 2

- salt and freshly ground black pepper
- 2 tablespoons finely chopped fresh parsley
- 3 cloves garlic, finely chopped
- generous $1/3$ cup/100 g lard or fatty cooked ham, cut into strips
- 2 lb/1 kg beef rump
- 3 tablespoons extra-virgin olive oil
- 2 tablespoons lard or butter
- 1 red onion, finely chopped
- 1 stalk celery, finely chopped
- $1/8$ teaspoon freshly grated nutmeg
- 3 cloves, crushed
- generous $3/4$ cup/200 ml dry red wine
- 1 cup/250 g peeled plum tomatoes, pressed through a fine mesh strainer (passata)
- water or beef stock

ABRUZZO & MOLISE

Fiery and warming, these are among the hottest of Italian regional cuisines because of the inhabitants' enthusiasm for chile peppers. Try *Tagliatelle alla chitarra*, which is made by rolling egg pasta over a *chitarra*, a wooden box with strings. This is served with bell pepper or tomato sauces. *Scrippelle* (crepes) are served in homemade stock and sprinkled with local hard cheeses. Meat sauces are usually based on mutton or lamb. For a summer treat, serve vermicelli with zucchini flowers for Sunday lunch.

Lasagna, Abruzzo style (see page 152)

Sauces, Soups & Baked Pasta

LAMB AND BELL PEPPER SAUCE

Ragù di agnello e peperoni

- 2 cloves garlic, lightly crushed but whole
- 1 red onion, finely chopped
- 2 bay leaves
- 8 oz/200 g lean lamb, cut into small chunks
- 5 tablespoons extra-virgin olive oil
- generous $^1/_3$ cup/100 ml white wine
- 1 green bell pepper/capsicum, seeded, and cut into thin strips
- 1 yellow bell pepper/capsicum, seeded, and cut into thin strips
- 2 firm-ripe tomatoes, peeled, seeded, and coarsely chopped
- salt and freshly ground black pepper

Sauté the garlic, onion, bay leaves, and lamb in the oil in a large saucepan over medium heat for about 5 minutes until the meat has browned. • Pour over half the wine and cook until evaporated. • Lower the heat and pour over the remaining wine, cover, and cook for 40 minutes, or until the meat is tender. • Add the bell peppers and tomatoes and cook for 30 minutes more. Season with salt and pepper. • Use this meat sauce to flavor any type of dried pasta or gnocchi.

Serves 4 • Prep: 30 min • Cooking: 90 min • Level: 1

SPAGHETTI WITH FISH STOCK

Minestra di brodo di pesce

- 2 cloves garlic, lightly crushed but whole
- $^1/_8$ teaspoon red pepper flakes
- $^1/_4$ cup/60 g extra-virgin olive oil
- 1 lb/500 g peeled plum tomatoes, pressed through a fine mesh strainer (passata)
- 2 lb/1 kg white-fleshed fish, such as sea bass or snapper, cleaned
- 6 cups/1.5 liters water, boiling
- salt
- 8 oz/200 g dried spaghetti, broken up into short lengths

Sauté the garlic and red pepper flakes in the oil in a large frying pan over low heat for 3 minutes, until the garlic is pale gold. • Stir in the tomatoes and bring to a boil. • Cook for 5 minutes, then lay the fish carefully in the pan. • Pour in the water and season with salt. Cover and cook over very low heat for about 20 minutes, or until the fish flakes away from the bone. • Remove the fish carefully from the saucepan and fillet it. Reserve the filleted flesh to serve as a main course. • Strain the stock. • Cook the spaghetti in the boiling strained stock until al dente. • Serve immediately.

Serves 4 • Prep: 30 min • Cooking: 40 min • Level: 1

LASAGNA, ABRUZZO STYLE

Lasagne Abruzzesi

Pasta Dough: Sift the flour and salt onto a work surface and make a well in the center. Break the eggs into the well and mix in to make a smooth dough. Knead for 15–20 minutes, until smooth and elastic. Shape the dough into a ball, wrap in plastic wrap (cling film), and let rest for 30 minutes. • Roll out the dough on a lightly floured surface until very thin. Cut into 6 x 4-inch (15 x 10-cm) rectangles. Blanch the dough for 1 minute and lay it out on a damp cloth (see page 222). • Meat Sauce: Heat the oil in a large saucepan over medium heat. Add the beef and ham and sauté over high heat for 3–4 minutes, until browned all over. • Pour in the wine and let it evaporate for about 3 minutes. • Stir in the tomato sauce and season with salt and pepper. Cook over low heat for at least 1 hour. • Preheat the oven to 400°F/200°C/gas 6. • Oil a baking dish. • Meatballs: Mix the veal, eggs, and Pecorino in a large bowl. Season with salt and pepper and form into balls the size of hazelnuts. • Add the meatballs to the meat sauce and cook for 10 minutes. • Lay the first layer of lasagna in the prepared baking dish along the bottom and against the sides of the dish, extending far enough so that you can lay it back over the top layer. Cover with some of the meat sauce, the Fior di Latte, hard-cooked eggs, and Pecorino. Continue to layer the ingredients for a total of five layers. Fold the extra pasta over the top. Dot with the butter and sprinkle with any remaining Pecorino. • Bake for 35–40 minutes, or until golden brown. • Let rest at room temperature for 20 minutes before serving.

Serves 6 • Prep: 60 min + 30 min to rest the dough • Cooking: 2 hr • Level: 2

Pasta Dough
- 2 cups/300 g all-purpose/plain flour
- $^1/_4$ teaspoon salt
- 3 large eggs

Meat Sauce
- 2 tablespoons extra-virgin olive oil
- 8 oz/200 g lean ground/minced beef
- 4 oz/100 g fatty and lean cooked ham, finely chopped
- generous $^1/_3$ cup/100 ml dry red wine
- 4 cups/1 liter store-bought tomato sauce
- salt and freshly ground black pepper

Meatballs
- 12 oz/300 g ground/minced veal or beef
- 2 large eggs
- 2 tablespoons freshly grated Pecorino cheese
- salt and freshly ground black pepper
- 8 oz/300 g Fior di Latte or fresh Mozzarella cheese, sliced
- 3 hard-cooked eggs, finely chopped
- $^3/_4$ cup/90 g freshly grated Pecorino cheese
- 2 tablespoons butter, cut into flakes

TAGLIATELLE IN STOCK
Brodosini

Pasta Dough
- 2 cups/300 g all-purpose/plain flour
- $1/4$ teaspoon salt
- 3 large eggs
- $3/4$ cup/90 g diced lard or fatty pancetta

To serve
- 6 cups/1.5 liters meat stock or broth

Pasta Dough: Sift the flour and salt onto a surface and make a well in the center. Break the eggs into the well and mix in to make a smooth dough. Knead for 15–20 minutes, until smooth and elastic. Shape the dough into a ball, wrap in plastic wrap (cling film), and let rest for 30 minutes. • Roll out the dough on a lightly floured surface until thin, about $1/8$ inch (3 mm) thick. Cut into 4 x $3/4$-inch (10 x 2-cm) strips. • Fry the lard in a nonstick frying pan over medium heat for 3 minutes, until slightly golden. • Bring the stock to a boil in a large saucepan and add the lard. • Cook the pasta in the boiling stock for about 10 minutes, or until al dente. • Serve hot.

Serves 6 • Prep: 1 hr + 30 min to rest the dough • Cooking: 20 min • Level: 2

LENTIL AND VEGETABLE SOUP
Virtù

Bring 2 quarts (2 liters) water to a boil in a large saucepan with the lentils and beans. Skim off any foam. Reduce the heat and simmer for about 90 minutes, or until the beans are almost tender. • Drain, reserving the stock. The cooking time varies for each bean. • Sauté the pancetta in the oil in a Dutch oven (casserole) over low heat for 5 minutes. • Add the onion and cook for 5 minutes. • Add the herbs and tomatoes and cook for 3 minutes. • Add the remaining 2 quarts (2 liters) of water and the ham bone and bring to a boil. Season with salt and add all the vegetables. • Cook over medium heat for 30 minutes. • Add the drained beans and lentils and about half of the reserved stock. Chop the garlic and lard and add to the pot. • Cook for about 30 minutes, or until the vegetables are tender. • Cook the pasta in the boiling soup until al dente. If there is not enough liquid, add more of the boiling reserved stock as needed. • Sprinkle with Pecorino, grind black pepper over, and serve hot or warm.

Serves 4 • Prep: 60 min + 12 hr to soak the beans Cooking: 3 hr • Level: 1

- 4 oz/125 g dried beans, such as fava/broad beans or chickpeas/garbanzo beans, soaked overnight and drained
- 4 oz/125 g lentils
- 4 quarts/4 liters water
- $1/2$ cup/60 g finely chopped pancetta (or bacon) or cooked ham
- $1/4$ cup/60 ml extra-virgin olive oil
- 1 onion, finely chopped
- 3 tablespoons finely chopped mixed fresh herbs (such as marjoram, thyme, parsley, and sage)
- $2/3$ cup/150 ml peeled plum tomatoes, pressed through a fine mesh strainer (passata)
- 1 ham bone
- salt
- 1 lb/500 g vegetables in season, such as carrots, celery, spinach, Swiss chard, potatoes, or zucchini/courgettes, finely chopped
- 2 cloves garlic
- $1/4$ cup/30 g lard or butter, cut up
- 8 oz/200 g dried mixed short pasta, such as ditalini
- $1/4$ cup/30 g freshly grated Pecorino cheese
- freshly ground black pepper

Tagliatelle in stock

Long spiral pasta with vegetable sauce

LONG SPIRAL PASTA WITH VEGETABLE SAUCE

Fusilli al sugo (finto)

- 6 tablespoons extra-virgin olive oil
- 1 large red onion, finely chopped
- 1 carrot, finely chopped
- 1 stalk celery, finely chopped
- salt and freshly ground black pepper
- 2 cloves garlic, finely chopped
- 1 tablespoon finely chopped fresh mint
- 1¹/₂ lb/700 g firm-ripe tomatoes, peeled and chopped
- 12 oz/350 g dried long fusilli or bucati
- 2 tablespoons freshly grated Pecorino Romano cheese

Heat the oil in a large frying pan over medium heat. Add the onion, carrot, and celery and season with salt and pepper. Cover and cook over medium-low heat for 30 minutes. • Add the garlic and mint and cook over high heat for 3 minutes. • Stir in the tomatoes and cook over medium heat for 30 minutes more. • Season with salt and remove from the heat. • Cook the pasta in a large pot of salted boiling water for about 10 minutes, or until al dente. • Drain and add to the sauce. Sprinkle with Pecorino and serve.

Serves 4 • Prep: 40 min • Cooking: 70 min • Level: 1

CREPES IN STOCK

Scrippelle in brodo

Sift the flour and salt into a large bowl. • Add the eggs, beating until just blended. • Pour in the milk and add the parsley. Use a balloon whisk to beat the mixture well until smooth. Let rest in a cool place for at least 1 hour. • Heat a small amount of the oil in an 8¹/₂-inch (22-cm) nonstick crepe pan or frying pan over medium heat. Stir the batter and pour in about 2 tablespoons, tilting the pan so the batter forms a thin, even layer. Cook until the top is set and the bottom is golden, about 1 minute. Turn the crepe over and cook on the second side until lightly browned, about 30 seconds. Repeat, oiling the pan each time, until all the batter is used. Stack the cooked crepes between sheets of waxed paper. • Sprinkle each crepe with Pecorino and roll it up. Lay two of the crepes in each of six bowls and pour over the boiling stock. Serve hot.

Serves 6 • Prep: 40 min + 60 min to rest the batter • Cooking: 30 min • Level: 1

- 1¹/₃ cups/200 g all-purpose/plain flour
- ¹/₈ teaspoon salt
- 4 large eggs
- 1 cup/250 ml milk
- 1 tablespoon finely chopped fresh parsley
- 3–4 tablespoons extra-virgin olive oil
- ¹/₂ cup/60 g freshly grated Pecorino cheese
- 8 cups/2 liters chicken or beef stock or broth, boiling

Homemade spaghetti with tomatoes and arugula

HOMEMADE SPAGHETTI WITH TOMATOES AND ARUGULA

Tagliatelle alla chitarra con rucola

Pasta Dough
- 2²/₃ cups/400 g all-purpose/plain flour
- ¹/₄ teaspoon salt
- 4 large eggs, lightly beaten

Sauce
- 2 cloves garlic, finely chopped
- 1 dried chile pepper, crumbled
- 5 tablespoons extra-virgin olive oil
- 2 cups/500 ml peeled and chopped tomatoes
- 2 large bunches arugula/rocket, finely shredded
- 1 stalk celery, coarsely chopped
- 2 oz/60 g Parmesan cheese, in flakes
- 1 tablespoon finely chopped fresh parsley

Pasta Dough: Sift the flour and salt onto a surface and make a well in the center. Break the eggs into the well and mix in to make a smooth dough. Knead for 15–20 minutes until smooth and elastic. Shape the dough into a ball, wrap in plastic wrap (cling film), and let rest for 30 minutes. • Roll out the dough on a lightly floured surface until thin. Use a chitarra to cut the pasta into strips (see photos on this page). • Sauce: Sauté the garlic and chile in the oil in a large frying pan over medium heat for 2 minutes until the garlic is pale gold. • Stir in the tomatoes and cook for 15 minutes over high heat. • Cook the pasta in a large pot of salted boiling water until al dente. • Drain and add to the sauce. Add the arugula, celery, Parmesan, and parsley. • Toss well and serve.

Serves 4 • Prep: 40 min + 30 min to rest the dough • Cooking: 30 min • Level: 2

HOMEMADE SPAGHETTI WITH MEATBALLS

Tagliatelle alla chitarra con polpettine

Sauce: Sauté the onion and carrot in the oil in a large frying pan over medium heat for 5 minutes, or until softened. • Add the beef and cook, turning often, until browned all over. • Stir in the tomatoes. Simmer over low heat for 3 hours. Season with salt. • Meatballs: Mix the veal, egg, Parmesan, bread crumbs, and nutmeg in a large bowl until well blended. Form the mixture into small balls ¹/₂ inch (1 cm) in diameter. • Heat the olive oil in a large frying pan until very hot. Fry the meatballs in small batches for 5–7 minutes, or until golden brown. Drain well and pat dry on paper towels. • Cook the pasta in a large pot of salted boiling water until al dente. • Drain and add to the pan with the sauce. Toss well and serve with the meatballs.

Serves 4 • Prep: 40 min • Cooking: 3 h 20 min • Level: 2

Sauce
- 1 small onion, finely chopped
- 1 carrot, finely chopped
- ³/₄ cup/180 ml extra-virgin olive oil
- 8 oz/250 g beef, in a single cut
- 2 cups/500 g chopped tomatoes
- salt to taste

Meatballs
- 8 oz/250 g ground/minced veal or beef
- 1 egg
- 2 cups/250 g freshly grated Parmesan cheese
- 4 cups/250 g fresh bread crumbs
- ¹/₈ tsp freshly grated nutmeg
- 1 cup/250 ml olive oil, for frying
- 1 recipe Homemade spaghetti (see recipe left)

MAKING TAGLIATELLE ALLA CHITARRA

1. Run all the pieces of dough through the pasta machine, first at the widest setting, then the second-widest, and so on. Let dry on a floured cloth for 20 minutes.

2 When the dough has dried slightly, run it through the cutting rollers to make tagliatelle or taglierini.

3. For *tagliatelle alla chitarra*, you will need a sheet of pasta dough the same width as the *chitarra*. Lay the sheet of dough over the very taut strings and use the rolling pin to press down on the dough until it cuts through.

PASTA AND BREAD GNOCCHI

Gnocchi di pasta e pane

Bread Dough

- 2²/₃ cups/400 g all-purpose/ plain flour
- generous ³/₄ cup/ 200 ml water
- scant 2 tablespoons/ 20 g active yeast
- pinch of salt

Sauce

- 1 cup/250 ml Ligurian meat sauce (see page 17)
- 1 cup/125 g freshly grated Pecorino cheese

Bread Dough: Sift two-thirds of the flour and the salt into a bowl. Dissolve the yeast in the water. Add the yeast mixture to the bowl and mix until blended. Gradually add as much of the remaining flour as is needed to make a smooth dough. Knead the dough on a lightly floured surface for about 10 minutes, until elastic. Place the dough in a oiled bowl and let rise for about 1 hour. • Place the dough on a lightly floured surface and knead for another 3 minutes. Break off pieces of dough. Form into ¹/₂-inch (1-cm) thick lengths and cut into ¹/₂-inch (1-cm) long pieces. Arrange on a floured cloth and let rise for 30 minutes. • Cook the gnocchi in a large pot of salted boiling water for 3–5 minutes until they rise to the surface. • Sauce: Heat the sauce in a frying pan over low heat. Transfer the gnocchi to the frying pan. • Sprinkle with Pecorino. Serve hot.

Serves 4 • Prep: 60 min + 90 min for the dough to rise • Cooking: 15 min • Level: 2

FRESH PASTA WITH PANCETTA AND TOMATO SAUCE

Patellette

In Abruzzo, patellette *is used to indicate pieces of pasta or lasagna. The cornmeal gives this pasta a crunchy consistency.*

Pasta Dough: Sift the flour, cornmeal, and salt onto a surface and make a well in the center. Mix in enough water to make a smooth dough. Knead for 15–20 minutes, until smooth and elastic. Shape the dough into a ball, wrap in plastic wrap (cling film), and let rest for 30 minutes. • Roll out the dough to a thickness of ¹/₈ inch (3 mm). Cut into ³/₄-inch (2-cm) squares. • Sauce: Sauté the onion and pancetta in the oil in a small frying pan over low heat for about 10 minutes, or until the onion has softened. • Stir in the tomatoes and cook over medium heat for 5 minutes. • Season with salt and pepper and simmer over low heat for 20 minutes. • Cook the pasta in a large pot of salted boiling water for about 5 minutes, until al dente. • Drain and add to the sauce. Sprinkle with Pecorino and serve.

Serves 4 • Prep: 40 min + 30 min to rest the dough • Cooking: 40 min • Level: 2

Pasta Dough

- 2 cups/300 g all-purpose/plain flour
- ²/₃ cup/100 g fine ground cornmeal
- ¹/₄ teaspoon salt
- ²/₃ cup/150 ml lukewarm water + more as needed

Sauce

- 1 red onion, finely chopped
- 5 oz/150 g pancetta or bacon
- 2 tablespoons extra-virgin olive oil
- 1 lb/500 g peeled plum tomatoes, pressed through a fine mesh strainer (passata)
- salt and freshly ground black pepper
- ¹/₄ cup/30 g freshly grated aged Pecorino cheese

Pasta and bread gnocchi

Sweet fried ravioli

SPAGHETTI WITH GARLIC, OIL, AND PEPPERS

Spaghetti aglio, olio, e peperoncino

- 12 oz/350 g dried spaghetti
- 2 cloves garlic, finely chopped
- 2 dried chile peppers, finely chopped
- $^1/_4$ cup/60 ml extra-virgin olive oil
- 1 tablespoon finely chopped fresh parsley

This is perhaps the most classic of sauces in Italy for dry pasta. It is prepared in many versions depending on the region and on personal tastes.

Sauté the chile and garlic in the oil in a large frying pan over medium heat for 2 minutes, until the garlic is pale gold. • Remove from the heat and set aside. • Cook the pasta in a large pot of salted boiling water until not quite al dente. • Drain and add to the frying pan. • Sauté over medium heat for 2 minutes and sprinkle with the parsley.

Serves 4 • Prep: 5 min • Cooking: 20 min • Level: 1

SWEET FRIED RAVIOLI

Ravioli abruzzesi

<u>Pasta Dough</u>: Sift the flour and salt onto a surface and make a well in the center. Break the eggs into the well and mix in to form a stiff dough. Knead for 15–20 minutes, until smooth and elastic. • Press the dough into a disk, wrap in plastic wrap (cling film), and let rest for 30 minutes. • <u>Ricotta Filling</u>: Mix the Ricotta, egg and egg yolk, sugar, and cinnamon in a large bowl. • Roll out the dough on a lightly floured work surface until very thin. Cut into 8-inch (20-cm) long strips and arrange pellets of filling near one edge about $^3/_4$ inch (2 cm) apart. Fold each strip of dough lengthwise to cover the filling. Seal, then cut into squares with a saw-toothed ravioli cutter. • Heat the oil in a large frying pan until very hot (375°F/190°C). Fry the ravioli, in small batches, until golden brown. • Drain and pat dry on paper towels. • Sprinkle with confectioners' sugar and serve hot.

Serves 4 • Prep: 40 min + 30 min to rest the dough • Cooking: 30 min • Level: 3

Pasta Dough
- $1^1/_3$ cups/200 g all-purpose/plain flour
- $^1/_4$ teaspoon salt
- 2 large eggs

Ricotta Filling
- $1^3/_4$ cups/480 g Ricotta cheese, well-drained
- 1 large egg + 1 egg yolk, beaten
- 1 tablespoon granulated sugar
- $^1/_4$ teaspoon ground cinnamon

To serve
- 1 cup/250 ml peanut oil, for frying
- $^1/_2$ cup/75 g confectioners' sugar, to sprinkle

Vermicelli with zucchini flowers

VERMICELLI WITH ZUCCHINI FLOWERS

Vermicelli con fiori di zucca

- 1 red onion
- 2 bunches fresh parsley
- 20 squash flowers (reserve four to decorate)
- $1/4$ cup/60 ml extra-virgin olive oil
- salt and freshly ground black pepper
- pinch of saffron threads mixed with 1 tablespoon warm water
- $3/4$ cup/180 ml meat stock or broth
- 12 oz/350 g dried vermicelli
- 1 egg yolk
- 2 tablespoons freshly grated Pecorino cheese

Among the most representative ingredients of Abruzzo is saffron obtained from the stigmas of the crocus that is grown on the highland of Navelli, in the province of L'Aquila. In this case, we use whole stigmas, or threads, to enhance the aroma of the sauce.

Finely chop the onion, parsley, and 16 squash flowers to make a fine mixture. • Sauté the chopped mixture in the oil in a large frying pan over low heat for 2 minutes until aromatic. • Season with salt and pepper and add the saffron mixture. Cook for 15–20 minutes over medium heat, stirring often and adding stock if the mixture becomes too thick. • Cook the pasta in a large pot of salted boiling water until al dente. • Drain and transfer to the pan with the sauce. Stir in the egg yolk and 2 tablespoons stock. Cook over low heat, stirring constantly, until the egg mixture has set and is cooked. • Sprinkle with Pecorino. • Cut the reserved squash flowers in half. • Garnish the pasta with the squash flowers and serve.

Serves 4 • Prep: 30 min • Cooking: 30 min • Level: 1

BAKED CREPES WITH MEAT SAUCE

Timballo di scrippelle

Meat Sauce: Heat the oil in a large saucepan over high heat. Add the beef, sausage, and ham and cook for 2–3 minutes until browned all over. • Pour in the wine and let it evaporate. • Stir in the tomato sauce and season with salt and pepper. Simmer over low heat for about 1 hour. • Meatballs: Mix the veal, eggs, and Pecorino in a large bowl. Season with salt and pepper and form into balls the size of hazelnuts. • Place the meatballs in the meat sauce and cook for 10 minutes. • Crepes: Sift the flour and salt into a medium bowl. • Add the eggs, beating until just blended. • Pour in the milk. Use a balloon whisk to beat the mixture until smooth. Let rest in a cool place for at least 1 hour. • Heat a small amount of the oil in an $8^{1}/_{2}$-inch (22-cm) nonstick crepe pan or frying pan over medium heat. Stir the batter and pour in about 2 tablespoons, tilting the pan so the batter forms a thin, even layer. Cook until the top is set and the bottom is golden, about 1 minute. Turn the crepe over and cook on the second side until lightly browned, about 30 seconds. Repeat, oiling the pan each time, until all the batter is used. Stack the cooked crepes between sheets of waxed paper. • Preheat the oven to 400°F/200°C/gas 6. • Grease a baking dish with oil and lay a crepe on the bottom. Cover with a little of the meat sauce. Sprinkle with pieces of Fior di Latte, hard-cooked eggs, peas, and Pecorino. Continue to layer until all the ingredients have been used. Dot with the butter and sprinkle with any remaining Pecorino. • Bake for 35–40 minutes, or until golden brown. • Let rest at room temperature for 20 minutes before serving.

Serves 6 • Prep: 1 hr + 1 hr to rest the batter • Cooking: 2 hr • Level: 1

Meat Sauce
- 8 oz/200 g lean ground/minced beef
- 3 oz/100 g fatty and lean cooked ham, finely chopped
- 2 sausages, casings removed and crumbled
- generous $1/3$ cup/100 ml dry red wine
- 2 cups/500 ml peeled plum tomatoes, pressed through a fine mesh strainer (passata)
- 2 tablespoons extra-virgin olive oil
- salt and freshly ground black pepper

Meatballs
- 10 oz/300 g lean ground/minced veal or beef
- 2 large eggs
- 2 tablespoons freshly grated Pecorino cheese
- salt and freshly ground black pepper

Crepes
- $1^{1}/_{3}$ cups/200 g all-purpose/plain flour
- $1/8$ teaspoon salt
- 4 large eggs
- 1 cup/250 ml milk
- $1/4$ cup/60 ml extra-virgin olive oil, to grease the frying pan

Topping
- 2 oz/60 g Fior di Latte or Mozzarella cheese, cut into cubes
- 2 hard-cooked eggs, shelled and thinly sliced
- $1/2$ cup/60 g fresh or frozen peas
- 1 cup/125 g freshly grated Pecorino cheese
- $1/4$ cup/60 g butter

PUGLIA

At the heel of the Italian boot, Puglia has always benefited from fertile farmland and its vicinity to the sea. Mussels, anchovies, and clams all feature in home cooking and in restaurants close to the Riviera. Homemade semolina pasta, such as *orecchiette*, an ear-shaped pasta, and *cavatieddi*, thin shell-shapes, are served with fresh farm vegetables and dried tomatoes. Try lagane, sheets of fresh egg pasta, enjoyed with garbanzo beans inland and eel sauce along the coast. Spice up your pasta with fresh red-hot chile peppers or dried red pepper flakes.

Baked pasta with meatballs
(see page 166)

Sauces

SPAGHETTI WITH TOMATOES

Spaghetti alla pizzaiola

- 5 tablespoons extra-virgin olive oil
- 12 oz/300 g beef, sliced, (from the round or rump)
- 12 oz/300 g firm-ripe tomatoes, coarsely chopped
- 3 bunches parsley, coarsely chopped
- 2 cloves garlic
- 1 tablespoon salt-cured capers, rinsed
- salt
- 12 oz/350 g dried spaghetti

Heat the oil in a large saucepan over medium heat and add the beef, tomatoes, parsley, garlic, and capers. Cook over low heat for 1 hour. • Season with salt. • Cook the pasta in a large pot of salted boiling water until al dente. • Drain and add to the saucepan with the meat sauce. The meat itself can be served as a second course, accompanied by vegetables.

Serves 4 • Prep: 15 min • Cooking: 1 hr • Level: 1

PASTA WITH ANCHOVIES AND CAPERS

Pasta alla sangiovannello

- $^1/_2$ cup/125 ml extra-virgin olive oil
- 3 salt-cured anchovies or 6 anchovy fillets packed in oil, rinsed and finely chopped
- 3 cloves garlic, finely chopped
- 2 tablespoons salt-cured capers, rinsed
- 1 dried chile pepper, crumbled
- 12 oz/350 g short dried pasta such as penne

Heat 2 tablespoons of the oil in a small saucepan over low heat. Add the anchovies and cook for 5–10 minutes until they dissolve and become a paste. Remove from the heat and set aside. • Sauté the garlic, capers, and chile in the remaining 6 tablespoons oil in a large frying pan over medium heat for 2–3 minutes, until the garlic is pale gold. • Cook the pasta in a large pot of salted boiling water until al dente. • Drain and add to the frying pan. Mix in the anchovies and serve hot.

Serves 4 • Prep: 15 min • Cooking: 20 min • Level: 1

PASTA WITH MUSSELS

Lagane con le cozze

Soak the mussels in a large bowl of warm salted water for 1 hour. Pull off the beards. • Insert a thin knife and twist the knife until the mussels open up. • <u>Pasta Dough</u>: Sift the flour and salt onto a surface and make a well in the center. Mix in the oil and enough water to make a fairly stiff dough. Knead for 15–20 minutes, until smooth and elastic. Shape the dough into a ball, wrap in plastic wrap (cling film), and let rest for 30 minutes. • Roll the dough out on a lightly floured surface until thin. Cut into $^1/_3$ x 8-inch (1 x 20-cm) strips. • <u>Sauce</u>: Beat the eggs, Pecorino, parsley, chopped garlic, and pepper in a large bowl until well blended. Mix in enough bread crumbs to make a doughlike consistency. • Fill each half of the opened mussels with the filling. • Sauté the whole clove of garlic in the oil in a large frying pan over low heat for 5 minutes, until pale gold. • Discard the garlic. Increase the heat and add the tomatoes. Season with salt and pepper and simmer for 5 minutes. • Add the mussels and cook, covered, over medium heat, for about 10 minutes. • Cook the pasta in a large pot of salted boiling water until al dente. • Drain and add to the sauce. Serve hot.

Serves 6 • Prep: 40 min + 1 hr to soak the mussels + 30 min to rest the dough • Cooking: 30 min • Level: 2

- 2 lb/1 kg mussels, in shell

Pasta Dough
- 1$^1/_3$ cups/200 g all-purpose/plain flour
- $^1/_4$ teaspoon salt
- 2 tablespoons extra-virgin olive oil
- lukewarm water

Sauce
- 2 large eggs
- 2 tablespoons freshly grated Pecorino cheese
- 2 tablespoons finely chopped fresh parsley
- 1 clove garlic, finely chopped + 1 clove, lightly crushed but whole
- freshly ground white pepper
- $^1/_4$ cup/30 g fine dry bread crumbs + more as needed
- 1 lb/400 g peeled plum tomatoes, pressed through a fine mesh strainer (passata)
- 2 tablespoons extra-virgin olive oil
- salt

Sauces & Baked Pasta

PASTA WITH BROCCOLI

Pasta e broccoli

- 2 cloves garlic, finely chopped
- 2 salt-cured anchovies, rinsed and filleted
- ¹/₄ cup/60 ml extra-virgin olive oil
- 3 broccoli heads, weighing a total of about 2 lb/1 kg
- salt
- 12 oz/350 g short pasta (such as penne, shells, or orecchiette)
- ¹/₈ teaspoon red pepper flakes

Sauté the garlic and anchovies in the oil in a frying pan over low heat until the anchovies have dissolved. • Remove from the heat and let cool. • Divide the broccoli into florets and stems. Peel and chop the stems coarsely. • Bring a large pot of salted water to a boil. Add the broccoli stems and cook for 2 minutes. Add the florets and cook until tender, 4–6 minutes. Remove with a slotted spoon and set aside. Bring the water back to a boil. • Add the pasta and cook until al dente. • Drain the pasta and add to the sauce with the broccoli. Season with red pepper flakes and serve.

Serves 4 • Prep: 15 min • Cooking: 40 min • Level: 1

Pasta with broccoli

BAKED PASTA WITH MEATBALLS

Pasta al forno

Meatballs: Mix the beef, sausage, parsley, egg, Pecorino, garlic, and salt and pepper in a large bowl. Stir in the bread crumbs and form into balls the size of walnuts. • Heat the oil in a deep frying pan until very hot. Fry the meatballs in small batches for 5–7 minutes, or until browned and crispy. • Drain and pat dry on paper towels. • Sauce: Sauté the onion in the oil in a medium saucepan over low heat. Cover and cook for about 20 minutes, or until softened. • Add the tomatoes and basil and season with salt and pepper. • Cook, uncovered, over medium heat for 30 minutes, or until the oil separates from the tomatoes. • Preheat the oven to 350°F/180°C/gas 4. • Cook the pasta in a large pot of salted boiling water for half the time indicated on the package (see page 222). • Drain. In a large bowl, toss the pasta with half the sauce. Transfer half of the pasta mixture to a baking dish. Top with half the Mozzarella and half the meatballs. Cover with the remaining pasta mixture. Cover with the remaining meatballs and Mozzarella. Finish with the remaining sauce and sprinkle with Pecorino. • Bake for 40–45 minutes, or until the cheese is golden brown. • Serve warm.

Serves 6–8 • Prep: 65 min • Cooking: 1 hr 40 min • Level: 1

Meatballs

- 8 oz/200 g lean ground/minced beef
- 2 Italian sausages, casing removed and crumbled
- 1 tablespoon finely chopped fresh parsley
- 1 large egg
- 2 tablespoons freshly grated aged Pecorino cheese
- 1 clove garlic, finely chopped
- salt and freshly ground black pepper
- 2 tablespoons fresh bread crumbs
- 1 cup/250 ml olive oil, for frying

Sauce

- 1 large red onion, finely chopped
- ¹/₄ cup/60 ml extra-virgin olive oil
- 2 lb/1 kg peeled plum tomatoes, pressed through a fine mesh strainer (passata)
- 1 sprig fresh basil
- salt and freshly ground black pepper
- 1 lb/500 g dried penne
- 1 lb/500 g Mozzarella cheese, thinly sliced
- 2 tablespoons freshly grated Pecorino cheese

Penne with cauliflower

ORECCHIETTE WITH ROMANESCO BROCCOLI

Orecchiette con cavolfiore verde e lardo

- 2 lb/1 kg Romanesco broccoli or green cauliflower, divided into florets
- 2 cloves garlic, finely chopped
- 1 dried chile pepper, crumbled
- $^2/_3$ cup/150 ml extra-virgin olive oil
- scant $^1/_2$ cup/100 g lard or butter, cut up
- 8 cherry tomatoes, finely sliced
- 1 lb/400 g fresh pasta, such as orecchiette (see page 168)
- 5 tablespoons freshly grated Parmesan cheese
- 3 tablespoons freshly grated Pecorino cheese

Cook the broccoli in salted boiling water for 8–12 minutes, or until tender. • Use a slotted spoon to remove the broccoli, reserving the cooking water. • Sauté the garlic and chile in the oil and lard over low heat for 3 minutes, until the lard has melted. • Increase the heat and add the cherry tomatoes. Cook for a few minutes and add the broccoli. • Bring the cooking water from the broccoli to a boil and cook the orecchiette until al dente. • Drain and add to the sauce. • Sprinkle with Parmesan and Pecorino and serve.

Serves 4 • Prep: 20 min • Cooking: 30 min • Level: 1

PENNE WITH CAULIFLOWER

Pasta al cavolfiore

Sauté the garlic in the oil in a frying pan over medium heat for 2 minutes until the garlic is pale gold. • Remove from the heat and let cool. • Divide the cauliflower into florets. Cook in a large pot of salted boiling water until tender, about 5 minutes. Remove with a slotted spoon. Bring the water back to a boil. • Add the pasta and cook until al dente. • Drain the pasta and add to the sauce with the cauliflower and parsley. Season with a grinding of black pepper and serve.

Serves 4 • Prep: 15 min • Cooking: 40 min • Level: 1

- 1 medium cauliflower , weighing about 1 lb/ 500 g
- 12 oz/350 g dried short pasta (such as penne or orecchiette)
- 2 cloves garlic, finely chopped
- $^1/_4$ cup/60 ml extra-virgin olive oil
- 2 tablespoons finely chopped fresh parsley
- salt and freshly ground black pepper

Sauces & Fresh Pasta

ORECCHIETTE WITH TOMATOES AND RICOTTA

Orecchiette con pomodori e ricotta

- 1 lb/400 g fresh orecchiette (see below), or 10 oz/300 g dried
- 3 tablespoons freshly grated Ricotta Salata, Pugliese if available
- 1 lb/500 g peeled plum tomatoes, pressed through a fine mesh strainer (passata)
- 1/4 cup/60 ml extra-virgin olive oil

Cook the pasta in a large pot of salted boiling water until al dente. • Drain and toss with the Ricotta, tomatoes, and the oil. • Serve immediately.

Serves 4 • Prep: 20 min • Cooking: 20 min • Level: 1

ORECCHIETTE

Orecchiette means little ears and it is a classic pasta.

Sift both types of flour onto a surface and make a well in the center. Mix in the oil, if desired, and enough water to make a smooth dough. Knead for 15–20 minutes until smooth and elastic. • Shape the dough into thin cylinders and cut them into 1/2 inch (1 cm) lengths. Make the orecchiette, pressing down on them with a knife with a rounded blade. Turn over each shell you make onto your finger to make the ear shape • Arrange the orecchiette on a kitchen cloth sprinkled with semolina and let dry for about 30 minutes. When the orecchiette are completely dried, they can be kept for as long as 2 weeks.

Serves 4 • Prep: 1 hr + time to dry • Level: 2

- 1 1/3 cups/200 g semolina flour
- 1 1/3 cups/200 g all-purpose/plain flour
- lukewarm water
- extra-virgin olive oil (optional)

MAKING ORECCHIETTE

1. Sift the semolina flour onto a pastry board, make a well, and pour in the warm water.

2. Begin to mix the flour from the interior of the well until you have incorporated the flour.

3. Mix until you have a smooth dough.

4. Knead and roll the dough on the pastry board, folding it over onto itself for about 15–20 minutes, until smooth and elastic. Form the dough into long, thin cylinders

5. Cut the cylinders into short lengths, about ½ inch (1 cm) long. Use round-bladed knife to drag each section along the wooden pastry board.

6. Turn over each shell you make onto your finger to make the orecchiette.

ORECCHIETTE
WITH ARUGULA AND POTATOES

Orecchiette con rucola e patate

- 1 lb/400 g potatoes, peeled and cut into ¼-inch/0.5-cm thick slices
- 4 cloves garlic, lightly crushed but whole
- 1 lb/400 g fresh orecchiette (see page 168)
- 12 oz/350 g arugula/rocket, shredded
- ⅛ teaspoon red pepper flakes
- 5 tablespoons extra-virgin olive oil
- salt

Cook the potatoes in salted boiling water for 15 minutes. • Add 2 cloves garlic and cook for 10 minutes more. • Add the orecchiette and arugula and cook until the pasta is al dente. • Sauté the remaining 2 cloves garlic and chile in the oil in a large frying pan over low heat for 3–4 minutes until aromatic. • Drain the pasta with the arugula and potatoes and transfer to the pan. • Discard the garlic, toss to mix, and serve.

Serves 4 • Prep: 20 min • Cooking: 40 min • Level: 1

ORECCHIETTE
WITH GREENS

Orecchiette con cime di rapa

Cook the turnip greens in boiling water for 12–15 minutes, or until tender. • Use a slotted spoon to remove the greens, reserving the cooking water. • Sauté the garlic in the oil in a large frying pan over medium heat for 2 minutes until the garlic is pale gold. • Add the anchovies and let them dissolve over low heat for 5–10 minutes. • Add the greens and simmer for 3 minutes. Season with salt. • Bring the cooking water from the greens to a boil and cook the orecchiette until al dente. • Drain and add to the sauce. • Serve hot.

Serves 4 • Prep: 30 min • Cooking: 1 hr • Level: 2

- 2 lb/1 kg turnip greens, coarsely chopped
- 4 cloves garlic, lightly crushed but whole
- 6 tablespoons extra-virgin olive oil
- 3 salt-cured anchovies, rinsed and filleted
- 1 lb/400 g fresh orecchiette (see page 168)
- salt

Orecchiette with arugula and potatoes

Penne with asparagus

Penne with asparagus

Penne con asparagi

- 12 oz/350 g asparagus, peeled and cut into 1-inch (2.5-cm) lengths
- 2 cloves garlic, finely chopped
- ¹/₄ cup/60 ml extra-virgin olive oil
- 3 tomatoes, peeled and coarsely chopped
- salt and freshly ground white pepper
- 2 large egg yolks
- 5 tablespoons freshly grated Pecorino cheese
- 12 oz/350 g dried ridged penne

The best season to make this dish is spring, when wild asparagus is available. It is also good with farmed asparagus, which have especially meaty tips.

Cook the asparagus in a large pot of salted boiling water until tender, 4–5 minutes. Remove with a slotted spoon and return the water to a boil. • Sauté the garlic in the oil in a large frying pan over medium heat for 2 minutes until pale gold. • Add the tomatoes and cook for 12–15 minutes, or until the tomatoes have broken down. • Season with salt and pepper. • Mix the egg yolks and Pecorino in a large bowl. Place over barely simmering water and cook over low heat, stirring constantly, until the eggs register 160°F (80°C) on an instant-read thermometer. Plunge into a bowl of ice water and season with pepper. • Cook the pasta in a large pot of salted boiling water until al dente. • Drain and transfer to the bowl with the eggs. Toss well and transfer into the frying pan with the asparagus and the tomato sauce. • Toss well and serve.

Serves 4 • Prep: 20 min • Cooking: 20 min • Level: 1

Pasta with cold tomato sauce

Pasta con la pomarola fredda

Cut the tomatoes in half, squeeze them gently to remove the seeds and the liquid, and run them through a food mill. Alternately, process the tomatoes in a food processor or blender until pureed. • Transfer to a large bowl, season with salt, and refrigerate for 1 hour. • Use a skimmer to remove the fluid that has separated from the puree. • Mix in the garlic, onion, basil, oil, chile, and the sugar if the tomatoes are not in season. • Cook the pasta in a large pot of salted boiling water until al dente. • Drain and add to the tomato sauce.

Serves 4 • Prep: 30 min + 1 hr to chill the puree • Cooking: 15 min • Level: 1

- 1¹/₂ lb/700 g firm-ripe tomatoes, preferably San Marzano or Roma
- salt
- 2 cloves garlic, finely chopped
- 1¹/₂ oz/40 g red onion, very finely chopped
- 6 leaves fresh basil, torn
- 5 tablespoons extra-virgin olive oil
- 1 dried spicy chile pepper
- ¹/₈ teaspoon sugar (optional)
- 12 oz/350 g penne or other short pasta

Baked Pasta & Sauces

Baked seafood spaghetti

Spaghetti di mare al cartoccio

- 1¹/₂ lb/700 g clams, in shell
- 1¹/₂ lb/700 g mussels, in shell
- 14 oz/400 g small squid, cleaned
- 1 lb/500 g firm-ripe tomatoes, peeled and seeded
- 2 cloves garlic, finely chopped
- 1 dried red spicy chile pepper
- 2 tablespoons finely chopped fresh parsley
- 6 tablespoons extra-virgin olive oil
- generous ¹/₃ cup/ 100 ml dry white wine
- 12 oz/350 g shelled crayfish
- 12 oz/350 g spaghetti
- salt to taste

Soak the clams and mussels in separate large bowls for 1 hour. • Drain and set aside. Pull off the beards from the mussels. • Remove the mottled skin from the squids and cut the bodies into small chunks. Cut the tentacles in half. • Squeeze the tomatoes to remove the excess liquid, and slice them thinly. • Preheat the 350°F/180°C/gas 4. • Sauté the garlic, chile, and parsley in the oil in a small saucepan over high heat until the garlic is pale gold. • Pour in the wine and let it evaporate. • Add the tomatoes and cook for 1 minute. • Add the squid, clams, mussels, and crayfish. Cover and cook over medium heat until the clams and mussels open up. • Remove from the heat and discard any seafood that haven't opened. • Shell half the seafood. • Cook the spaghetti in salted boiling water for half the time indicated on the package. • Drain and add to the seafood sauce. • Cut four large pieces of aluminum foil and fold each in half to double the thickness. • Divide the pasta into four portions and place in the center of the pieces of aluminum foil, adding 3 tablespoons of cooking water from the pasta to each portion. Close, sealing the foil well. There should be an air pocket in each of the packages. • Transfer to a large baking sheet. • Bake for 12–15 minutes, or until the parcels have puffed up slightly. • The parcels should be served on individual plates and brought to the table. The diners can open the foil and eat directly from them.

Serves 4 • Prep: 1 hr + 1 hr to purge the seafood • Cooking: 30 min • Level: 2

Cavatelli with arugula

Cavatelli con la rucola

You can use any kind of pasta made by hand with semolina flour. Wild arugula (rocket) gives a more pungent flavor to the sauce.

Blanch the arugula in salted, simmering water for 5 minutes. • Add the cavatelli and cook until al dente. • Drain, reserving a little cooking water. • Sauté the garlic in the oil in a large frying pan over medium heat for 2 minutes, until pale gold. • Add the pasta and arugula, with a little of the cooking water. • Sprinkle with Pecorino and top with the tomato sauce. • Toss well and serve.

Serves 4 • Prep: 15 min • Cooking: 30 min • Level: 1

- 1 lb/500 g arugula/ rocket
- 12 oz/350 g fresh cavatelli pasta (see below)
- 2 cloves garlic, finely chopped
- ¹/₄ cup/60 ml extra-virgin olive oil
- ¹/₂ cup/60 g freshly grated Pecorino cheese
- 6 tablespoons store-bought unseasoned tomato sauce

Making Cavatelli

1. Form the semolina flour pasta dough (see page 168) into long, thin logs. Cut into short sections, about ¹/₄ inch (2 cm) long.

2. Use the back of a spatula or a knife to drag each section along the wooden pastry board so that it becomes thinner and curls up.

Sauces

BAVETTE WITH MUSHROOMS

Bavette ai funghi

- 1 lb/500 g mixed small mushrooms (porcini, champignons, finferli, chiodini)
- 1 onion, finely chopped
- $^1/_4$ cup/60 ml extra-virgin olive oil
- salt
- 2 cloves garlic, finely chopped
- 1 dried hot chile pepper, crumbled
- $^1/_4$ cup/60 ml dry white wine
- 8 cherry tomatoes, coarsely chopped
- Leaves from 1 bunch fresh basil, torn
- 1 tablespoon finely chopped fresh parsley
- 12 oz/350 g bavette or other long pasta

Clean the mushrooms very carefully and cut the larger ones into small pieces. • Cook the onion in the oil in a frying pan, covered, over low heat for 20 minutes. Season with salt and add the garlic and chile. • Increase the heat and pour in the wine. • Add the mushrooms and sauté over high heat for a few minutes. • Stir in the tomatoes, basil, and parsley and cook for about 10 minutes, or until the mushrooms are tender. Season with salt. • Cook the pasta in a large pot of salted boiling water until al dente. • Drain and add to the sauce. Serve hot.

Serves 4 • Prep: 30 min • Cooking: 40 min • Level: 1

PASTA AND LENTILS

Pasta e lenticchie

Soak the lentils in cold water for 2 hours. • Drain, rinsing them under cold running water, and place in a large saucepan with the celery, garlic, and 2 tablespoons of the oil. • Pour in the water to cover the lentils with double the volume of water. • Simmer, partially covered, for about 60 minutes, or until the lentils are tender. Season with salt. • Cook the pasta in the pot with the boiling lentil mixture, adding more water if needed, until al dente. • Drain and drizzle with the remaining 2 tablespoons of oil and a grinding of black pepper.

Serves 4 • Prep: 30 min + 2 hr to soak the lentils • Cooking: 75 min • Level: 1

- 8 oz/200 g lentils
- 1 stalk celery, finely chopped
- 2 cloves garlic, finely chopped
- $^1/_4$ cup/60 ml extra-virgin olive oil
- 8 cups/2 liters water + more as needed
- salt
- 8 oz/200 g dried tagliatelle or other long pasta, broken up into short lengths
- freshly ground black pepper

PASTA WITH MUSSELS

Pasta alle cozze

- 4 lb/2 kg mussels, in shell
- $^3/_4$ cup/180 ml dry white wine
- 2 cloves garlic, finely chopped
- 1 fresh red chile pepper, finely chopped
- 1 tablespoon finely chopped fresh parsley
- 6 tablespoons extra-virgin olive oil
- 3 lb/1.5 kg firm-ripe tomatoes, peeled and coarsely chopped
- salt
- 12 oz/350 g pasta (any type)

Soak the mussels in a large bowl of warm salted water for 1 hour. Pull off the beards. • Pour $^1/_2$ cup (60 ml) of the wine into a large saucepan and place the mussels in the pan. Cover and cook over high heat, shaking the pot occasionally, for about 10 minutes, until they open up. • Discard any that do not open. Let the mussels cool completely and remove most of the mussels from the shells. Leave some mussels in the shells to garnish. • Sauté the garlic, chile, and parsley in the oil in a large frying pan over medium heat for 2 minutes, until the garlic is pale gold. • Increase the heat, pour in the remaining $^1/_4$ cup (60 ml) wine, and let it evaporate. • Stir in the tomatoes and cook over high heat until the tomatoes have broken down, about 5 minutes. • Season with salt and remove from the heat. • Add the shelled mussels and cook for 5 minutes more. • Cook the pasta in a large pot of salted boiling water until al dente. • Drain and transfer to a serving dish. Add the sauce and toss well. Garnish with the mussels in their shells and serve.

Serves 4 • Prep: 30 min + 1 hr to soak the mussels • Cooking: 30 min • Level: 1

Fresh pasta with garbanzo beans

Lagane e ceci

- 3 cups/300 g garbanzo beans/chickpeas, soaked overnight and drained
- 3 quarts/3 liters water
- 1 stalk celery, finely chopped
- 1 onion, finely chopped
- 3 cloves garlic, lightly crushed but whole
- 1 bay leaf
- 2 tablespoons extra-virgin olive oil + 3 tablespoons to serve
- salt
- freshly ground black pepper

Lagane are large tagliatelle made of fresh pasta. This recipe can also be prepared with dried short pasta or broken long pasta.

Bring the water to a boil over medium-low heat in a large saucepan with the beans, celery, onion, garlic, bay leaf, and oil. Skim off the froth. Cook over low heat for about 90 minutes, or until the beans are very soft. • Season with salt, cook for 10 minutes. and remove from the heat (there should still be plenty of cooking water). • Pasta Dough: Sift the flour and salt onto a surface and make a well in the center. Mix in the oil and enough water to make a smooth dough.

Knead for 15–20 minutes, until smooth and elastic. Shape the dough into a ball, wrap in plastic wrap (cling film), and let rest for 30 minutes. • Roll out the dough on a lightly floured surface until very thin and cut it into 1 x 4-inch (2 x 10-cm) strips. • Bring the beans back to a boil and add the pasta. Cook until the pasta is al dente, adding more water, if needed. • Drizzle with the remaining 3 tablespoons oil and a grinding of black pepper.

Serves 6 • Prep: 1 hr + 30 min. for the dough to rest • Cooking: 2 hr 30 min • Level: 2

Pasta Dough

- 1 1/3 cups/200 g all-purpose/plain flour
- 1/4 teaspoon salt
- 2 tablespoons extra-virgin olive oil
- lukewarm water as required

Fresh pasta with garbanzo beans

Fresh pasta with eel sauce

FRESH PASTA WITH EEL SAUCE

Lasagne con anguilla

The term lasagne, in Puglia, is used to describe fettuccine or thin tagliatelle made with a dough similar to that of orecchiette.

Pasta Dough: Sift the flour and salt onto a surface and make a well in the center. Add enough water to make a smooth dough. Knead for 15–20 minutes, until smooth and elastic. Shape the dough into a ball, wrap in plastic wrap (cling film), and let rest for 30 minutes. • Roll out the dough on a lightly floured surface until very thin and let stand for 20 minutes on a kitchen cloth. • Cut into $1/4$-inch (3-mm) wide strips. Wrap the strips into nests and place them on a dry cloth. • Eel Sauce: Sauté the garlic and parsley in the oil in a saucepan over medium heat for 2 minutes, until the garlic is pale gold. • Increase the heat and pour in the wine. • Add the eel, cover, and cook over low heat for 10 minutes. • Stir in the tomatoes and cook over high heat for 2 minutes. • Season with salt and remove from the heat. • Cook the pasta in a large pot of salted boiling water until al dente. • Drain and add to the sauce. Serve hot.

Serves 4 • Prep: 90 min + 30 min to rest the dough • Cooking: 30 min • Level: 2

Pasta Dough

- $2^2/_3$ cups/400 g all-purpose/plain flour
- $1/_4$ teaspoon salt
- 6 tablespoons water + more as needed

Eel Sauce

- 2 cloves garlic, chopped
- 1 tablespoon finely chopped parsley
- 6 tablespoons extra-virgin olive oil
- $3/_4$ cup/180 ml dry white wine
- 1 lb/500 g eel, cleaned and cut into large chunks
- 5 tomatoes, peeled and thinly sliced
- salt

MACARONI WITH BELL PEPPERS

Maccheroni ai peperoni

- 3 yellow bell peppers/capsicums
- 6 tablespoons extra-virgin olive oil
- salt
- 2 cloves garlic, finely chopped
- 1 lb/500 g tomatoes, peeled and thinly sliced
- 1 tablespoon finely chopped fresh parsley
- 12 oz/350 g dried macaroni

Broil (grill) the bell peppers until the skins are blackened all over. Wrap them in a paper bag for 5 minutes, then remove the skins and seeds. Slice thinly. • Sauté the bell peppers in 3 tablespoons of the oil in a frying pan over high heat for 2 minutes. Season with salt and remove from the heat. • Sauté the garlic in the remaining 3 tablespoons of the oil in a large frying pan over medium heat for 2 minutes until pale gold. • Stir in the tomatoes and cook over high heat for 5 minutes. • Season with salt and add the parsley. Remove from the heat. • Cook the pasta in a large pot of salted boiling water until al dente. • Drain. Add the pasta and peppers to the frying pan containing the tomato mixture and toss. • Serve hot.

Serves 4 • Prep: 40 min • Cooking: 20 min • Level: 1

BASILICATA & CAMPANIA

Overshadowed by the foreboding Mt. Vesuvius, Campania reaps the most benefit from its climate, volcanic sands, and vegetation. The hot summer sun produces San Marzano plum tomatoes, giant bell peppers, and olives. Mozzarella, goat cheese, and Scamorza are the favorite cheeses. Basilicata is the area farther inland at the top of the heel of the peninsula. *Lagane* (pasta strips that are similar to lasagna) with beans is a classic Basilicata dish, emphasizing the rustic nature of southern Italian cuisine.

Campanian tomato sauce
(see page 180)

Sauces

RIGATONI WITH FRESH BASIL

Rigatoni al basilico

- Leaves from 3 bunches basil
- 1 clove garlic
- salt
- 2 tablespoons lard or butter
- 3 tablespoons extra-virgin olive oil
- freshly ground white pepper
- 12 oz/350 g dried rigatoni pasta
- 3 tablespoons freshly grated Parmesan cheese
- 2 tablespoons grated Pecorino cheese

This is a quick dish that is ideal for summer, the basil season.

Finely chop the basil with the garlic and a pinch of salt. • Melt the lard and oil in a large frying pan over low heat and add the chopped basil mixture. Sauté for 2 minutes and season with salt and pepper. • Cook the pasta in a large pot of salted boiling water until al dente. • Drain and transfer to the pan with the basil mixture. Sprinkle with Parmesan and Pecorino and serve.

Serves 4 • Prep: 10 min • Cooking: 20 min • Level: 1

SPAGHETTI WITH OLIVES, TOMATOES, AND ANCHOVIES

Spaghetti alla puttanesca

Sauté the onion and chile in the oil in a large frying pan over medium heat for 5 minutes. • Add the garlic and anchovies and cook over low heat until the anchovies dissolve, 5–10 minutes. • Stir in the tomatoes and cook for 10 minutes. • Add the olives and capers and simmer for 3 minutes. • Cook the pasta in a large pot of salted boiling water until al dente. • Drain and add to the sauce. Sprinkle with the parsley and serve.

Serves 4 • Prep: 30 min • Cooking: 20 min • Level: 1

- 1/2 red onion, chopped
- 1 dried chile pepper
- 1/4 cup/60 ml extra-virgin olive oil
- 2 cloves garlic, chopped
- 2 salt-cured anchovies, rinsed and filleted
- 1 lb/500 g tomatoes, finely chopped
- 1 cup/100 g black olives
- 1 tablespoon salt-cured capers, chopped
- 12 oz/350 g dried spaghetti
- 1 tablespoon chopped fresh parsley

ZITI WITH PESTO AND FRESH BASIL

Zite alla napoletana

- 12 oz/350 g dried ziti, broken up into pieces, about 2 1/2-inches/6-cm long
- 1/3 cup/80 g Genoese Pesto (see page 16)
- Leaves from 1 small bunch fresh basil, torn
- 1 cup/125 g freshly grated Caciocavallo cheese or Provolone cheese

Warm a large soup tureen. • Cook the pasta in a large pot of salted boiling water until al dente, 10 minutes. • Drain and arrange one layer in the tureen. • Add a little pesto, basil, and Caciocavallo. • Add more layers until all the pasta has been used. • Serve hot.

Serves 4 • Prep: 10 min • Cooking: 10 min • Level: 1

CAMPANIAN TOMATO SAUCE

Salsa di pomodoro, pomarola

This sauce is the emblem of Italian cooking and can be prepared in countless ways, all quite similar but with nuances that slightly modify the final outcome. This typical Campanian version lends itself to many uses, first and foremost, as a pasta sauce. This quantity is sufficient to serve pasta for six people.

Cook the tomatoes with 1/8 teaspoon salt in a covered saucepan over medium heat for 5 minutes. • Transfer to a colander with large holes and let drain for 1 hour. • Return to the saucepan and add the onion, garlic, basil, oil, sugar, and salt. Cover and bring to a boil over medium heat. Simmer for about 40 minutes, or until the sauce has thickened. • Remove from the heat and run through a food mill or process in a food processor or blender until smooth.

Makes 2 cups/500 ml • Prep: 20 min + 1 hr to drain the tomatoes • Cooking: 50 min • Level: 1

- 3 lb/1.5 kg firm-ripe plum tomatoes, preferably San Marzano, coarsely chopped
- salt
- 1 red onion, thinly sliced
- 2 cloves garlic, finely chopped
- Leaves from 1 small bunch fresh basil, torn
- 2 tablespoons extra-virgin olive oil
- 1/8 teaspoon sugar

RAVIOLI WITH MEAT SAUCE

Ravioli di ricotta e ragù potentino

Sauce

- 1 lb/400 g beef or pork, in a single cut
- 3 tablespoons freshly grated Pecorino cheese
- 1 clove garlic, finely chopped
- 1/8 teaspoon red pepper flakes
- 1 tablespoon finely chopped fresh parsley
- 2 slices of pancetta or bacon, cut into short lengths
- 1/4 cup/60 ml extra-virgin olive oil
- 6 tablespoons dry white wine
- 1 lb/500 g peeled plum tomatoes, pressed through a fine mesh strainer (passata)
- salt and freshly ground black pepper
- Leaves from 1 small bunch fresh basil, torn

Pasta Dough

- 2 cups/300 g all-purpose/plain flour
- 1/4 teaspoon salt
- 2 large eggs
- lukewarm water

Filling

- 1²/₃ cups/400 g Ricotta cheese
- 2 large eggs
- 1/2 cup/60 g freshly grated Pecorino cheese
- 2 tablespoons finely chopped fresh parsley
- salt and freshly ground white pepper

Sauce: Use a meat pounder to tenderize the beef until flattened. • Sprinkle with Pecorino, garlic, red pepper flakes, and parsley. Roll it up and tie with kitchen string. • Sauté the pancetta in the oil in a large frying pan over medium heat for 5 minutes until crispy. • Carefully place the roll of beef in the pan and cook over high heat on all sides for about 5 minutes. • Pour in the wine and let it evaporate. • Stir in the tomatoes, season with salt and pepper, and add the basil. Simmer, covered, for about 2 hours, or until the meat is tender. The meat should be served as a main course. • **Pasta Dough**: Sift the flour and salt onto a surface and make a well in the center. Break the eggs into the well and mix in with enough water to make a smooth dough. Knead for 15–20 minutes, until smooth and elastic. Shape the dough into a ball, wrap in plastic wrap (cling film), and let rest for 30 minutes. • **Filling**: Mix the Ricotta, eggs, Pecorino, parsley, and salt and pepper in a large bowl and refrigerate for 30 minutes. • Roll out the dough on a lightly floured surface until very thin. Cut it into 1¹/₂-inch (4-cm) squares and drop a small nugget of filling into the centers. Fold into rectangles, sealing the edges with a fork. • Cook the pasta in small batches in a large pot of salted boiling water for 2 minutes. • Transfer to a serving dish with a slotted spoon and top with the sauce.

Serves 6 • Prep: 1 hr + 30 min to rest the dough + 30 min to chill the filling • Cooking: 2 hr 30 min • Level: 3

WHEAT WITH MEAT SAUCE

Grano al ragù

Measure the wheat berries. Put in a large saucepan along with double their volume of lukewarm water. Bring to a boil and cook for about 2 hours, or until tender. • **Meat Sauce**: Sauté the garlic and red pepper flakes in the oil in a Dutch oven (casserole) over medium heat for 3–5 minutes, until the garlic is pale gold. • Discard the garlic. Add the lamb and beef and cook over high heat for 2 minutes, until browned all over. • Add the tomatoes and salt. Cover, and simmer gently over low heat for about 2 hours, or until the meat is tender. • Drain the wheat berries and top with the meat sauce and Ricotta Salata.

Serves 6 • Prep: 30 min + overnight to soak the wheat • Cooking: 2 hr 30 min • Level: 1

- 4 cups/400 g wheat berries, soaked overnight and drained
- water

Meat Sauce

- 2 cloves garlic, lightly crushed but whole
- red pepper flakes
- 2 tablespoons extra-virgin olive oil
- 8 oz/200 g ground/minced lamb
- 8 oz/200 g ground/minced beef
- 1 lb/500 g peeled plum tomatoes, pressed through a fine mesh strainer (passata)
- salt
- 4 oz/100 g Ricotta Salata cheese, in flakes

Ravioli with meat sauce

Baked Ricotta crepes

BAKED RICOTTA CREPES
Crespelle con la ricotta

Crepes
- ²/₃ cup/100 g all-purpose/plain flour
- ¹/₈ teaspoon salt
- 4 large eggs
- 1 cup/250 ml milk
- 2 tablespoons extra-virgin olive oil

Filling
- 1¹/₄ cups/310 g Ricotta cheese
- ¹/₄ cup/30 g freshly grated Parmesan cheese
- 7–8 oz/250 g fresh Mozzarella, preferably buffalo milk, cut into small cubes
- 1 tablespoon finely chopped fresh parsley
- 4–6 leaves fresh basil, torn
- salt and freshly ground white pepper
- 1 cup/250 ml store-bought unseasoned tomato sauce
- ¹/₄ cup/30 g freshly grated Parmesan cheese

Preheat the oven to 400°F/200°C/gas 6. Set out a baking dish. • Crepes: Sift the flour and salt into a medium bowl. • Add the eggs, beating until just blended. • Pour in the milk and use a balloon whisk to beat the mixture until smooth. Let rest in a cool place for at least 1 hour. • Filling: Mix the Ricotta, Parmesan, Mozzarella, parsley, and basil in a large bowl. Season with salt and pepper. • Heat a small amount of the oil in an 8¹/₂-inch (22-cm) nonstick crepe pan or frying pan over medium heat. Stir the batter and pour in about 2 tablespoons, tilting the pan so the batter forms a thin, even layer. Cook until the top is set and the bottom is golden, about 1 minute. Turn the crepe over and cook on the second side until lightly browned, about 30 seconds. Repeat, oiling the pan each time, until all the batter is used. Stack the cooked crepes between sheets of waxed paper. • Spread the filling evenly over the crepes, roll up and arrange them, seam side down, in the baking dish. Partly cover with the tomato sauce and sprinkle with Parmesan. • Bake for 12–15 minutes, or until the cheese is golden brown. • Serve hot.

Serves 6 • Prep: 40 min + 1 hr to rest the batter • Cooking: 40 min • Level: 2

Sauces & Baked Pasta

PENNE, NAPLES STYLE

Penne alla napoletana

- $^1/_2$ red onion, finely chopped
- 6 tablespoons butter, cut up
- 2 tablespoons extra-virgin olive oil
- 2 lb/1 kg plum tomatoes, preferably San Marzano tomatoes, peeled, seeded, and finely chopped
- 5 leaves fresh basil, torn
- salt and freshly ground black pepper
- 12 oz/350 g smooth dried penne
- $^3/_4$ cup/90 g freshly grated Caciocavallo cheese or Provolone

Sauté the onion in 4 tablespoons of the butter and the oil in a large saucepan over low heat. • Add the tomatoes and basil and cook for about 5 minutes, until the tomatoes have broken down. • Season with salt and pepper and add the remaining 2 tablespoons butter. • Remove from heat and mix until the butter has melted. • Cook the pasta in a large pot of salted boiling water until al dente. • Drain and transfer to the saucepan with the tomato sauce. Sprinkle with the Caciocavallo and serve.

Serves 4 • Prep: 20 min • Cooking: 20 min • Level: 1

PASTA WITH TWO CHEESES AND EGG

Maccheroni cacio e uova

- 2 large eggs
- $^1/_8$ teaspoon salt
- $^1/_8$ teaspoon freshly ground black pepper
- 2 tablespoons freshly grated mature Pecorino cheese
- 2 tablespoons freshly grated Parmesan cheese
- 2 tablespoons finely chopped fresh parsley
- 2 tablespoons butter
- 12 oz/350 g short dried pasta (such as smooth ditalini)
- cold water (optional)

Beat the eggs with the salt, pepper, Pecorino, Parmesan, and 1 tablespoon of parsley in a small bowl. • Melt the butter in a large frying pan and remove from heat. • Cook the pasta in a large pot of salted boiling water until al dente. • Drain and add to the frying pan. • Pour in the egg mixture and cook over high heat until the eggs are creamy, taking care not to break them up. If this starts to happen, add cold water to stop the eggs from cooking. • Sprinkle with the remaining parsley and serve.

Serves 4 • Prep: 5 min • Cooking: 15 min • Level: 1

LASAGNA, CARNIVAL STYLE

Lasagne di carnevale

Pasta Dough: Sift the flour and salt onto a surface and make a well in the center. Break the eggs into the well and mix in to make a smooth dough. Knead for 15–20 minutes, until smooth and elastic. Shape the dough into a ball, wrap in plastic wrap (cling film), and let rest for 30 minutes. • Roll out the pasta on a lightly floured surface to paper-thin. Cut into 6 x 4-inch (10 x 15-cm) rectangles. • Blanch the pasta for 1 minute and lay it out on a damp cloth (see page 222). • Meatballs: Mix the veal, eggs, and Pecorino in a large bowl. Season with salt and pepper. • Form into balls the size of a hazelnut. • Heat the oil in a frying pan over medium heat until very hot. Fry the meatballs in small batches for 7–10 minutes, or until browned. • Drain well and pat dry on paper towels. • Cut the sausage into chunks and prick well all over. • Cook the sausages with the wine in a medium saucepan for 5 minutes, or until tender. Skim off the fat and set aside. • Preheat the oven to 400°F/200°C/gas 6. • Grease a baking dish with oil. • Lay the first layer of pasta along the bottom and sides of the prepared baking dish, so that the pasta overlaps the dish and can be folded over to cover the top layer. • Top with a little Ricotta, sauce, white cheese, sausage, Pecorino, and some of the meatballs. • Continue for a total of 5 layers. • Fold over the overlapping pasta. • Cover with dots of butter and Pecorino. • Bake for 40–45 minutes, or until golden. • Set aside for 20 minutes before serving.

Serves 8 • Prep: 1 hr + 30 min to rest the pasta
Cooking: 80 min • Level: 3

Pasta Dough
- $2^2/_3$ cups/400 g buckwheat flour
- $^1/_4$ teaspoon salt
- 4 large eggs

Meatballs
- 2 oz/350 g ground/minced veal or beef
- 2 large eggs
- 2 tablespoons freshly grated Pecorino cheese
- salt and freshly ground black pepper
- 2 cups/500 ml olive oil
- 12 oz/300 g fresh Italian sausage, cut into small chunks
- $^1/_2$ cup/125 ml dry white wine
- $1^1/_4$ cups/310 g Ricotta cheese
- 1 quantity Meat Sauce, Naples Style (see page 187)
- $1^1/_4$ cups/310 g diced soft white cheese, such as fresh Mozzarella
- 1 cup/125 g freshly grated Pecorino cheese
- 2 tablespoons butter, cut up

PASTA WITH POTATOES

Pasta e patate

- 4 tablespoons lard or butter, cut up
- 1 small carrot, finely chopped
- 1 stalk celery, finely chopped
- $1/2$ tablespoon finely chopped parsley
- 1 onion, finely chopped
- $1/4$ cup/60 ml extra-virgin olive oil
- $1^{1}/_{2}$ lb/750 g potatoes, peeled and cut into small cubes
- rind of Parmesan cheese (optional)
- $1/2$ tablespoon tomato paste/concentrate dissolved in 1 tablespoon warm water
- cold water
- salt and freshly ground white pepper
- 4 oz/125 g each of three different types of short pasta, such as penne, farfalle, and shells, kept separate (12 oz/375 g total)
- 1 cup/125 g freshly grated Parmesan cheese

Cook the lard, carrot, celery, parsley, and onion in the oil in a large saucepan over a low heat for 10 minutes. • Add the potatoes and the Parmesan rind, if using. • Stir in the tomato paste mixture. • Pour in enough cold water to cover and place over medium heat. Season with salt and pepper and bring to a boil. Cook for 15–20 minutes, or until the potatoes are tender. • Remove a quarter of the vegetables, run them through a food mill, and return the puree to the saucepan. • Add more water, if needed to cook the pasta, and season with salt and pepper. • Cook the pasta, beginning with the type requiring the longest cooking time, and adding the other types in order of longest to shortest cooking times. • When all the pasta is al dente, the mixture should be fairly dry. • Sprinkle with Parmesan and serve.

Serves 6 • Prep: 30 min • Cooking: 40 min • Level: 1

SPAGHETTI WITH SIMPLE TOMATO SAUCE

Spaghetti di maratea

Place the tomatoes, garlic, oil, salt, and pepper in a large, heat-resistant serving bowl. Let marinate while the pasta cooks. • Cook the pasta in a large pot of salted boiling water until not quite al dente. • Use a slotted spoon to remove the pasta and transfer it to the bowl containing the tomatoes. • Place the serving bowl on top of the saucepan still full with the cooking water. Cook in this double boiler arrangement for about 15 minutes, or until the tomatoes break down slightly. Serve hot.

Serves 4 • Prep: 20 min • Cooking: 25 min • Level: 1

- 1 lb/500 g firm-ripe tomatoes, peeled, seeded, and coarsely chopped
- 2 cloves garlic, finely chopped
- $1/4$ cup/60 ml extra-virgin olive oil
- salt and freshly ground black pepper
- 12 oz/350 g dried spaghetti

Pasta with potatoes

Meat sauce, Naples style

MEAT SAUCE, NAPLES STYLE

Ragù napoletano

- 3 lb/1.5 kg beef or pork
- 2 oz/50 g pancetta, cut into thin strips
- 3 oz/80 g prosciutto/ Parma ham, sliced into thin strips
- 1 tablespoon finely chopped parsley
- freshly ground black pepper
- 3 onions
- 9 tablespoons lard or butter, cut up
- $^1/_3$ cup/40 g finely chopped pancetta
- 3 cloves garlic
- $^2/_3$ cup/150 ml extra-virgin olive oil
- freshly ground black pepper

First lard the meat by cutting holes in the direction of the grain with a long, thin knife and inserting strips of pancetta and prosciutto with the parsley and a pinch of pepper. • Chop the onions, 3 tablespoons lard, pancetta, and garlic. Melt the remaining 6 tablespoons lard and the oil in a large heavy-based saucepan over low heat. • Place the chopped mixture in the saucepan and season with pepper. Add the larded meat and cover and cook over low heat, turning the meat from time to time until the onion has turned golden brown, about 1 hour. • Pour in a little red wine and cook until evaporated. • Continue to add the red wine in small amounts, allowing it to evaporate each time. • This will take about 1 hour, at which point there should be no liquid at all left in the pan. • Mix 2

tablespoons of the tomato paste with the Marsala and the warm water. • Increase the heat and add about 6 tablespoons of the tomato paste mixture. Simmer until the tomato turns dark. • Add a little more diluted tomato paste and continue until you have used up all the tomato, allowing the sauce to become quite dark before you add more. • This will take about 2 hours. Season with salt. • Add the stock, basil, and cinnamon stick. Bring to a boil and remove the meat (this can be used as a second course). • Lower the heat and cook, covered, for about 2 hours, adding more stock or water if the sauce becomes too thick. • Let the meat sauce stand overnight. Skim off the top layer of grease, remove the cinnamon stick, and serve the meat sauce on pasta.

Serves 6–8 • Prep: 30 min + overnight to rest the sauce•
Cooking: 6 hr (requires continuous attention) • Level: 2

- 1 cup/250 ml dry red wine
- generous $^3/_4$ cup/200 g tomato paste/ concentrate
- $^2/_3$ cup/150 ml Marsala wine or dry sherry
- $^1/_4$ cup/60 ml warm water
- $1^1/_3$ cups/310 ml meat stock or broth
- salt
- Leaves from 1 bunch fresh basil, torn
- 1 stick cinnamon

Sauces & Gnocchi

FUSILLI, NAPLES STYLE

Fusilli alla napoletana

- 3 red onions, finely chopped
- 2 carrots, finely chopped
- 2 stalks celery, finely chopped
- 2 cloves garlic, lightly crushed but whole
- 1^1/$_2$ cups/180 g diced pancetta
- ^{1}/$_4$ cup/60 ml extra-virgin olive oil
- 2 lb/1 kg stew beef, such as topround, in a single piece
- ^{2}/$_3$ cup/150 ml dry white wine
- ^{1}/$_4$ cup/60 ml tomato paste/concentrate dissolved in ^{1}/$_4$ cup/60 ml dry white wine
- 3 lb/1.5 kg peeled plum tomatoes, pressed through a fine mesh strainer (passata)
- Leaves from 1 small bunch fresh basil, torn
- salt and freshly ground black pepper
- scant 1 cup/200 ml meat stock or broth (optional)
- 1 lb/500 g long fusilli pasta
- 1^1/$_2$ cups/180 g diced salami, preferably Neapolitan
- 1^2/$_3$ cups/400 g Ricotta cheese
- 6 tablespoons freshly grated aged Pecorino cheese

Sauté the onions, carrots, celery, garlic, and pancetta in the oil in a Dutch oven (casserole) over high heat for 2–3 minutes, until lightly golden. • Add the meat and sear all over. • Cook over low heat for 90 minutes. • Increase the heat, pour in the wine and tomato paste mixture, and let it evaporate. • Add the tomatoes and basil and season with salt and pepper. • Simmer, partially covered, over low heat for about 2 hours, or until the meat is tender, adding the stock if the sauce becomes too thick. • Cook the pasta in a large pot of salted boiling water until al dente. • Drain and transfer to a large bowl with the salami and half the sauce. • Arrange one-third of the pasta in a baking dish and spread over one-third of the Ricotta. Sprinkle with Pecorino and more sauce. Continue to layer the pasta, sauce, Ricotta, sauce, and Pecorino until all the ingredients are used. The meat should be served as a main course. Serve hot.

Serves 6 • Prep: 40 min • Cooking: 3 hr 40 min • Level: 1

POTATO GNOCCHETTI WITH MEAT SAUCE

Gnocchetti di casa

Pasta Dough: Boil the potatoes in salted boiling water for 15–20 minutes, or until tender. • Drain, peel, and transfer to a large bowl. Use a fork or potato masher to mash the potatoes until smooth. • Sift the whole-wheat and buckwheat flours and salt into a large bowl. • Mix in the mashed potatoes. Season with salt and add enough water to form a fairly firm dough. • Roll out small pieces of dough on a lightly floured work surface into ^{2}/$_3$ inch (1.5 cm) diameter rounds. Cut into ^{3}/$_4$-inch (2-cm) pieces and use a knife or your thumb to press into shell-shaped gnocchetti. • Lay the gnocchetti out on a kitchen cloth dusted with flour. • Cook the pasta in a large pot of salted boiling water until al dente, about 10 minutes. • Drain and serve with the sauce and Pecorino.

Serves 4 • Prep: 1 hr • Cooking: 25–30 min • Level: 2

Pasta Dough
- 2 medium baking/floury potatoes
- ^{2}/$_3$ cup/100 g whole-wheat flour
- 1^1/$_3$ cups/200 g buckwheat flour
- ^{1}/$_8$ teaspoon salt
- warm water (optional)

- Meat Sauce, Naples Style (see page 187)
- ^{3}/$_4$ cup/90 g freshly grated Pecorino romano cheese

RIGATONI WITH ONION SAUCE

Maccheroni alla moda di torano

Melt the butter in a small saucepan over low heat. • Add the onion and cook for 10–15 minutes, or until softened. • Increase the heat, pour in the wine, and let it evaporate, about 5 minutes. • Cook the pasta in a large pot of salted boiling water until al dente. • Drain and add to the pan with the sauce. Season with salt and pepper. Sprinkle with Pecorino and serve hot.

Serves 4 • Prep: 10 min • Cooking: 20 min • Level: 1

- ^{2}/$_3$ cup/150 g butter or diced pork lard
- 1 onion, finely chopped
- ^{1}/$_4$ cup/60 ml dry white wine
- 12 oz/350 g rigatoni pasta
- salt and freshly ground black pepper to taste
- 4 tablespoons freshly grated Pecorino cheese

Bucatini with hot chile oil

BUCATINI WITH HOT CHILE OIL

Bucatini o maccheroni di fuoco

- 4 fresh red chile peppers, chopped
- 4 cloves garlic, chopped
- 6 tablespoons extra-virgin olive oil
- salt
- 12 oz/350 g bucatini or other dried long pasta

Change the amount of chiles according to your taste.

Process the chiles with the garlic and oil in a food processor or blender until very finely chopped. • Heat the oil in a large frying pan over medium heat and add the chile mixture. • As soon it begins to sizzle, remove from the heat and season with salt. • Cook the pasta in a large pot of salted boiling water until al dente. • Drain and add to the chile oil. Toss well and serve.

Serves 4 • Prep: 5 min • Cooking: 10 min • Level: 1

HARD PASTA

Minnicchi—Pasta di grano duro

Pasta Dough: Sift the flour and salt onto a surface and make a well in the center. Mix in enough water to make a smooth dough. Knead for 15–20 minutes until smooth and elastic. Shape the dough into a ball, wrap in plastic wrap (cling film), and let rest for 30 minutes. • Form the dough into logs, $^1/_2$-inch (1-cm) diameter. • Use a ferretto about $^1/_{16}$ (1-mm) to each side (or a knitting needle) to make hollow cylinders, like bucatini, about 2 inches (5 cm) long. Lay the pasta on a kitchen cloth dusted with semolina. • Cook the pasta in a large pot of salted boiling water for 3–5 minutes, until al dente. • Drain and serve with the sauce. Sprinkle with the Pecorino.

Serves 6 • Prep: 1 hr • Cooking: 15 min • Level: 2

Pasta Dough
- $2^2/_3$ cups/400 g semolina flour
- $^1/_4$ teaspoon salt
- lukewarm water

Sauce
- 2 cups/500 ml Campanian Tomato Sauce (see page 180)
- $^1/_2$ cup/60 g freshly grated Pecorino cheese

VERMICELLI WITH ONIONS AND BREAD CRUMBS

Vermicelli alla carrettiera

- 1 onion, finely chopped
- $^1/_4$ cup/60 ml extra-virgin olive oil
- 2 cloves garlic, finely chopped
- 1 teaspoon finely chopped fresh oregano
- salt and freshly ground black pepper
- 2 tablespoons fresh bread crumbs
- 12 oz/350 g dried vermicelli pasta
- 1 tablespoon finely chopped fresh parsley

Sauté the onion in 2 tablespoons of the oil in a large frying pan over medium heat for 10 minutes, or until softened. • Add the garlic and oregano and cook for 1 minute. • Season with salt and pepper and remove from the heat. • Toast the bread crumbs in the remaining 2 tablespoons of the oil in a small frying pan over medium heat until golden brown. • Cook the pasta in a large pot of salted boiling water until al dente. • Drain and add to the onion. Sprinkle with the toasted bread crumbs and parsley. Serve hot.

Serves 4 • Prep: 15 min • Cooking: 10 min • Level: 1

LARD-BASED PASTA

Pasta strascinata

The special feature of this pasta is that the dough contains lard, giving the pasta a very particular flavor and texture.

Pasta Dough: Sift the flour and salt onto a work surface and make a well in the center. Mix in the lard and enough water to make a smooth dough. Knead for 15–20 minutes, until smooth and elastic. Shape the dough into a ball, wrap in plastic wrap (cling film), and let rest for 30 minutes. • Form the dough into logs $^2/_3$ inch (1.5 cm) in diameter and cut them into 4-inch (10-cm) lengths. • Alternatively you can roll out the dough and then cut it into rectangles, like lasagne. • Lay the pasta on a kitchen cloth dusted with semolina. • Cook the pasta in a large pot of salted boiling water for about 15 minutes, or until al dente. • Drain and serve with the tomato sauce and Pecorino.

Serves 6 • Prep: 30 min + 30 min to rest the dough • Cooking: 15 min • Level: 2

Pasta Dough
- 2$^2/_3$ cups/400 g all-purpose/plain flour
- $^1/_4$ teaspoon salt
- 1 tablespoon lard, chopped
- lukewarm water

Sauce
- 2 cups/500 ml Campanian Tomato Sauce (see page 180), heated
- $^1/_2$ cup/60 g freshly grated Pecorino cheese

Vermicelli with onions and bread crumbs

Sauces

SPAGHETTI WITH MUSSELS

Spaghetti alle cozze

- 2 lb/1 kg mussels
- ¹/₄ cup/60 ml dry white wine
- 2 cloves garlic, finely chopped
- 1 small bunch parsley, finely chopped
- ¹/₂ cup/125 ml extra-virgin olive oil
- salt and freshly ground black pepper to taste
- 12 oz/350 g dried spaghetti

Soak the mussels in a large bowl of warm salted water for 1 hour. Pull off the beards and discard • Transfer the mussels to a large saucepan, drizzle with the wine, and cook over high heat for about 10 minutes, shaking the pot occasionally, until they open up. Discard any that do not open. Strain the liquid and set aside. • Leave eight mussels in their shells. Shell the rest and chop the flesh coarsely. • Sauté the garlic, parsley, and shelled mussels in the oil in a frying pan over medium heat. Season generously with salt and pepper and let simmer for 4–5 minutes until the garlic is golden. • Remove the mussel mixture and set aside covered with a plate to keep it warm. Add the strained liquid from cooking the mussels and bring to a boil. • Cook the pasta in a large pot of salted boiling water until not quite al dente. • Drain and finish cooking in the boiling cooking liquid from the mussels. • Add all the mussels, mix well, and serve hot.

Serves 4 • Prep: 15 min • Cooking: 30 min • Level: 1

LASAGNA WITH BEANS

Lasagne e fagioli

- 10 oz/300 g fresh beans, such as borlotti or cranberry, rinsed
- 1 bay leaf
- 1 clove garlic
- 2 tablespoons extra-virgin olive oil
- salt
- 2 cloves garlic, finely chopped
- 1 dried chile pepper, ground
- ¹/₄ cup/60 ml extra-virgin olive oil

Pasta Dough
- 1¹/₃ cups/200 g semolina flour
- ¹/₄ teaspoon salt
- ¹/₄ cup/60 ml lukewarm water + more as needed

In Basilicata, there are numerous simple recipes for pasta and beans. The version described here can also be prepared with garbanzo beans (chickpeas) or lentils.

Place the beans in a very large saucepan. Add enough water to cover the beans to double the volume. Add the bay leaf, garlic, and oil and bring slowly to a boil over low heat. • Simmer for about 60 minutes, or until tender. • Season with salt and cook for 10 minutes more. • Pasta Dough: Sift the flour and salt onto a surface and make a well in the center. Mix in enough water to make a smooth dough. Knead for 15–20 minutes, until smooth and elastic. Shape the dough into a ball, wrap in plastic wrap (cling film), and let rest for 20 minutes. • Knead briefly, then rest for 30 minutes more. • Sauté the garlic and chile in the oil in a small frying pan over low heat for 5 minutes, until the garlic is pale gold. • Remove from the heat. • Roll the dough out on a lightly floured surface until very thin. Cut into 1 x 4-inch (3 x 10-cm) wide lasagna shapes. • Cook the pasta in a large pot of salted boiling water until al dente. • Drain and add to the beans. Top with the garlic and chile oil and serve.

Serves 4 • Prep: 1 hr + 50 min to rest the dough • Cooking: 2 hr • Level: 1

CALABRIA

Miles of unspoiled coastline stretch down to the Messina Strait, the sea separating Calabria from Sicily. Despite its natural beauty, Calabria remains unaffected by tourism. Fresh fish and seafood abound in homes and in restaurants. Home-pressed olive oil is drizzled over locally produced pasta, and almost all pasta dishes are spiced up with *peperoncini* (chile peppers). Pasta is treated with reverence by Calabrians, who have a curious instinct for matching sauces with pasta types.

Macaroni, Calabrian style
(see page 197)

SPAGHETTI WITH SQUID

Spaghetti al ragù di totano

- 1³/₄ lb/800 g small squid/calamari, bodies cut into rings, tentacles left whole
- salt
- ¹/₂ cup/125 ml extra-virgin olive oil
- 1 red onion, finely chopped
- 1 clove garlic, lightly crushed but whole
- 1 tablespoon store-bought unseasoned tomato sauce
- ¹/₈ teaspoon sugar
- ¹/₈ teaspoon finely chopped dried chile pepper
- water (optional)
- 12 oz/350 g dried spaghetti
- 4 leaves fresh basil, torn

Cook the squid in a saucepan with a pinch of salt over very low heat until transparent. • Pour in the oil and add the onion and garlic. Cook for 5 minutes until the onion has softened. Do not allow the garlic to brown as it will become bitter. • Stir in the tomato sauce, sugar, and chile pepper. Cook over low heat for 20 minutes, stirring and adding water if the sauce becomes too thick. • Remove the squid and garlic. The rings can be dipped in flour and fried as a side dish. • Cook the pasta in a large pot of salted boiling water until al dente. Drain and serve with the squid sauce and garnish with basil. Top with the cooked tentacles.

Serves 4 • Prep: 20 min • Cooking: 30 min • Level: 1

BAKED RIGATONI PASTA

Schiaffettoni

- 1 large onion, finely chopped
- 4 tablespoons extra-virgin olive oil
- salt and freshly ground black pepper to taste
- 2 sausages, weighing about 7 oz/200 g
- 1 cup/150 g diced salami
- 1 lb/500 g ground/minced beef
- 1 cup/250 ml meat stock or broth (optional)
- 3 hard-cooked eggs, crumbled
- 1 lb/500 g large rigatoni pasta
- 1 quart/1 liter store-bought tomato sauce
- 1 cup/125 g freshly grated aged Pecorino cheese

Sauté the onion in the oil in a large frying pan over medium heat for 10 minutes. Season with salt. • Pierce the sausages and blanch in hot water for 3 minutes. Drain, remove the casings, and crumble the meat. • Add the sausage meat, salami, and beef to the onion. Cook over medium heat for 30 minutes, adding some stock if the mixture starts to stick to the pan. • Add the eggs and season with salt and pepper. • Cook the pasta for half the time on the package. • Drain and let cool. • Preheat the oven to 350°F/180°C/ gas 4. • Butter a baking dish and sprinkle with bread crumbs. • Fill the pasta with the meat sauce. • Arrange the pasta in the baking dish with the sauce and Pecorino. • Cover with the remaining sauce and Pecorino. • Bake for 40–45 minutes, or until golden. • Serve hot.

Serves 6–8 • Prep: 1 hr • Cooking: 80 min • Level: 2

MACARONI, CALABRIAN STYLE

Maccheroni alla calabrese

Capocollo is a deli meat cured with a mixture of aromatic herbs and spices. It is vivid in color with a strong aroma. If you are unable to locate it, use a spicy salami or prosciutto (Parma ham) instead.

Heat 3 tablespoons of oil and 1 tablespoon lard in a medium saucepan over low heat with the garlic. Add the onion and sauté for 5 minutes, until softened. • Add the capocollo, parsley, and basil. Add the tomatoes and season with salt and pepper. Cook for about 30 minutes, or until the tomatoes have broken down. • Puree the mixture in a blender and set aside. • Cook the pasta in a large pot of salted boiling water until al dente. • Drain well. Melt the remaining lard over the top of the pasta and drizzle with the remaining 2 tablespoons oil. Season with pepper. • Preheat the oven to 400°F/200°C/gas 6. • Spoon half the pasta into a baking dish, top with half the meat sauce, and sprinkle with half the Pecorino. • Cover with the remaining pasta, meat sauce, and Pecorino. • Bake for 15–20 minutes, or until the cheese is bubbling. • Cool for 15 minutes before serving.

Serves 4 • Prep: 30 min • Cooking: 1 hr • Level: 2

- 5 tablespoons extra-virgin olive oil
- 6 tablespoons lard or butter
- 1 clove garlic, lightly crushed but whole
- ¹/₂ red onion, finely sliced
- 3 oz/90 g capocollo (or coppa or prosciutto), finely chopped
- Leaves from 1 bunch fresh parsley, finely chopped
- Leaves from 1 bunch fresh basil, finely chopped
- 6 firm-ripe tomatoes, peeled and seeded
- salt and freshly ground black pepper
- 12 oz/350 g dried ziti, broken into quarters or elbow macaroni
- ¹/₄ cup/30 g freshly grated Pecorino cheese

CALABRIAN BEAN AND PASTA SOUP

Millecoselle

- 8 oz/200 g mixed dried beans, including lentils, fava/broad beans, and garbanzo beans/chickpeas, soaked overnight and drained
- water
- salt
- 2 cloves garlic, finely chopped
- 1/2 cup/60 g diced pancetta (or bacon)
- 1/4 cup/60 ml extra-virgin olive oil
- 1 onion, finely chopped
- 1 stalk celery, finely chopped
- 1/2 small Savoy cabbage, finely shredded
- 1/2 oz/15 g dried mushrooms, soaked in warm water for 15 minutes and drained
- 8 oz/200 g dried short pasta, such as ditalini
- freshly ground black pepper
- 1/4 cup/30 g freshly grated Pecorino cheese, preferably Calabrian

This dish is generally made in the spring with the dried beans leftover from the winter.

Rinse the beans under cold running water and place in a large saucepan. • Pour in water to cover the beans with double the volume of the beans. • Boil gently for about 60 minutes, or until the beans are tender. Season with salt. • Drain, reserving the cooking liquid. • Sauté the garlic and pancetta in the oil in a large frying pan over low heat for 5 minutes. • Add the onion, celery, and cabbage and simmer for 3 minutes. • Drain the mushrooms, straining the water through a coffee filter or paper towel to remove grit. Finely chop the mushrooms and add to the pan. • Pour in enough of the reserved cooking water from the beans to cover the vegetables. Cook for about 30 minutes, or until all the vegetables are tender. • Add the beans and cook for 10 minutes more. • Add the pasta and cook until al dente, adding more of the cooking water from the beans if needed. • Season with salt. • Serve warm, sprinkled with pepper and Pecorino.

Serves 4 • Prep: 1 hr + overnight to soak the beans • Cooking: 3 hr • Level: 1

PASTA WITH GARLIC AND BREAD CRUMBS

Pasta con la mollica

Sauté the garlic in the oil in a large frying pan over low heat for 1 minute. • Add the bread crumbs and oregano and cook for 3 minutes, until the bread crumbs have browned. Remove from the heat. • Cook the pasta in a large pot of salted boiling water until al dente. • Drain and add to the bread crumbs. • Cook over low heat for 1 minute, until the sauce sticks to the pasta. • Season with pepper and serve.

Serves 4 • Prep: 10 min • Cooking: 10 min • Level: 1

- 3 cloves garlic, finely chopped
- 1/2 cup/125 ml extra-virgin olive oil
- 2 3/4 cups/150 g day-old bread, crumbled
- 1 tablespoon finely chopped fresh oregano or 2 teaspoons dried oregano
- 12 oz/350 g long dried pasta, such as spaghetti or vermicelli
- freshly ground black pepper

Calabrian bean and pasta soup

Pasta with roasted meat sauce

PASTA WITH ROASTED MEAT SAUCE

Pasta e arrosto

- $^1/_2$ cup/125 ml extra-virgin olive oil
- 4 quails
- 8 oz/300 g lean pork (or beef or veal)
- 1 bunch fresh sage
- 2 sprigs fresh rosemary
- salt and freshly ground white pepper
- generous $^1/_3$ cup/100 ml red wine
- 12 oz/350 g dried ziti

Preheat the oven to 375°F/190°C/gas 5. • Drizzle $^1/_4$ cup (60 ml) of the oil into a small baking dish. • Arrange the quails, pork, sage, and rosemary in the prepared baking dish. Season with salt and pepper and drizzle with the remaining $^1/_4$ cup (60 ml) oil. • Roast for 20 minutes. • Remove the baking dish from the oven and drizzle the meat with $^1/_4$ cup (60 ml) of the wine. Lower the oven temperature to 325°F/170°C/gas 3. • Return the meat to the oven and roast for 1 more hour, turning the meat occasionally and drizzling it with the remaining wine. • Remove the quails and pork. Strain the juices and pour them into a large frying pan. • Bone the quails and set aside the breasts. • Chop the pork and quail meat coarsely and add to the pan. Season with salt. • Cook the pasta in a large pot of salted boiling water until al dente. Drain and add to the pan with the meat sauce. • Serve, garnished with the quail breasts.

Serves 4 • Prep: 30 min • Cooking: 90 min • Level: 2

Rigatoni with cheese sauce

RIGATONI WITH CHEESE SAUCE

Rigatoni alla pastora

- 4 oz/100 g fresh luganega sausage (a long thin sausage without herbs), casing removed and crumbled
- 1/3 cup/100 ml water
- 8 oz/200 g fresh sheep's milk Ricotta cheese, strained through a fine mesh
- salt and freshly ground white pepper
- 12 oz/350 g dried tube pasta, such as rigatoni
- 3 tablespoons freshly grated spicy Pecorino cheese

This is a very simple recipe that depends entirely on the quality of the Ricotta. If you wish to make the dish richer, increase the amount of sausage, crumble it thoroughly during the cooking, and use all the meat as well as the grease, instead of reserving pieces of the meat for another use.

Cook the sausage with the water in a small saucepan over very low heat for 5 minutes, stirring with a fork occasionally until all of the grease has melted. • Remove the larger pieces of sausage. • Mix the Ricotta into the saucepan with the remaining sausage and liquid. Season with salt and pepper. • Cook the pasta in a large pot of salted boiling water until al dente. Drain, reserving 1 cup (250 ml) of the cooking liquid, and add to the saucepan with the Ricotta. Sprinkle with the Pecorino and a little cooking water from the pasta if it seems too dry. Mix well and serve hot.

Serves 4 • Prep: 5 min • Cooking: 20 min • Level: 1

PASTA WITH WILD FENNEL

Pasta e finocchietto selvatico

Clean the fennel removing the larger tougher stalks. • Cook the fennel in a large pot of salted, boiling water for 15–20 minutes, or until tender. • Remove the fennel from the saucepan, set it aside, and reserve the cooking liquid. • Sauté the garlic in the oil in a large frying pan over medium heat for 2 minutes until pale gold. • Add the drained fennel and paprika. Sauté over high heat for 5 minutes. • Bring the reserved cooking liquid to a boil, add the pasta, and cook until al dente. • Drain and add to the fennel mixture. Serve hot.

Serves 4 • Prep: 15 min • Cooking: 30 min • Level: 1

- 1 large bunch of common or herb fennel, weighing about 10 oz/300 g
- 2 cloves garlic, finely chopped
- 1/2 cup/125 ml extra-virgin olive oil
- 1/8 teaspoon sweet paprika
- 12 oz/350 g long dried pasta, such as bucatini, spaghetti, or vermicelli

CAVATELLI PASTA
WITH SPICY TOMATO SAUCE

Cavatelli al pomodoro

Pasta Dough
- 2 2/3 cups/400 g all-purpose/plain flour
- 1/4 teaspoon salt
- about 2/3 cup/150 ml water, boiling

Sauce
- 2 cloves garlic, finely chopped
- 1 fresh chile pepper, finely chopped

The boiling water in the dough gives the pasta a particularly gummy consistency, which helps it keep its shape when cooking.

Pasta Dough: Sift the flour and salt onto a work surface and make a well in the center. Mix in enough water to make a smooth dough. Knead for 15–20 minutes, until smooth and elastic. Shape the dough into a ball, wrap in plastic wrap, and let rest for 10 minutes. • Clean the board and roll out logs about 2/3 inch (1.5 cm) in diameter. • Cut into 3/4-inch (2-cm) lengths and use two fingertips to push down and turn, hollowing them out into a curved shell. Keep your hands and the pastry board well floured all the time. • Sauce: Sauté the garlic, chile, and bell peppers in the oil in a large frying pan over medium heat for 2 minutes, until the garlic is pale gold. • Stir in the tomatoes and cook over high heat for 5 minutes, or until the tomatoes have broken down. Season with salt and remove from the heat. • Cook the pasta in a large pot of salted boiling water until al dente. • Drain and add to the sauce. Cook over high heat for 1 minute until the sauce sticks to the pasta. Sprinkle with parsley and Parmesan.

Serves 4 • Prep: 90 min + 10 min to rest the dough • Cooking: 30 min • Level: 2

- 12 oz/300 g sweet green bell peppers/capsicums, seeded and coarsely chopped
- 6 tablespoons extra-virgin olive oil
- 2 lb/1 kg firm-ripe tomatoes, peeled and coarsely chopped
- salt
- 1 tablespoon finely chopped fresh parsley
- 3/4 cup/90 g freshly grated Parmesan cheese

SPAGHETTI WITH ARTICHOKE SAUCE

Spaghetti ai carciofi

- 2 medium artichokes
- 1 lemon
- $^1/_4$ cup/60 ml extra-virgin olive oil
- 2 cloves garlic, finely chopped
- 2 tablespoons finely chopped fresh parsley
- salt and freshly ground black pepper
- 6 tablespoons water
- $^1/_4$ cup/60 ml dry white wine
- 12 oz/350 g dried spaghetti
- 2 large eggs
- $^1/_4$ cup/60 ml freshly grated aged Pecorino cheese

Remove the tough outer leaves from the artichokes by snapping them off at the base Cut off the top third of the remaining leaves. Cut the artichokes in half, removing any fuzzy choke with a sharp knife. Rub with the lemon. • Chop the artichokes coarsely. • Heat the oil in a frying pan over medium heat and add the garlic, artichokes, parsley, salt, pepper, and water. Cook for 5 minutes, until the water has evaporated. • Increase the heat and pour in the wine. Cook for 15 minutes more, or until the artichokes have softened. • Cook the pasta in a large pot of salted boiling water until al dente. • Drain and add to the sauce. • Beat the eggs in a medium bowl with salt, pepper, and Pecorino. Cook the pasta in the sauce for 30 seconds, then pour in the eggs, stirring until the sauce thickens. • Serve hot.

Serves 4 • Prep: 15 min • Cooking: 15 min • Level: 2

PASTA WITH MEAT SAUCE

Pasta alla genovese

This sauce is made in both Calabria and Campania, and has no relation to the town of Genoa. It appears to have been made popular by the sea-going traders who traveled to Naples centuries ago

Heat the oil and lard in a Dutch oven (casserole) over medium heat. Add the onions, pancetta, bay leaf, and the beef. Cover and cook over medium-low heat for about 30 minutes, stirring often. • Increase the heat and pour in the wine and stock. Add the basil, parsley, and salt and pepper and bring to a boil. • Lower the heat and simmer, partially covered, for at least 2 hours, adding more stock if the sauce becomes too thick. • Cook the pasta in a large pot of salted boiling water until al dente. • Drain and add to the sauce. Sprinkle with Pecorino and serve hot. • The meat should be served, sliced, as a main course.

Serves 6 • Prep: 1 hr • Cooking: 2 hr 40 min • Level: 1

- $^1/_4$ cup/60 ml extra-virgin olive oil
- 2 tablespoons lard or butter
- 2 onions, finely chopped
- $1^3/_4$ cups/200 g diced pancetta or bacon
- 1 bay leaf
- 2 lb/1 kg stewing beef, in a single piece
- $^2/_3$ cup/150 ml dry white wine
- $^2/_3$ cup/150 ml meat stock or broth, boiling + more as needed
- Leaves from 1 small bunch fresh basil, torn
- 1 tablespoon finely chopped fresh parsley
- salt and freshly ground black pepper
- 1 lb/500 g long dried fusilli pasta
- 6 tablespoons freshly grated aged Pecorino cheese

Spaghetti with artichoke sauce

Vermicelli with mushrooms

Vermicelli with mushrooms

Vermicelli ai funghi

- 1 lb/500 g small mixed mushrooms (porcini, button, chanterelle, etc.)
- 1/4 cup/60 ml extra-virgin olive oil
- 1 onion, finely chopped
- salt
- 8 tomatoes, peeled, seeded, and diced
- 1/8 teaspoon cayenne pepper
- 12 oz/350 g dried vermicelli or other long pasta
- 1 tablespoon finely chopped fresh parsley

Clean the mushrooms and cut the large ones into pieces. • Heat the oil in a large frying pan over low heat and add the onion. Season with salt. • Cover and cook over low heat for 20 minutes. • Add the tomatoes and cayenne. Partially cover and cook over medium heat for about 5 minutes, or until the sauce has reduced a little. • Season with salt and add the mushrooms. Cook over high heat for 15 minutes more, or until the mushrooms are cooked. • Cook the pasta in a large pot of salted boiling water until al dente. • Drain and add to the mushroom sauce. Sprinkle with parsley and serve.

Serves 4 • Prep: 40 min • Cooking: 1 hr • Level: 1

Short pasta with fava beans

Pasta e fave

Heat the oil and lard in a Dutch oven (casserole) over low heat. • Add the pancetta and sauté for 5 minutes. • Add the onion and cook for 10 minutes. • Stir in the fava beans and pour in the water. • Bring to a boil and simmer gently for about 40 minutes. • Add the pasta, season with salt, and cook until the pasta is just al dente. If, as you cook the pasta, there is not enough liquid, add more water. • Season with pepper and sprinkle with Pecorino.

Serves 4 • Prep: 20 min • Cooking: 1 hr • Level: 1

- 2 tablespoons extra-virgin olive oil
- 2 tablespoons lard or butter
- 1/2 cup/60 g diced pancetta or bacon
- 1 onion, finely chopped
- 2 cups/200 g fresh shelled fava/broad beans
- 2 cups/500 ml cold water + more as needed
- 8 oz/200 g dried short pasta, such as ditali
- salt
- freshly ground black pepper
- 1/4 cup/30 g freshly grated Pecorino cheese, preferably Calabrian

SPAGHETTI WITH CHILE OIL

Pasta con l'olio santo

Olio Santo
- spicy fresh red chile peppers
- extra-virgin olive oil

- 12 oz/350 g dried spaghetti
- $^{1}/_{4}$ cup/60 ml extra-virgin olive oil
- 3 cloves garlic, lightly crushed but whole
- 4 tablespoons fresh bread crumbs

Olio Santo: Remove the stems from the chile peppers without breaking them. Rinse and dry them. • Place the chiles in a glass container, filling it three-quarters full. Add oil to cover to the rim. Cover with a cloth and allow to steep for 2–3 months. • If you want to make the olio santo in a few days, grind the chile peppers before placing them in the glass container. • Sauté the garlic in the oil in a large frying pan over medium heat for 2 minutes, until pale gold. • Cook the pasta in a large pot of salted boiling water until al dente. • Drain and add to the pan. • Add 2 tablespoons of the olio santo and the bread crumbs. • Mix well and serve immediately.

Serves 4 • Prep: 10 min • Cooking: 10 min (plus the time to prepare and steep the olio santo) • Level: 1

FUSILLI PASTA WITH SNAILS

Fusilli e lumache

- 1 onion, finely chopped
- 1 stalk celery, finely chopped
- $^{1}/_{4}$ cup/60 ml extra-virgin olive oil
- salt
- $^{1}/_{8}$ teaspoon red pepper flakes
- 4 tomatoes, coarsely chopped
- 1 tablespoon finely chopped fresh parsley
- 7 oz/200 g canned snails
- 12 oz/350 g dried long pasta (such as fusilli or perciatelli)
- $^{1}/_{4}$ cup/30 g freshly grated Pecorino cheese, preferably Calabrian

Put the onion and celery in the oil in a Dutch oven (casserole) over low heat. • Cover and cook for 20 minutes with a pinch of salt, until very soft and aromatic. • Add the red pepper flakes, tomatoes, and parsley. Cook over high heat for 10 minutes, season with salt, and add the snails. • Lower the heat and cook for about 40 minutes, or until the snails are tender. • Cook the pasta in a large pot of salted boiling water until al dente. • Drain and add to the snails. Sprinkle with Pecorino and serve.

Serves 4 • Prep: 30 min • Cooking: 80 min • Level: 1

CAVATELLI PASTA WITH BEAN SOUP

Minestra di cavatelli e fagioli

Put the beans in a large saucepan and cover with 10 cups (2.5 liters) water and bring them to a boil. • Simmer for about 1 hour, or until the beans are tender. • Let the beans cool and puree them with their stock in a food processor. • Pasta Dough: Sift the flour and salt onto a surface and make a well in the center. Mix in enough water to make a smooth dough. Knead for 15–20 minutes until smooth and elastic. Shape the dough into a ball, wrap in plastic wrap (cling film), and let rest for 10 minutes. • Clean the surface and roll out the dough into logs about $^{2}/_{3}$ inch (1.5 cm) in diameter. • Cut into $^{3}/_{4}$-inch (2-cm) lengths and use two fingertips to push down and turn, hollowing them out into a curved shell. Keep your hands and the surface well floured all the time. • Soup: Cover and cook the onion, chile, and bay leaf in the oil in a Dutch oven (casserole) for 15 minutes. Season with salt. • Add the tomato paste and cook over high heat for 1 minute. • Stir in the bean puree and pour in the 6 cups (1.5 liters) of water. Season with salt and bring to a boil. • Cook the pasta in the boiling liquid for about 15 minutes, or until not quite al dente. They will absorb the bean stock and the pasta starch will make the dish creamy. • Remove from the heat and let rest for at least 5 minutes before serving.

Serves 4 • Prep: 75 min + overnight to soak the beans + 10 min to rest the dough • Cooking: 1 hr 50 min • Level: 2

- 5 cups/500 g white beans, such as cannellini, soaked overnight and drained
- 10 cups/2.5 liters water

Pasta Dough
- 1$^{1}/_{3}$ cups/200 g all-purpose/plain flour
- $^{1}/_{8}$ teaspoon salt
- $^{1}/_{2}$ cup/125 ml boiling water + more as needed

Soup
- 1 onion, finely chopped
- 1 fresh chile pepper, finely chopped
- 1 bay leaf
- 6 tablespoons extra-virgin olive oil
- salt
- 2 tablespoons tomato paste/concentrate
- 6 cups/1.5 liters water

SICILY

Aromatic and fragrant, Sicilian cuisine is hearty and filling. Served with an inexhaustible array of sauces, pasta is the staple food. *Pasta alla norma*, pasta with a tomato sauce topped with fried eggplant, is the island's renowned dish. Not surprisingly there is a wealth of fish on local menus, including tuna and sardines. Oven-baked pastas are popular in Sicily, often utilizing the fresh cheeses produced throughout the region.

Bucatini with sardines and eggplant
(see page 208)

Sauces

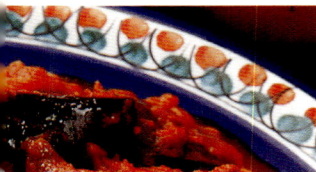

PASTA WITH ZUCCHINI

Pasta con le zucchine

- 1 lb/400 g zucchini/courgettes
- 2 cups/500 ml extra-virgin olive oil
- salt
- 1 lb/400 g dried spaghetti
- 6 tablespoons freshly grated Pecorino cheese, preferably Sicilian
- Leaves from 4 bunches fresh basil, torn

Wash the zucchini and cut into rounds or slice them lengthwise. • Heat the oil in a large deep frying pan until very hot. Fry the zucchini for 5–7 minutes, or until golden brown. Drain well and pat dry on paper towels. Season with salt and cover with a plate to keep them warm. • Cook the pasta in a large pot of salted boiling water until al dente. Drain and sprinkle with Pecorino. Top with the fried zucchini, basil, and a drizzle of oil.

Serves 4 • Prep: 10 min • Cooking: 20 min • Level: 1

BUCATINI WITH SARDINES AND EGGPLANT

Bucatini con sarde e melanzane

- 2 large eggplants/aubergines, thinly sliced
- coarse salt
- 1 cup/250 ml olive oil, for frying
- 6 tablespoons extra-virgin olive oil
- 2 cloves garlic, finely chopped
- 1 cup/250 ml peeled and chopped tomatoes
- salt and freshly ground black pepper
- 1 lb/400 g fresh sardines, cleaned and boned
- 1 lb/400 g dried bucatini pasta
- 4 tablespoons fine dry bread crumbs
- 6 tablespoons freshly grated Pecorino cheese, preferably Sicilian
- teaspoon finely chopped fresh oregano

Put the eggplant in a colander and sprinkle with salt. Let drain for 1 hour. • Heat the oil in a large frying pan until very hot. • Fry the eggplants in small batches for 5–7 minutes, or until golden brown. • Drain and pat dry on paper towels. • Sauté the garlic in 5 tablespoons of the extra-virgin olive oil in a large frying pan over medium heat for 2 minutes, until pale gold. • Stir in the tomatoes and season with salt and pepper. Cook for 5 minutes, or until the tomatoes have broken down. • Cut the sardines into small chunks and add to the sauce. Cook over low heat for 10 minutes. • Cook the pasta in a large pot of salted boiling water until al dente. • Drain and let cool to lukewarm. • Preheat the oven to 400°F/200°C/gas 6. • Grease a baking dish with the remaining 1 tablespoon of extra-virgin olive oil and sprinkle with bread crumbs. • Layer the pasta, sardine sauce, fried eggplant, and half the Pecorino in the baking dish. • Cover with the remaining Pecorino, oregano, salt and pepper, and bread crumbs. • Bake for 10–15 minutes, or until lightly golden. • Serve hot.

Serves 4 • Prep: 1 hr + 1 hr to drain the eggplant • Cooking: 50 min • Level: 1

PASTA WITH GREENS

Pasta con i tenerumi

The tenerumi (taddi in Sicilian dialect) are the green leaves of zucchini (courgettes) grown in the summer. They have a sweet flavor. You can substitute the same weight of Swiss chard.

Carefully wash the leaves and remove any tough stalks. • Bring the water to a boil in a large saucepan with the onion, potato, 1 tomato, and 1 clove garlic. Season with salt and add the leaves. Cook for about 30 minutes, or until the leaves are tender. Remove the leaves, reserving the stock, and chop them finely. • Sauté the remaining 2 cloves of garlic in the oil in a large frying pan over medium heat for 2 minutes, until pale gold. • Add the remaining 2 tomatoes and cook for 5 minutes, or until the sauce has reduced by half. • Season with salt and add the cooked leaves. Remove from the heat. • Bring the reserved stock to a boil and add the tomato mixture and pasta • Cook the pasta, until al dente, in the boiling stock, adding hot water if needed. • Sprinkle with Pecorino and grind with black pepper. Serve hot.

Serves 4 • Prep: 30 min • Cooking: 1 hr • Level: 1

- 1 lb/500 g green leaves from zucchini/courgettes or Swiss chard
- 8 cups/2 liters water
- 1 onion, coarsely chopped
- 1 medium waxy potato, peeled and coarsely chopped
- 3 tomatoes, coarsely chopped
- 3 cloves garlic, finely chopped
- salt
- ¹/₄ cup/60 ml extra-virgin olive oil
- 8 oz/200 g dried short tube pasta, such as ditalini
- ³/₄ cup/90 g freshly grated Pecorino cheese, preferably Sicilian, or Ricotta Salata
- freshly ground black pepper

Sauces

PASTA WITH SUN-DRIED TOMATOES

Pasta al pomodoro secco

- 1 cup/180 g sun-dried tomatoes packed in oil, finely sliced
- dried chile pepper
- salt
- 12 oz/350 g dried spaghetti
- Leaves from 4 sprigs fresh basil, torn
- 1/2 cup/60 g freshly grated Caciocavallo cheese or Provolone

Pour the oil from the sun-dried tomatoes, about 1/3 cup (80 ml), into a frying pan. Heat over low heat and add the tomatoes. Sauté briefly and season with chile pepper and salt. • Cook the pasta in a large pot of salted boiling water until al dente. Drain and add to the pan. Sprinkle with the basil. • Serve the spaghetti piping hot with the Caciocavallo.

Serves 4 • Prep: 5 min • Cooking: 15 min • Level: 1

PASTA WITH FRIED EGGPLANT AND TOMATO SAUCE

Pasta alla norma

Place the eggplant slices in a colander and sprinkle with salt. Let drain for 1 hour. • Heat the oil in a large deep frying pan until very hot. • Fry the eggplant in small batches for 5–7 minutes, or until golden brown. • Drain and pat dry on paper towels. • <u>Sauce</u>: Stir together the tomatoes, onion, garlic, basil, oil, sugar, and salt in a medium saucepan. Cover and simmer over medium heat for 15 minutes, or until the tomatoes have broken down. • Uncover and cook for about 40 minutes, or until the sauce had thickened. • Transfer to a food processor or blender and process until smooth. • Cook the pasta in a large pot of salted boiling water until al dente. • Drain and add to the sauce. Top with the fried eggplant and sprinkle with Parmesan.

Serves 4 • Prep: 1 hr + 1 hr to drain the eggplant • Cooking: 1 hr 20 min • Level: 1

- 1 large eggplant/ aubergine, weighing about 1 lb/400 g, thinly sliced
- coarse salt
- 1 cup/250 ml olive oil, for frying

Sauce

- 2 lb/1 kg firm-ripe tomatoes, peeled and coarsely chopped
- 1 red onion, thinly sliced
- 2 cloves garlic, finely chopped
- Leaves from 1 small bunch fresh basil, torn
- 2 tablespoons extra-virgin olive oil
- 1/8 teaspoon sugar
- salt
- 12 oz/350 g long dried pasta (such as spaghetti or bucatini)
- 1 cup/125 g freshly grated Parmesan cheese

Pasta with sun-dried tomatoes

Linguine with almonds

PASTA WITH TOMATO FISH SAUCE

Pasta con la neonata

- 2 cloves garlic, lightly crushed but whole
- 6 tablespoons extra-virgin olive oil
- 1¹/₂ lb/750 g peeled plum tomatoes, pressed through a fine mesh strainer (passata)
- 12 oz/300 g small fresh fish, such as sardines, whitebait, or anchovies, skinned and boned
- salt and freshly ground black pepper
- 12 oz/350 g dried spaghettini (thin spaghetti)
- 1 tablespoon finely chopped fresh parsley

The "newborn" or neonata is a combination of newborn fish of various species, including sardines, anchovies, and mullet. It is gelatinous in appearance and exquisitely flavorful.

Sauté the garlic in the oil in a large frying pan over medium heat for 2 minutes, until pale gold. • Stir in the tomatoes and cook over high heat for about 5 minutes, or until the tomatoes have broken down. • Add the fish and season with salt and pepper. Cook for 5 minutes, shaking the pan. • Discard the garlic and remove from the heat. • Cook the pasta in a large pot of salted boiling water until al dente. • Drain and add to the sauce. Cook over high heat for 1 minute, until the sauce sticks to the pasta. Sprinkle with the parsley and serve.

Serves 4 • Prep: 20 min • Cooking: 20 min • Level: 1

LINGUINE WITH ALMONDS

Linguine con mandorle

Chop the almonds very finely with the garlic and basil. Transfer to a pestle and mortar or food processor and crush or process until the mixture is creamy. • Add the tomato sauce, Parmesan, and 2 tablespoons of the oil, and mix well. • Cook the pasta in a large pot of salted boiling water until al dente. • While the pasta is cooking, dilute the sauce with 2–3 tablespoons of cooking water. Season with salt. • Drain the pasta and serve with the almond sauce, adding a drizzle of the remaining tablespoon oil and more cooking water if needed.

Serves 4 • Prep: 20 min • Cooking: 15 min • Level: 1

- 8 oz/200 g blanched almonds
- 3 cloves garlic
- Leaves from 1 small bunch basil
- 3 tablespoons store-bought unseasoned tomato sauce
- ³/₄ cup/90 g freshly grated Parmesan cheese
- 2–3 tablespoons extra-virgin olive oil
- 12 oz/350 g dried linguine
- salt

Sauces & Couscous

SPAGHETTI WITH BLACK INK

Spaghetti al nero di seppia

- 1 lb/500 g squid or cuttlefish
- 2 cloves garlic, finely chopped
- 1/4 cup/60 ml extra-virgin olive oil
- Leaves from 1 small bunch parsley, finely chopped
- 1/8 teaspoon red pepper flakes
- 1 tablespoon tomato paste/concentrate
- generous 1/3 cup/100 ml white wine
- salt
- 1/3 cup/100 ml hot water
- 12 oz/350 g spaghetti

Use as little or as much of the ink you like. Cuttlefish has more ink than squid, but squid is more readily available in North America.

To clean the squid, reach inside the body and pull everything out, taking care not to damage the small silver-gray sac—the ink bladder—located near the top of the body. Be sure to remove the transparent plasticlike quill running along the inside. Cut off the tentacles just below the eyes. Reserve the tentacles and the inksac and discard the rest of the innards. • Peel, wash, and cut the bodies into 1-inch (2-cm) squares and cut the tentacles into small pieces. • Sauté the garlic in the oil in a medium saucepan over medium heat for 2 minutes, until pale gold. Add the squid, parsley, and red pepper flakes. • Cook, covered, over low heat for 45 minutes. • Dissolve the tomato paste in 1/4 cup (60 ml) wine and add to the saucepan. Cook for 20 minutes. • Season with salt and add the hot water. Cook, covered, for 30 minutes more. • Remove the ink from the bladders, mix with the remaining wine, and add it to the sauce a few minutes before serving. • Cook the pasta in a large pot of salted boiling water until al dente. Drain and serve with the sauce, mixing well. Serve hot.

Serves 4 • Prep: 45 min • Cooking: 1 hr 45 min • Level: 2

SICILIAN COUSCOUS

Cuscus

Boil the fish stock with the onion, garlic, oil, parsley, saffron, cinnamon, lemon, and salt for about 30 minutes. • Set aside the stock. • Carefully clean the fish, fillet it, and remove all the small bones. • Sauté the onion, bay leaf, and cinnamon in 1/4 cup (60 ml) of the oil in a Dutch oven (casserole) over low heat for 10 minutes. • Add the garlic, tomato paste, lemon zest, and 1 cup (250 ml) water. Bring to a boil and gently add the filleted fish. • Pour in enough water to cover the fish completely. Season with salt, cover, and cook over very low heat for about 1 hour. • Strain the fish stock and bring it back to a boil. Place the couscous in a large saucepan and pour over the hot fish stock. Stir, making sure that the couscous is completely covered. Cover and let rest for 10 minutes. Place over low heat and add the remaining 1/4 cup (60 ml) of oil to prevent clumping. Stir for 5 minutes, then transfer to a large, deep serving dish. Pour in enough of the fish stock to cover the couscous completely. Stir and cover with a kitchen cloth. Let rest for about 20 minutes before serving.

Serves 6–8 • Prep: 60 min + 30 min to rest • Cooking: 60 min • Level: 1

- 6 cups/1.5 liters fish stock or broth
- 1 onion, cut into quarters
- 2 cloves garlic, lightly crushed but whole
- 1/4 cup/60 ml extra-virgin olive oil
- 1 tablespoon finely chopped fresh parsley
- 1/2 teaspoon saffron threads, crumbled
- 1 small stick cinnamon
- 1/2 lemon, chopped
- salt
- 3 lb/1.5 kg mixed fish, such as mullet, snapper, grouper, and cod
- 1 red onion, finely chopped
- 1 bay leaf
- 1 small stick cinnamon
- 1/2 cup/125 ml extra-virgin olive oil
- 2 cloves garlic, finely chopped
- 2 tablespoons tomato paste/concentrate
- grated zest of 1/2 lemon
- 3 cups/750 ml water + more as needed
- salt
- 2 lb/1 kg instant couscous

SPAGHETTI WITH OLIVES

Spaghetti alla disperata

- 1 tablespoon dried mushrooms, soaked for 15 minutes in warm water
- 1 oz/25 g salt-cured capers
- 1 large onion, finely chopped
- 5 tablespoons extra-virgin olive oil
- 1 firm-ripe tomato, peeled and cut into small cubes
- 10 green olives, pitted
- 3 salt-cured anchovies, rinsed and boned
- ¼ teaspoon dried oregano
- salt and freshly ground white pepper
- 12 oz/350 g dried spaghetti
- 6 tablespoons freshly grated Pecorino cheese, preferably Sicilian

Drain the mushrooms, reserving the soaking liquid, and finely chop. • Strain the soaking liquid. • Rinse the capers under cold running water and transfer to a small saucepan. Add enough water to cover and place over medium heat. Bring to a boil, drain the capers, rinse them again, and pat dry on paper towels. • Sauté the onion in the oil in a small saucepan over medium heat for 2 minutes, until softened. • Add the mushrooms and tomato and cook for 8-10 minutes, adding 2–3 tablespoons of the strained soaking water from the mushrooms.

• Meanwhile, finely chop the olives, capers, and anchovies. Add to the sauce and season with oregano, salt, and pepper. Cook over low heat for 5 minutes. The sauce should not come to a boil. It should remain fairly liquid. Add more of the liquid from the mushrooms, if needed. • Cook the pasta in a large pot of salted boiling water until al dente. • Drain and sprinkle with Pecorino. Top with the sauce and serve.

Serves 4 • Prep: 20 min + 15 min to soak the mushrooms • Cooking: 20 min • Level: 1

Spaghetti with olives

Spaghetti with tuna and capers

SPAGHETTI WITH TUNA AND CAPERS

Spaghetti con tonno

- 1 cup/100 g salt-cured capers
- 7 oz/150 g tuna packed in oil, drained
- Leaves from 1 bunch fresh mint
- ⅛ teaspoon red pepper flakes (optional)
- 3 tablespoons extra-virgin olive oil
- salt
- 12 oz/350 g dried spaghetti

Rinse the capers under cold running water and cover with fresh water in a small saucepan. Place over medium heat. Bring to a boil, drain the capers, rinse them again, and pat dry on paper towels. • Chop the tuna, capers, mint, and red pepper flakes, if using. • Transfer to a large bowl and mix in the oil. Season with salt. • Cook the pasta in a large pot of salted boiling water until al dente. Add ¼ cup (60 ml) of the cooking water to the sauce to make a creamy consistency. • Drain the pasta, reserving a little cooking water, and toss with the tuna sauce, adding more cooking water if needed. Serve immediately.

Serves 4 • Prep: 10 min • Cooking: 15 min • Level: 1

PASTA WITH ANCHOVIES, PINE NUTS, AND RAISINS

Pasta con l'anciova

Tripolini are a sort of wide trenette, about ½ inch (1 cm), with one smooth edge and one jagged edge. The anciova, in the dialects spoken in certain parts of Sicily, is the anchovy.

Sauté the garlic in the oil in a large frying pan over medium heat for 2 minutes, until pale gold. • Add the pine nuts and raisins and toast them for 2 minutes, until the pine nuts are golden. • Stir in the tomato paste mixture. Add the anchovies and let them dissolve, 5–10 minutes. • Season with salt and remove from the heat. • Cook the pasta in a large pot of salted boiling water until al dente. • Drain, reserving some of the cooking liquid, and add to the sauce, adding some of the cooking water if needed. • Sprinkle with the parsley and serve.

Serves 4 • Prep: 15 min • Cooking: 20 min • Level: 1

- 1 clove garlic, finely chopped
- 6 tablespoons extra-virgin olive oil
- 2 tablespoons pine nuts
- 2 tablespoons golden raisins/sultanas
- 2–3 tablespoons tomato paste/concentrate dissolved in ¼ cup/ 60 ml lukewarm water
- 4 salt cured anchovies, rinsed and boned
- salt
- 12 oz/350 g dried long pasta (such as tripolini)
- 1 teaspoon finely chopped fresh parsley

Ziti in tuna sauce

ZITI IN TUNA SAUCE

Zite al ragù di tonno

- 2 onions, chopped
- 4 cloves garlic, lightly crushed but whole
- 1/4 cup/60 ml extra-virgin olive oil
- 2/3 cup/150 ml dry white wine
- 1 1/4 lb/575 g peeled plum tomatoes, pressed through a fine mesh strainer (passata)
- 1 lb/500 g fresh tuna, skin removed
- 1 small bunch common or herb fennel leaves, finely chopped, and/or 1 tablespoon fresh mint, finely chopped
- salt and freshly ground black pepper
- fish stock or water (optional)
- 1 lb/500 g dried ziti
- 3/4 cup/90 g freshly grated Caciocavallo or Ricotta Salata cheese

Add some dried chile pepper to give the dish some piquancy.

Sauté the onions and garlic in the oil in a large saucepan over low heat for 10 minutes until the onion has softened. • Pour in the wine and add the tomatoes, tuna, wild fennel and/or the mint. Season with salt and pepper and bring to a boil. Lower the heat and simmer, partially covered, for at least 1 hour, adding fish stock or hot water if the sauce begins to stick to the pan. • Remove the tuna and crumble it coarsely with a fork. Return the tuna meat to the sauce. • Cook the pasta in a large pot of salted boiling water until al dente. Drain and serve with the tuna sauce. Sprinkle with Caciocavallo. Serve hot.

Serves 6 • Prep: 30 min • Cooking: 90 min • Level: 1

GNOCCHETTI, SICILY STYLE

Gnocculi

Gnocchetti Dough: Sift the flour and salt onto a surface and make a well in the center. • Mix in enough water to form a very dry and well-combined dough. Knead for 15–20 minutes, until smooth and elastic. • Shape the dough into a ball, wrap in plastic wrap, and let rest for 30 minutes. • Break off pieces of dough and form into logs about 1/4 inch (1 cm) in diameter. Slice the dough into 1/2-inch (0.5-cm) lengths and make gnocchetti with your fingers, using a fork to press a ridged pattern on the tops of the gnocchetti. Let dry for about 30 minutes, covered with a kitchen cloth. • Cook the gnocchetti in a large pot of salted boiling water for about 10 minutes, or until al dente. • Drain and cover with sauce. Sprinkle with Caciocavallo and serve.

Serves 4 • Prep: 1 hr + 1 hr to rest and dry the pasta • Cooking: 10 min • Level: 2

Gnocchetti Dough
- 2 2/3 cups/400 g semolina flour
- 1/8 teaspoon salt
- lukewarm water

Sauce
- Meat Sauce (see Oven-Baked Pasta, page 221), or Tomato Sauce (see Pasta with Fried Eggplant and Tomato Sauce, page 210) or Pork Sauce (see Homemade Macaroni with Meat Sauce, page 226)
- 1 cup/125 g freshly grated Caciocavallo or Ricotta Salata cheese

PASTA WITH TUNA

Pasta fredda al tonno

- 12 oz/300 g fresh tuna, in a single cut, skinned, boned, and chopped
- juice of 1 lemon
- 3/4 cup/180 ml extra-virgin olive oil
- 20 black olives, pitted and finely chopped
- 2 cloves garlic, lightly crushed but whole
- 1 lb/500 g firm-ripe tomatoes, peeled and seeded
- salt and freshly ground white pepper
- 12 oz/350 g penne pasta
- 4–5 leaves fresh basil, torn

Place the tuna in a bowl. Drizzle with the lemon juice and 4 tablespoons of oil. Add the olives. Let marinate for 30 minutes. • Sauté the garlic in 4 tablespoons of oil in a frying pan over low heat for a few seconds. Remove from the heat and let cool. Discard the garlic. • Chop the tomatoes, salt them, and place them in a colander. Let drain for 15 minutes. • Mix the tomatoes and garlic-infused oil into the tuna. Season with salt and pepper. • Cook the pasta in a large pot of salted boiling water until al dente. • Drain and let cool under running cold water. • Transfer to a serving bowl and drizzle with the remaining oil. Add the tuna sauce and basil. Toss well and serve.

Serves 4 • Prep: 40 min + 45 minutes to marinate and drain • Cooking: 15 min • Level: 1

COLD PASTA SALAD WITH CAVIAR

Pasta fredda al caviale

Mix the scallion, chives, and caviar in a large bowl. Drizzle with the oil and season with salt and pepper. • Cook the pasta in a large pot of salted boiling water until al dente. • Drain and add the caviar mixture. Toss well and serve.

Serves 4 • Prep: 10 min • Cooking: 15 min • Level: 1

- 1 scallion/spring onion, finely chopped
- 1 bunch chives, finely chopped
- 2 oz/50 g caviar (salmon, sturgeon, or lumpfish)
- 1/3 cup/80 g extra-virgin olive oil
- salt and freshly ground white pepper
- 12 oz/350 g dried spaghettini

Sauces & Baked Pasta

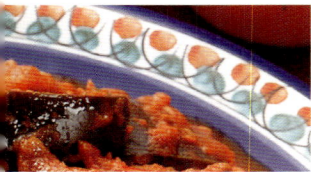

PASTA, SIRACUSA STYLE

Pasta alla siracusana

- 2 salt-cured anchovies, rinsed
- 2 tablespoons salt-cured capers, rinsed
- 1/3 cup/40 g green olives
- 2 cloves garlic, lightly crushed but whole
- 6 tablespoons extra-virgin olive oil
- 2 eggplants/aubergines, cut into cubes
- 1 lb/500 g peeled plum tomatoes, pressed through a fine mesh strainer (passata)
- salt and freshly ground black pepper
- 2 yellow bell peppers/capsicums, seeded and cut into thin strips
- Leaves from 1 bunch fresh basil, torn
- 1 lb/400 g dried smooth or ridged medium macaroni
- 1/2 cup/60 g freshly grated peppered Pecorino cheese

Chop the anchovies finely with the capers. • Pit the olives and crush them slightly. • Sauté the garlic in the oil in a large frying pan over medium heat for 3 minutes until pale gold. • Discard the garlic and add the eggplant to the oil. Sauté for 15 minutes. • Add the tomatoes and season with salt and pepper. Let reduce for 10 minutes. • Add the bell peppers, olives, the chopped capers and anchovies, and the basil. • Simmer briefly and remove from the heat. • Cook the pasta in a large pot of salted boiling water until al dente. • Drain and serve with the sauce and sprinkled with Pecorino.

Serves 4 • Prep: 30 min • Cooking: 40 min • Level: 1

BAKED PASTA WITH EGGPLANT

Sformato di maccheroni e melanzane

Place the eggplant slices in a colander and sprinkle with salt. Let drain for 1 hour. • Preheat the oven to 400°F/200°C/gas 6. • Butter a 10-inch (25-cm) springform mold and sprinkle with 1/4 cup (30 g) of the bread crumbs. • Heat the oil in a large deep frying pan until very hot. Fry the eggplant in small batches over medium heat for 5–7 minutes, or until golden brown. • Drain well and pat dry on paper towels. • Arrange the eggplant in a single layer on the bottom and along the sides of the prepared pan, letting the edges of the eggplant overhang. • Cook the pasta in a large pot of salted boiling water until al dente. • Drain and transfer to a large bowl. Mix in the meat sauce, oregano, basil, the cheeses, and pepper. • Spoon the pasta into the pan, taking care not to disturb the eggplant. Fold over the overhanging eggplant and top with the remaining slices of eggplant. • Sprinkle with bread crumbs and dot with butter. • Bake for 25–30 minutes, or until golden brown on top. • Remove from the oven and let rest for 10 minutes before turning out of the mold. • Serve warm.

Serves 6 • Prep: 40 min + 1 hr to drain the eggplants + 10 min to rest • Cooking: 1 hr • Level: 1

- 3 eggplants, each weighing about 1 lb/500 g, thinly sliced
- coarse salt
- 3/4 cup/60 g fine dry bread crumbs
- 1 cup/250 ml olive oil, for frying
- 1 lb/500 g dried bucatini
- 1²/3 cups/400 ml Meat sauce (see Oven-Baked Pasta, page 221)
- 1/8 teaspoon dried oregano
- Leaves from 1 small bunch fresh basil, torn
- 1¹/4 cups/150 g freshly grated mixed firm cheeses, such as Caciocavallo, Parmesan, and Pecorino
- freshly ground black pepper
- 1/4 cup/60 g butter, cut into flakes

PASTA WITH ARTICHOKES, FAVA BEANS, AND PEAS

Pasta con la frittedda

- 3 artichokes
- 1 lemon
- 1 lb/500 g fava/broad beans in the shell
- 8 oz/250 g peas in the pod
- 1 onion, finely chopped
- $^1/_4$ cup/60 ml extra-virgin olive oil
- salt and freshly ground white pepper
- hot water (optional)
- Leaves from 1 sprig fresh mint, finely chopped
- 1 tablespoon white wine vinegar
- 1 lb/500 g dried bucatini

Remove the tough outer leaves from the artichokes by snapping them off at the base. Cut off the top third of the remaining leaves. Cut the artichokes into six sections, removing any fuzzy choke with a sharp knife. Rub with the lemon. • Shell the fava beans and peas. • Sauté the onion in the oil in a large frying pan over medium heat for about 10 minutes until softened. • Add the peas and beans and season with salt and pepper. Cover and cook for 15 minutes, adding water in small amounts during the cooking. • Add the artichokes and cook for about 40 minutes, or until all the the vegetables have softened. • Add the mint and vinegar and cook for 1 minute. Remove from the heat and set aside. • Use a fork to mash some of the vegetables, making it thicker and creamier. • Cook the pasta in a large pot of salted, boiling water until al dente. • Drain and add to the vegetables.

Serves 6 • Prep: 30 min • Cooking: 70 min • Level: 1

PASTA WITH RICOTTA AND PECORINO

Pasta con ricotta e pecorino

Mix the Ricotta, butter, Ricotta Salata, chile pepper, and salt in a large bowl. • Cook the pasta in a large pot of salted boiling water until al dente. • Drain, reserving 2 tablespoons of the cooking water. Transfer the pasta to the Ricotta mixture, adding the reserved cooking water. • Toss well, sprinkle with Pecorino, and serve.

Serves 6 • Prep: 10 min • Cooking: 12 min • Level: 1

- $^3/_4$ cup/180 g fresh Ricotta cheese
- $^1/_4$ cup/60 g butter, cut up
- $^1/_2$ cup/60 g freshly grated Ricotta Salata cheese
- 1 dried chile pepper, crumbled
- salt
- 1 lb/500 g dried spaghettini
- $^1/_2$ cup/60 g freshly grated Pecorino cheese

Pasta with artichokes, fava beans, and peas

Oven-baked pasta

OVEN-BAKED PASTA

Pasta al forno

- 1 eggplant/aubergine, cut into thin strips (peeled or unpeeled)

Meat Sauce
- 1 lb/500 g ground/minced lean beef
- 1 large red onion, finely chopped
- 1/4 cup/60 ml extra-virgin olive oil
- generous 1/3 cup/100 ml dry red wine
- 2 lb/1 kg peeled plum tomatoes, pressed through a fine mesh strainer (passata)
- 1 tablespoon tomato paste/concentrate
- 1 stick cinnamon
- 1 clove
- Leaves from 1 small bunch basil, torn

This dish is very popular in Palermo, all through the year and at all hours of the day and night. It can be enjoyed at home or at the beach. Odd as it may seem, this is a typical component of picnics on the beach. If you want to serve this dish for an important dinner, cook it in a ring-shaped mold lined with thin slices of fried eggplant (aubergine), and turn it out onto the serving dish after letting it cool for 30 minutes.

Soak the strips of eggplant in a large bowl of salted cold water for 1 hour. This will remove any bitter taste. • <u>Meat Sauce</u>: Sauté the beef and onion in the olive oil in a medium saucepan over high heat for about 10 minutes until the beef has browned all over. Drizzle with the wine, add the tomato, tomato paste, cinnamon stick, clove, basil, and oregano. Season with salt and pepper. Cook for about 2 hours, adding water or stock if the sauce begins to stick to the pan, until the sauce has reduced by half. Discard the cinnamon and clove. • Drain the eggplant, rinse under cold running water, and pat dry on paper towels. • Heat the peanut oil in a large deep frying pan until very hot. Fry the strips of eggplant in small batches for 5–7 minutes, or until golden brown. Drain well and pat dry on paper towels. • Cook the pasta in a large pot of salted boiling water for half the time indicated on the package. Drain and run under cold water to stop the cooking. • Preheat the oven to 350°F/180°C/gas 4. • Grease a baking dish with oil. • Toss the pasta with two-thirds of the meat sauce, the fried eggplant, and Caciocavallo. • Beat the eggs with the Pecorino in a small bowl until frothy. • Arrange half the pasta in the prepared baking dish, spreading it out evenly. Pour over the remaining meat sauce and arrange the hard-boiled eggs on top. Top with the remaining pasta, spreading it out. Pour over the egg and Pecorino mixture. • Bake for 40–45 minutes, or until golden brown on top.

Serves 6–8 • Prep: 40–45 min • Cooking: 3 hr • Level: 1

- 1/8 teaspoon dried oregano
- salt and freshly ground black pepper
- water or stock (optional)
- 1 cup/250 ml peanut oil, for frying
- 1 lb/500 g dried pasta, such as anellini or small pasta rings
- 3 oz/100 g Caciocavallo or Ricotta Salata cheese, cut into small cubes
- 2 large eggs, lightly beaten
- 2 hard-boiled eggs, thinly sliced
- 1/2 cup/60 g freshly grated Pecorino cheese, preferably Sicilian

Oven-baked pasta

Baked Pasta

CANNELLONI, SICILY STYLE

Cannelloni alla siciliana

Meat Sauce
- 3/4 cup/100 g diced pancetta
- 6 tablespoons extra-virgin olive oil
- 1 lb/500 g stewing beef, in a single piece
- 1 red onion, chopped
- 1 stalk celery, chopped
- 2 cloves garlic, chopped
- 2 tablespoons finely chopped fresh parsley
- 1 stick cinnamon
- 1 sprig rosemary
- 1 bay leaf
- 1/4 cup/60 ml red wine
- 3 lb/1.5 kg peeled plum tomatoes, pressed through a fine mesh strainer (passata)

Meat Sauce: Sauté the pancetta in the oil in a Dutch oven (casserole) over medium heat for 5 minutes until crispy. • Add the beef, onion, celery, garlic, parsley, cinnamon, rosemary, and bay leaf. • Pour in the wine and the tomatoes and basil. Season with salt and pepper and bring to a boil. Cover and simmer over low heat for 2 hours, or until the meat is tender, adding water if the sauce begins to stick to the pan. • Discard the cinnamon stick, rosemary, and bay leaf. • Remove from the heat and process the meat with 3 tablespoons of the cooking juices in a food processor until chopped. • **Pasta Dough:** Sift the flour and salt onto a surface and make a well in the center Mix in the egg yolks and enough water to make a smooth dough. Knead for 15–20 minutes, until elastic. • Shape the dough into a

ball, wrap in plastic wrap (cling film), and let rest for 30 minutes. • Roll out the dough on a lightly floured surface until thin. Cut into 6 x 8-inch (15 x 20-cm) strips. • Preheat the oven to 375°F/190°C/gas 5. • Blanch the dough for 1 minute and lay on a damp cloth (see below). • Spread the meat sauce over the pasta and roll up tightly into rolls from the long side. • Arrange the cannelloni in a baking dish and cover with the meat sauce. • Beat the eggs with the salt and pepper and 2 tablespoons Caciocavallo. Sprinkle the remaining Caciocavallo over the meat sauce. Pour the eggs over the top. • Bake for 30–35 minutes, or until the top is brown. • Serve hot.

Serves 6 • Prep: 2½ hr + 30 min to rest the dough • Cooking: 2 hr 30 min • Level: 3

- 1 sprig fresh basil
- salt and freshly ground black pepper
- hot water (optional)

Pasta Dough
- 2 2/3 cups/300 g all-purpose/plain flour
- 1/4 teaspoon salt
- 3 large egg yolks
- lukewarm water

Topping
- 2 large eggs
- salt and freshly ground black pepper
- 1 3/4 cups/215 g freshly grated Caciocavallo or Ricotta Salata cheese

ROLLING OUT AND BLANCHING PASTA DOUGH

1. When the dough has rested for the time indicated in the recipe, place it on the pastry board and use a rolling pin to roll it out, maintaining a rounded shape as much as possible.

2. As the sheet of pasta dough becomes larger, allow it to stick to the rolling pin and turn it over on the pastry board.

3. As you roll the pasta dough up onto the rolling pin, flatten it with your hands in order to make it even thinner.

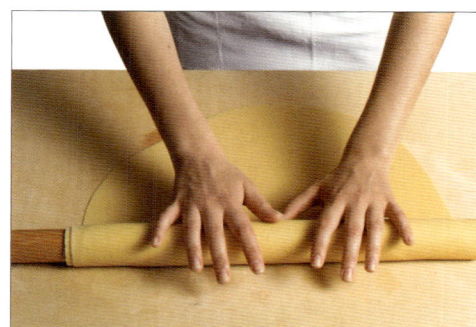

4. Bring a large pot of salted water to a boil and add the pasta. For dried pasta, cook for half the time indicated on the package. For fresh pasta, cook for 1–2 minutes.

5. Use a slotted spoon to remove the pasta from the water.

6. Lay out the pasta sheets on clean kitchen towels until ready to use.

Baked Pasta

ST. JOSEPH'S DAY TIMBALE

Tiano di S. Giuseppe

- 12 oz/300 g asparagus, peeled and coarsely chopped
- 1 lb/500 g broccoli, separated into florets and stalks
- 8 oz/200 g common or herb fennel, stalks removed and chopped
- $^{1}/_{2}$ cup/125 ml extra-virgin olive oil
- 3 salt-cured anchovies, rinsed and filleted
- 1 onion, finely chopped
- salt
- 2 tablespoons golden raisins/sultanas
- 2 tablespoons pine nuts
- 1 tablespoon tomato paste/concentrate dissolved in $^{3}/_{4}$ cup/ 180 ml water
- 1 tablespoon finely chopped fresh parsley
- freshly ground black pepper
- 3 tablespoons fresh bread crumbs
- 1 lb/500 g dried macaroni or bucatini
- 3 oz/90 g Caciocavallo cheese, cut into small cubes, or $^{3}/_{4}$ cup/90 g freshly grated Pecorino cheese, preferably Sicilian
- $^{1}/_{4}$ cup/60 g butter, cut into flakes
- 2 tablespoons finely chopped almonds, toasted

Cook the asparagus, broccoli, and fennel separately in salted boiling water for 5–7 minutes until tender. • Heat $^{1}/_{4}$ cup (60 ml) of the oil in a large frying pan over low heat and sauté the anchovies until they have dissolved. • Add the cooked vegetables and sauté over high heat for 3 minutes until lightly golden. Remove from the heat and set aside. • Sauté the onion in 1 tablespoon of the oil in a separate frying pan over low heat, covered, with $^{1}/_{8}$ teaspoon of salt, for 10 minutes, or until softened. • Stir in the raisins and pine nuts and toast over high heat for 3 minutes, until golden. • Pour in the tomato paste mixture and add the parsley. Season with salt and pepper. Cook for 5 minutes more. • Toast the bread crumbs in the remaining 2 tablespoons of the oil in a small frying pan over high heat for 2 minutes, until golden brown. • Cook the pasta in a large pan of salted boiling water for half the time indicated on the package. • Drain and rinse under cold running water. Drizzle with the remaining 1 tablespoon of oil to prevent sticking. • Preheat the oven to 350°F/180°C/gas 4. • Butter a large baking dish. • Arrange one-third of the pasta in the prepared baking dish. Cover with some of the sauce, sprinkle with Caciocavallo, bread crumbs, almonds, and the sautéed vegetables. Continue to make two more layers, finishing with Caciocavallo and butter. • Bake for 40–45 minutes, or until the top is golden brown. • Serve hot.

Serves 6–8 • Prep: 2 hr • Cooking: 3 hr • Level: 2

BAKED PASTA WITH MEAT SAUCE

Pasta con la carne gratinata

- 1 lb/500 g beef, in a single piece
- 1 large red onion, finely chopped
- $^{1}/_{4}$ cup/60 ml extra-virgin olive oil
- 1 cup/250 ml dry red wine
- 2 lb/1 kg peeled plum tomatoes, pressed through a fine mesh strainer (passata)
- 1 tablespoon tomato paste/concentrate
- 1 small stick cinnamon
- 1 clove
- Leaves from 1 small bunch fresh basil, torn
- 1 tablespoon finely
- chopped fresh parsley
- $^{1}/_{8}$ teaspoon dried oregano
- salt and freshly ground black pepper
- beef stock or broth (optional)
- 1 lb/500 g dried macaroni
- 8 oz/200 g Caciocavallo or Ricotta Salata cheese, cut into small cubes
- $^{1}/_{2}$ cup/60 g freshly grated Pecorino cheese, preferably Sicilian
- $^{1}/_{4}$ cup/60 g butter, cut into flakes

Sauté the beef and onion in the oil in a Dutch oven (casserole) over high heat for about 10 minutes until the beef has browned all over. • Pour in the wine and add the tomatoes, tomato paste, cinnamon, clove, basil, parsley, and oregano. Season with salt and pepper. Cook over low heat for about 2 hours, adding stock if the sauce starts to stick to the pan. The sauce should be flavorful but fairly liquid. • Remove the meat from the sauce and chop it finely. Return the meat to the sauce. Discard the cinnamon and clove. Season with salt. • Cook the pasta in a large pan of salted boiling water for half the time indicated on the package. • Drain and rinse under cold running water. • Preheat the oven to 350°F/180°C/gas 4. • Butter a large baking dish. • Mix the pasta in half of the meat sauce. • Arrange one-third of pasta in the prepared baking dish, cover with a little meat sauce, and sprinkle with some Pecorino. Top with one-third of the Caciocavallo. Continue to layer the ingredients, finishing with Pecorino and butter. • Bake for 40–45 minutes, or until the top is golden brown. • Serve hot.

Serves 6–8 • Prep: 1 hr • Cooking: 3 hr • Level: 1

Homemade pasta
with meat sauce

HOMEMADE PASTA WITH MEAT SAUCE

Maccaruna di casa

Sauce

- 1 red onion, finely chopped
- 2 tablespoons extra-virgin olive oil
- salt
- 1 clove garlic, finely chopped
- 12 oz/300 g lean ground/minced pork
- 1 Italian sausage, casing removed and crumbled
- generous $^1/_3$ cup/100 ml dry red wine
- 1 lb/500 g peeled plum tomatoes, pressed through a fine mesh strainer (passata)
- freshly ground black pepper

Sauce: Sauté the onion in the oil in a large frying pan over low heat for 10 minutes, or until softened. Season with salt. • Increase the heat and add the garlic, pork, and sausage. Sauté the meat for 5 minutes until browned all over. • Pour in the wine and stir in the tomatoes. Season with salt and pepper, cover, and cook for 90 minutes. • Pasta Dough: Sift the flour and salt onto a surface and make a well in the center. Break the egg into the well and mix in with enough water to make a smooth dough. Knead for 15–20 minutes, until smooth and elastic. • Shape the dough into a ball, wrap in plastic wrap (cling film), and let rest for 30 minutes. • Break off pieces of dough and form into logs about $^1/_2$ inch (1 cm) in

diameter. Slice into $^3/_4$-inch (2-cm) lengths and line up two or three lengths. Use a ferretto (or knitting needle) to shape into hollow cylinders, pressing down and turning at the same time to make hollow tubes. Carefully remove them from the needle and lay them on a flour-dusted cloth. Repeat until you have used up the dough. • Cook the pasta in a large pot of salted boiling water for about 10 minutes, or until al dente. • Drain and add to the sauce. Sprinkle with Caciocavallo and serve.

Serves 4 • Prep: 1 hr + 30 min to rest the dough • Cooking: 2 hr • Level: 2

Pasta Dough

- $2^2/_3$ cups/400 g semolina flour
- $^1/_8$ teaspoon salt
- 1 large egg
- lukewarm water

To serve

- 1 cup/125 g freshly grated Caciocavallo or Ricotta Salata cheese

BAKED PASTA WITH CHEESE

Pasta al graté

- 1 lb/500 g short hollow dried pasta, such as macaroni or penne
- 2 teaspoons extra-virgin olive oil

Béchamel Sauce
- ¹/₂ cup/125 g butter, cut up
- ²/₃ cup/100 g all-purpose/plain flour
- 2 cups/500 ml milk
- salt and freshly ground white pepper
- ¹/₈ teaspoon freshly grated nutmeg
- 1¹/₄ cups/150 g freshly grated Pecorino cheese, preferably Sicilian
- 5 oz/150 g Caciocavallo or Ricotta Salata cheese, thinly sliced

Preheat the oven to 400°F/200°C/gas 6. • Butter a large baking dish. • Cook the pasta in a large pot of salted boiling water with a drop of the oil for half the time indicated on the package. • Drain, running it under cold water to stop the cooking process, and transfer to a serving bowl. Drizzle with the remaining oil to prevent sticking. • Béchamel Sauce: Melt 6 tablespoons of the butter in a small saucepan over medium heat and add the flour. Cook for 3–4 minutes. Remove from the heat and add the milk all at once. Stir thoroughly, return to the heat, and bring to a boil, stirring constantly. As soon as the sauce comes to a boil, lower the heat, and season with salt, pepper, and nutmeg. Cover and cook over low heat for 10 minutes. Let cool to lukewarm. • Mix the pasta into the Béchamel sauce with nearly all of the Pecorino. • Arrange a layer of pasta in the baking dish and cover with the Caciocavallo. Top with the remaining pasta and sprinkle with Pecorino. Top with the remaining 2 tablespoons of butter. • Bake for 40–45 minutes, or until the top is golden brown. • Serve hot.

Serves 6 • Prep: 30 min • Cooking: 40–45 min • Level: 1

OVEN-BAKED TAGLIOLINI

Tagliolini cotti in forno

Preheat the oven to 400°F/200°C/gas 6. • Butter a baking dish and sprinkle with the bread crumbs. • Mix the Parmesan and cinnamon in a small bowl. • Arrange one-third of the pasta in the dish, dot with 1 tablespoon of butter, and sprinkle with one-third of the cinnamon-Parmesan mixture. Continue until all the pasta, butter, and Parmesan are used up. • Bake for 15–20 minutes, or until golden brown. • Remove from the oven and pour over the boiling stock. • Return to the oven and bake for 20–25 minutes, or until almost all of the liquid is absorbed, but taking care not to dry the pasta out. • Serve piping hot.

Serves 4 • Prep: 30 min • Cooking: 35–45 min • Level: 1

- ¹/₂ cup/60 g fine dry bread crumbs
- ²/₃ cup/80 g freshly grated Parmesan cheese
- ¹/₈ teaspoon ground cinnamon
- 12 oz/350 g very fine dried tagliolini (such as angel hair pasta)
- 3 tablespoons butter, in flakes
- 1¹/₄ cups/310 ml meat stock or broth, boiling

Baked pasta with cheese

FRIED SPAGHETTI PARCELS

Sformatini fritti di spaghetti

- 8 oz/200 g dried spaghettini (thin spaghetti)
- ¹/₄ cup/60 g butter
- ¹/₂ cup/60 g freshly grated Pecorino cheese, preferably Sicilian
- salt

Sauce
- 1 cup/125 g fresh or frozen peas
- 3 tablespoons water + more as needed
- 1¹/₂ tablespoons butter, cut up
- 1 tablespoon finely chopped onion + ¹/₂ onion, finely chopped
- ¹/₂ teaspoon sugar
- salt
- 5 oz/150 g ground/minced beef

For the more health-conscious, sprinkle the molds with grated Pecorino cheese and bread crumbs and bake at 400°F/200°C/gas 6 for about 40 minutes, or until golden brown. Turn out of the molds to serve.

Cook the pasta in a large pot of salted boiling water until just barely al dente. • Drain and toss with the butter and Pecorino until well mixed. • Butter four 2¹/₂–3-inch (6–7-cm) aluminum or soufflé molds. Spoon the pasta to cover the bottom and sides of the mold, leaving the center empty. Set aside the leftover pasta to seal the mold. • Sauce: Cook the peas with the water, butter, 1 tablespoon of the chopped onion, sugar, and ¹/₄ teaspoon of the salt in a large frying pan over medium heat, covered, for 5–10 minutes or until the peas are tender, shaking the pan often and adding more water if the mixture begins to stick to the pan. • Sauté the ¹/₂ onion and beef in the oil in a large frying pan over

high heat for 10 minutes until lightly browned. • Pour in the wine and let it evaporate. • Pour in the boiling stock and tomato paste mixture. Season with salt and pepper, add the oregano, and simmer over low heat for 30 minutes. • Stir in the pea mixture and let cool. • Fill the molds with a little of the meat sauce and the Provolone. Top with the remaining pasta, pressing it down, and carefully invert onto a chopping board. • Dip the forms carefully in the beaten egg, then in the bread crumbs, making sure they are well coated. (They can also be refrigerated for 1 day before frying.) • Heat the oil in a large, deep frying pan, preferably cast-iron, over medium heat and fry the forms, turning them once, for 5–7 minutes, until golden brown and crispy. • Drain and pat dry on paper towels. • Serve hot or warm, as part of a buffet or as a first course.

Serves 4 • Prep: 1 hr 30 min • Cooking: 1 hr 10 min • Level: 2

- 3 tablespoons extra-virgin olive oil
- ¹/₄ cup/60 ml dry red wine
- 1 tablespoon tomato paste/concentrate dissolved in 1 cup/250 ml beef stock or broth, boiling
- ¹/₈ teaspoon dried oregano
- freshly ground black pepper
- 2 oz/60 g Provolone or Caciocavallo cheese, cut into small cubes
- 3 large eggs, lightly beaten
- ³/₄ cup/90 g high-quality fine dry bread crumbs
- 1 cup/250 ml olive oil, for frying

BAKED LASAGNA WITH MEATBALLS

Sagna china

Pasta Dough
- 2 cups/300 g all-purpose/plain flour
- 2 eggs
- 3–4 tablespoons warm water

Meatballs
- 12 oz/300 g ground/minced beef
- 1 egg
- 1 tablespoon finely chopped fresh parsley
- salt and freshly ground black pepper
- 1¹/₄ cups/310 ml olive oil, for frying

Pasta Dough: Sift the flour onto a surface and make a well in the center. Mix in the eggs and enough water to make a smooth dough. Shape the dough into a ball, wrap in plastic wrap, and let rest for 30 minutes. • Roll the dough out until very thin. Cut into 6 x 4-inch (15 x 10-cm) strips. • Blanch the pasta (see step by step, page 222) and lay them out on a damp cloth. • Meatballs: Mix the beef, egg, parsley, and salt and pepper in a large bowl until well blended. Form into small balls the size of hazelnuts. • Heat the frying oil in a large frying pan until very hot. Fry the meatballs in small batches for 5–7 minutes, or until golden brown. • Drain and pat dry on paper towels. • Preheat the

oven to 400°F/200°C/gas 6. • Grease a baking dish with oil and sprinkle with bread crumbs. • Lay the first layer of pasta in the baking dish and top with the eggs, one-fifth of the sauce, and one-fifth of the meatballs. Continue until you have a total of five layers. Sprinkle with the cheeses. • Bake for 40–45 minutes, or until the top is golden brown. • Serve hot.

Serves 6 • Prep: 2 hr • Cooking: 60–80 min • Level: 2

- 3 hard-cooked eggs, finely chopped
- 2 cups/500 ml store-bought unseasoned tomato sauce
- 10 oz/300 g Caciocavallo or Ricotta Salata cheese, thinly sliced
- 7 oz/200 g Fiordilatte cheese, thinly sliced
- ³/₄ cup/90 g freshly grated Pecorino cheese, preferably Calabrian

SARDINIA

Isolated from the mainland, Sardinians demonstrate their independent mentality in their cuisine. Malloreddus, tiny ridged gnocchi, are the island's archetypical pasta, served traditionally with lamb sauce. A tiny soup pasta, fregola, is popular either boiled or baked with herbs and *arselle* (clams). Saffron, grown on the island and used sparingly, adds a pungent aroma to simple dishes. Along the coastline, chefs jazz up long pasta with the abundant fish and seafood.

Fregola with herbs (see page 233)

HOMEMADE RAVIOLI
Culingionis de casa

Pasta Dough
- 1²/₃ cups/250 g semolina flour
- ¹/₄ teaspoon salt
- 1 large egg
- generous ¹/₃ cup/100 ml lukewarm water

Filling
- ¹/₂ onion, finely chopped
- 3 tablespoons extra-virgin olive oil
- 1 cup/250 g cooked spinach or Swiss chard, squeezed dry and finely chopped
- 2 large eggs
- 4–6 threads saffron, crumbled
- 1 lb/500 g Ricotta cheese, strained through a fine mesh

- salt
- freshly grated nutmeg
- 3 tablespoons semolina flour

Tomato–Basil Sauce
- 1 onion, finely chopped
- 3 tablespoons extra-virgin olive oil
- 2 lb/1 kg peeled plum tomatoes, pressed through a fine-mesh strainer (passata)
- salt
- 5 leaves fresh basil, torn
- ¹/₃ cup/40 g freshly grated aged Pecorino cheese, preferably Sardinian

Also known as culurjones, or cullurzones, or culunzoni, or culirgioni but also angiulottus, these are the tortelli of Sardinia. Generally, they are meatless, though there are exceptions to the rule.

Pasta Dough: Sift the flour and salt onto a surface and make a well in the center. Break the egg into the well and mix in with enough water to make a smooth dough. Knead for 15–20 minutes. until smooth and elastic. Shape the dough into a ball, wrap in plastic wrap (cling film), and let rest for 30 minutes. • Filling: Sauté the onion in the oil in a frying pan over medium heat for 10 minutes until softened. • Add the spinach and simmer briefly. • Remove from the heat and let cool. • Add the eggs, saffron, and Ricotta. Season with salt and nutmeg. Add a few tablespoons of semolina flour. • Roll out the dough on a lightly floured surface until paper-thin. Cut into 5-inch (13-cm) wide strips and arrange small heaps of filling near one edge, about 1¹/₂ inches (4 cm) apart. Fold each strip of dough lengthwise to cover the filling. Seal, after making sure no air pockets remain, then cut into squares with a saw-toothed ravioli cutter. • Arrange the ravioli on a floured surface. • Tomato–Basil Sauce: Sauté the onion in the oil in a large frying pan over medium heat for 10 minutes until lightly browned. • Add the tomatoes and season with salt. Cook for 10 minutes until thickened. Add the basil and remove from the heat. • Cook the pasta in a large pot of salted boiling water for 4 minutes until they rise to the surface. Drain and serve in a bowl layered with the sauce and Pecorino.

Serves 4–6 • Prep: 2 hr • Cooking: 30 min • Level: 3

FREGOLA
Fregula

- 4 threads saffron, crumbled
- ¹/₂ teaspoon salt
- about ¹/₂ cup/125 ml water
- 1²/₃ cups/250 g semolina flour

Dissolve the saffron and salt in the water. • Sprinkle the semolina onto a large plate and wet it with the saffron water, kneading with your hands to make small grains. • Lay the pasta grains on a rough cloth to dry, turning them occasionally to help the drying process. In order to speed up this operation, the freshly made fregola can be placed in a hot oven, but only after the heat is turned off. • Once they are dry, about 10 minutes, sift the pasta to obtain fine and coarse fregola. You will make about 10 oz (300 g) of fregola.

Serves 6 • Prep: about 3 hr • Level: 2

FREGOLA WITH HERBS
Fregula stufada

Fregola is a type of pasta that has the same appearance as couscous. It is coarse-grained and firm.

Preheat the oven to 325°F/170°C/gas 3. • Grease a large baking dish with oil. • Sauté the onions and parsley in the oil in a small saucepan over medium heat for 12–15 minutes, or until aromatic. Season with salt and remove from the heat. • Cook the pasta in a large pot of salted boiling water for 4 minutes until al dente. • Drain the pasta and transfer it to the prepared baking dish, alternating layers of pasta with the onion and the Pecorino. Finish with a layer of fregola. • Cover the baking dish and bake for 10 minutes. • Uncover and continue baking for about 20 minutes. Serve piping hot.

Serves 4–6 • Prep: 10 min • Cooking: 40 min • Level: 1

- 2 onions, finely chopped
- 2 tablespoons finely chopped parsley
- 7 tablespoons extra-virgin olive oil
- salt
- 1¹/₂ lb/650 g large fregola pasta
- 1 cup/125 g freshly grated Pecorino cheese, preferably Sardinian

Spaghetti with lobster

Spaghetti with bottarga

SPAGHETTI WITH LOBSTER

Spaghetti con l'aragosta

- 1 onion, finely chopped
- $^1/_4$ cup/60 ml extra-virgin olive oil
- 1 tablespoon finely chopped parsley
- 8 oz/200 g peeled plum tomatoes, pressed through a fine mesh strainer (passata)
- salt
- 10 oz/300 g lobster meat, cut into large chunks (meat from 1 lobster, weighing $1^1/_2$ lb/750 g)
- 12 oz/350 g dried spaghetti

Sauté the onion in the oil in a large frying pan for 10 minutes. • Add 2 teaspoons of parsley and the tomatoes. Cook for 15–20 minutes, or until the tomatoes have broken down. • Season with salt and add the lobster meat. Simmer for 10 minutes. • Cook the pasta in a large pot of salted boiling water until al dente. Drain and add to the pan. • Serve in individual dishes and sprinkle with the remaining 1 teaspoon of parsley.

Serves 4 • Prep: 45 min • Cooking: 45 min • Level: 1

SPAGHETTI WITH BOTTARGA

Spaghetti alla bottarga

Soak the bottarga in 2 tablespoons of the oil in a small bowl for 30 minutes. • Sauté the garlic in the remaining 2 tablespoons oil in a large frying pan over low heat for 3 minutes until pale gold. • Discard the garlic and add the bread crumbs, mixing well. • Cook the pasta in a large pot of salted boiling water until al dente. Drain and add to the pan. • Remove from heat, add half the bottarga, and mix well. • Serve in individual dishes and sprinkle with the remaining bottarga.

Serves 4 • Prep: 30 min + 30 min to soak bottarga • Cooking: 15 min • Level: 1

- 1 tablespoon freshly grated bottarga (dried mullet or tuna roe)
- $^1/_4$ cup/60 ml extra-virgin olive oil
- 2 cloves garlic, lightly crushed but whole
- 2 teaspoons fine dry bread crumbs
- 12 oz/350 g dried spaghetti

Sauces

MALLOREDDUS

Pasta Dough

- 2²/₃ cups/400 g semolina flour
- ¹/₄ teaspoon salt
- ¹/₄ teaspoon saffron strands, crumbled and dissolved in ³/₄ cup/ 180 ml lukewarm water + more as needed

Sauce

- 2¹/₂ cups/300 g freshly grated Pecorino cheese, preferably Sardinian
- ³/₄ cup/180 ml hot water
- ¹/₄ teaspoon saffron strands, crumbled
- salt and freshly ground black pepper

Pasta Dough: Sift the flour and salt onto a surface and make a well in the center. Mix in enough saffron water to make a fairly stiff dough. Knead for 15–20 minutes, until smooth and elastic. Press the dough into a disk, wrap in plastic wrap (cling film), and let rest for 30 minutes. • Form into logs about ¹/₂ inch (1 cm) in diameter. Slice into ²/₃-inch (1.5-cm) lengths. • Use the flat of your thumb to press down on a flat or ridged surface, causing them to fold in on themselves until they become hollow. Arrange on a dry cloth and sprinkle with semolina. • Sauce: Place the Pecorino in a heated serving dish and pour over the hot water and saffron, stirring to melt the Pecorino. • Cook the pasta in a large pot of salted boiling water until al dente. • Drain and add to the Pecorino. • Season with salt and pepper and serve hot.

Serves 6 • Prep: 1 hr + 30 min to rest the pasta dough • Cooking: 12 min • Level: 2

MALLOREDDUS WITH LAMB SAUCE

Malloreddus con ragù di agnello

Lamb Sauce: Prepare the leg of lamb for cooking by slashing open the meat and inserting sprigs of rosemary and the garlic. Season generously with salt and pepper. Put the lamb in a large saucepan just large enough to hold it. Brush all over with a sprig of rosemary dipped in oil and let brown over medium heat, turning to brown all over, about 10 minutes. • Pour the wine over and let it evaporate, 5 minutes. • Add the scallion and tomatoes. Cook, covered, over low heat for about 2 hours, turning the meat occasionally, gradually adding the water or stock. • Remove the lamb and set aside to rest. Increase the heat and let the meat juices reduce. They should thicken. The lamb can be served as a separate course. • Cook the pasta in a large pot of salted boiling water until al dente. • Drain and serve with the lamb drippings and Pecorino.

Serves 4–6 • Prep: 15 min • Cooking: 2 hr 15 min • Level: 1

Lamb Sauce

- 2 lb/1 kg leg of lamb
- 7 sprigs rosemary
- 2 cloves garlic, thinly sliced into slivers
- salt and freshly ground black pepper
- 5 tablespoons extra-virgin olive oil
- generous ¹/₃ cup/100 ml dry white wine
- 1 scallion/spring onion, finely chopped
- 5 firm-ripe tomatoes, peeled, seeded, and coarsely chopped
- water or meat stock or broth, if needed

Pasta

- 1 lb/400 g fresh malloreddus pasta (see recipe left and below)
- ¹/₂ cup/60 g freshly grated Pecorino cheese, preferably Sardinian

MAKING MALLOREDDUS PASTA

1. Form the pasta dough (see recipe above left) into long, thin logs. Cut into short sections, about ³/₄ inch (2 cm) long.

2. Use your thumb to press them on a ridged basket (or over a ridged wooden board), making them hollow.

3. Allow them to drop onto a flour-dusted board.

Sauces & Fresh Pasta

FREGOLA WITH CLAMS

Fregula con le arselle

- 2 lb/1 kg clams, in shell
- 4 cloves garlic, lightly crushed but whole
- $^1/_2$ cup/125 ml extra-virgin olive oil
- 4 tablespoons tomato paste/concentrate
- 3 cups/750 ml hot water + more as needed
- salt
- 8 oz/200 g coarse fregola
- 2 tablespoons finely chopped fresh parsley
- 4 oz/100 g fine fregola

Soak the clams in a large bowl of warm salted water for 1 hour. • Transfer the clams to a large saucepan and cover and cook over high heat for about 7 minutes until they open up. • Discard any that do not open. • Shell the clams and strain the cooking liquid (it will be about $^3/_4$ cup/180 ml). • Sauté the garlic in the oil in a Dutch oven (casserole) over medium heat for about 3 minutes until pale gold. Discard the garlic. • Stir in the tomato paste and let it simmer for 2 minutes. • Pour in the strained cooking liquid from the clams and the hot water. Season with salt. • Add the coarse fregula and cook for about 4 minutes. • Add the clams, parsley, and the fine fregula. Cook for 3 minutes more. • Serve in individual serving bowls.

Serves 6 • Prep: 20 min + 1 hr to soak the clams • Cooking: 20 min • Level: 1

FUSILLI WITH SQUID

Fusilli con sugo di calamari

Remove the mottled skin from the squid and cut the bodies into small chunks. Cut the tentacles in half. • Sauté the squid in the oil in a large frying pan over high heat for 5 minutes until transparent. Season with salt and pepper. • Pour in the wine and parsley and cook over medium heat for 20 minutes, or until the wine has evaporated. • Cook the pasta in a large pot of salted boiling water until al dente. • Drain and add to the sauce. Serve immediately.

Serves 6 • Prep: 30 min • Cooking: 30 min • Level: 1

- 8 oz/200 g squid, cleaned
- $^1/_4$ cup/60 ml extra-virgin olive oil
- salt and freshly ground white pepper
- 1 cup/250 ml dry white wine
- 2 tablespoons finely chopped fresh parsley
- 1 lb/500 g long dried fusilli

Fregola with clams

Malloreddus

SPAGHETTINI WITH GARLIC AND PARSLEY

Pasta con l'aglio

- 4 cloves garlic, very finely chopped
- Leaves from 1 small bunch fresh parsley, finely chopped
- $^3/_4$ cup/180 ml extra-virgin olive oil
- salt and freshly ground white pepper
- 1 lb/500 g dried spaghettini
- 1 cup/125 g freshly grated Pecorino cheese

Sauté the garlic and parsley in the oil in a large frying pan over medium heat for 3 minutes until the garlic is pale gold. • Season with salt and pepper. Cook over low heat for 10 minutes, taking care that the garlic does not turn brown. • Cook the pasta in a large pot of salted boiling water until al dente. • Drain and add to the garlic and parsley. Sprinkle with Pecorino and serve.

Serves 6 • Prep: 15 min • Cooking: 25 min • Level: 1

MALLOREDDUS WITH FRESH SAUSAGE SAUCE

Malloreddus con la salsiccia fresca

Sauté the onion in the oil in a large frying pan over medium heat for about 10 minutes, until softened. • Add the sausage and cook over high heat for 5 minutes until browned all over. • Stir in the tomatoes and saffron. Season with salt. • Cook over medium heat for 20 minutes, stirring occasionally. • Add the basil and cook over low heat for 45 minutes more. • Cook the pasta in a large pot of salted boiling water until al dente. • Drain and add to the sauce. Sprinkle with Pecorino and serve.

Serves 6 • Prep: 20 min • Cooking: 75 min • Level: 1

- 1 onion, finely chopped
- 6 tablespoons extra-virgin olive oil
- 4 oz/125 g fresh Italian sausage, cut into small cubes
- 2 cups/500 g peeled, seeded, and chopped tomatoes
- 4–6 threads saffron, crumbled
- salt
- 4 leaves fresh basil, torn
- 1 lb/500 g fresh malloreddus pasta (see page 236)
- $^1/_2$ cup/60 g freshly grated Pecorino cheese

Saffron gnocchi in meat sauce

SAFFRON GNOCCHI IN MEAT SAUCE

Ciciones, gnocchetti allo zafferano

Pasta Dough

- 2²/₃ cups/400 g semolina flour
- ¹/₄ teaspoon salt
- ¹/₄ teaspoon saffron strands, crumbled and dissolved in ³/₄ cup/ 180 ml lukewarm water + more as needed
- ¹/₄ cup/60 ml extra-virgin olive oil
- 1 red onion, finely chopped
- 3 oz/90 g pancetta, bacon, or lard, finely chopped
- 12 oz/300 g lean ground/minced pork

Pasta Dough: Sift the flour and salt onto a surface and make a well in the center. Mix in enough saffron water to make a smooth dough. Knead for 15–20 minutes, until smooth and elastic. Shape the dough into a ball, wrap in plastic wrap (cling film), and let rest for 30 minutes. • Heat the oil in a Dutch oven (casserole) over low heat and add the onion and pancetta. Cover and cook for 10 minutes. • Add the pork and sauté over high heat for 7 minutes until browned all over. • Pour in the wine and let it evaporate, 5 minutes. • Stir in the tomatoes and basil and season with salt and pepper. Bring to a boil and simmer over low heat, partially covered, for at least 2 hours, adding stock or hot water if the sauce begins to stick to the pan. • Form the dough into logs ¹/₄ inch (5 mm) in diameter and cut into ¹/₂-inch (1-cm) lengths. • Lay them on a dry cloth dusted with semolina. • Cook the gnocchi in small batches in a large pot of salted boiling water until they rise to the surface, 2–3 minutes. • Drain and serve in the sauce, sprinkled with Pecorino.

Serves 6 • Prep: 1 hr + 30 min to rest the dough • Cooking: 40 min • Level: 2

- ¹/₂ cup/125 ml dry red wine
- 3 lb/1.5 kg peeled plum tomatoes, pressed through a fine mesh strainer (passata)
- 4 leaves fresh basil, torn
- salt and freshly ground black pepper
- 1 cup/125 g freshly grated aged Pecorino cheese, preferably Sardinian

PASTA WITH PECORINO AND LEMON

Maccarones con pecorino e limone

- 6 tablespoons butter, cut up
- juice of 2 lemons
- 4 threads saffron, crumbled
- 2 cups/250 g freshly grated Pecorino cheese
- 1 lb/500 g dried macaroni

Melt the butter in a medium frying pan over high heat. • Mix in the lemon juice, saffron, and Pecorino. Remove from the heat and set aside. • Cook the pasta in a large pot of salted boiling water until al dente. • Drain and add to the sauce. Serve hot.

Serves 6 • Prep: 15 min • Cooking: 12 min • Level: 1

BAKED PASTA WITH GREENS

Malloreddus al forno

Break the eggs, one at a time, into salted, simmering water. Add the vinegar and cook until the whites are set and the yolks are still slightly soft, about 15 minutes. • Use a slotted spoon to remove the eggs and set aside. • Preheat the oven to 350°F/180°C/gas 4. • Oil a baking dish. • Cook the Swiss chard and spinach in salted boiling water for 5–7 minutes, or until tender. • Remove with a slotted spoon. • Return to a boil and cook the pasta in the same cooking water until al dente. • Drain and transfer the pasta to the baking dish. Top with the Swiss chard and spinach and sprinkle with Pecorino. Continue to layer the ingredients, finishing with Pecorino. • Top with the eggs and pour over the cream. • Bake for 10–15 minutes, or until the egg whites begin to brown at the edges. • Serve warm.

Serves 6 • Prep: 40 min • Cooking: 45–60 min • Level: 2

- 6 large eggs
- 1 tablespoon malt vinegar
- 1 lb/400 g fresh Malloreddus pasta (see page 236)
- 8 oz/200 g Swiss chard leaves, shredded
- 8 oz/200 g spinach leaves, shredded
- 1 cup/125 g freshly grated Pecorino cheese
- ¹/₂ cup/125 ml light/single cream

Sauces

RICOTTA-FILLED RAVIOLI WITH TOMATO SAUCE

Ravioli galluresi

Pasta Dough
- 2²/₃ cups/400 g all-purpose/plain flour
- ¹/₄ teaspoon salt
- 2 large eggs
- 6 tablespoons water + more as needed

Filling
- 1²/₃ cups/400 g Ricotta cheese
- 2 large eggs
- 5 tablespoons sugar
- 1 tablespoon finely chopped fresh parsley
- grated zest of ¹/₂ lemon
- ¹/₈ teaspoon freshly grated nutmeg
- ¹/₈ teaspoon ground cinnamon
- salt and freshly ground white pepper

Tomato Sauce
- 1 clove garlic, lightly crushed but whole
- 3 tablespoons extra-virgin olive oil
- 2 lb/1 kg peeled plum tomatoes, pressed through a fine mesh strainer (passata)
- salt and freshly ground white pepper
- ¹/₄ teaspoon finely chopped fresh parsley
- 4 leaves fresh basil, torn
- 3 tablespoons butter
- 1 cup/125 g freshly grated Parmesan cheese

Pasta Dough: Sift the flour and salt onto a surface and make a well in the center. Break the eggs into the well and mix in with enough water to make a smooth dough. Knead for 15–20 minutes, until smooth and elastic. Shape the dough into a ball, wrap in plastic wrap (cling film), and let rest for 30 minutes. • Filling: Mix the Ricotta, eggs, sugar, parsley, lemon zest, nutmeg, cinnamon, salt, and pepper. • Roll out the dough on a lightly floured surface into a thin sheet and cut into 2¹/₂-inch (6-cm) strips. • Arrange 1 tablespoon of the filling on each strip at regular intervals. Top with another strip of dough and use a saw-toothed ravioli cutter to cut the pasta into 2¹/₂-inch (6-cm) square ravioli. Seal, after making sure no air pockets remain. • Tomato Sauce: Sauté the garlic in the oil in a frying pan over medium heat for 3 minutes until pale gold. Add the tomatoes and season with salt and pepper. • Cook for about 10 minutes, or until the oil separates from the tomatoes. • Discard the garlic and add the parsley, basil, and butter. • Cook the pasta in a large pot of salted boiling water until al dente, 2–3 minutes. • Drain and transfer to a serving tureen, with the sauce and Parmesan. Serve hot.

Serves 6 • Prep: 1 hr + 30 min to rest the dough • Cooking: 30 min • Level: 3

SPAGHETTI WITH MARINATED GAME SAUCE

Spaghetti con sugo di lepre

Game Sauce: Cut and rinse the hare thoroughly and cut it into large chunks, taking care not to splinter the bones excessively. • Place the pieces of meat in a glass or ceramic bowl with the vinegar and water. Cover with plastic wrap (cling film) and let marinate in the refrigerator for 4 hours. • Drain the meat thoroughly and pat dry. • Heat the oil and lard in a Dutch oven (casserole) and sauté the meat over high heat for about 10 minutes until browned all over. • Add the onion, garlic, bay leaves, cinnamon, cloves, and rosemary and sauté for 3 minutes. • Pour in the wine and the tomato paste mixture. • Simmer, covered, over low heat for at least 2 hours, or until the meat is tender, adding more water if the sauce begins to stick to the pan. (If you are cooking rabbit, it will take about 1 hour.) • Cook the pasta in a large pot of salted boiling water until al dente. • Drain and add to the sauce. • Serve hot.

Serves 6 • Prep: 1 hr + 4 hr to marinate • Cooking: 2 hr • Level: 1

Game Sauce
- 1 young hare or 1 rabbit, weighing about 3 lb/ 1.5 kg
- 2 cups/500 ml white wine vinegar
- 2 cups/500 ml water + more as needed
- ¹/₄ cup/60 ml extra-virgin olive oil
- 1¹/₄ cups/150 g diced lard or pancetta (or bacon)
- 1 large red onion, finely chopped
- 2 cloves garlic, lightly crushed but whole
- 2 bay leaves
- 1 sprig rosemary
- 1 small stick cinnamon
- 2 cloves
- 2 cups/500 ml dry red wine (use dry white wine if rabbit)
- 1 tablespoon tomato paste/concentrate dissolved in ³/₄ cup/ 180 ml meat stock or broth
- salt and freshly ground black pepper

Pasta
- 1 lb/500 g dried spaghetti

MODERN CLASSICS

Italian cooks and chefs, encouraged by the worldwide popularity of Italian cuisine, are striving to modernize some traditional dishes. Pesto made from Tuscan kale or sun-dried tomatoes varies the recipe without altering the method. Italians know better than to change age-old ways of working on a modern culinary whim. In this chapter, you'll find a variety of recipes, such as the delightful pasta salads. They're sure to please for an easy light dinner with a glass of your favorite *vino*.

Nests of tagliatelle
(see page 246)

Asparagus tortelli with tomato and orange

Tortelli di asparagi con pomodoro e arancio

Pasta Dough
- 1¹/₃ cups/200 g all-purpose/plain flour
- ¹/₄ teaspoon salt
- 2 large eggs
- 1 tablespoon warm water

Filling
- 8 oz/300 g asparagus, cut into short lengths
- 8 oz/300 g floury/mealy potatoes
- 1 clove garlic, chopped
- ¹/₄ cup/60 g butter
- 1 tablespoon onion seeds
- salt and freshly ground white pepper

Tomato–orange sauce
- ¹/₂ cup/125 ml extra-virgin olive oil
- 2 bay leaves
- 4 leaves fresh basil, torn
- 2 cloves garlic, chopped
- 1 sprig fresh thyme
- zest and juice of 1 orange
- 1¹/₂ lb/700 g firm-ripe tomatoes, chopped
- salt

Pasta Dough: Sift the flour and salt onto a surface and make a well in the center. Mix in the eggs and water to make a smooth dough. Knead for 15–20 minutes until elastic. Shape into a ball, wrap in plastic wrap, and let rest for 30 minutes. • Filling: Cook the asparagus in salted boiling water for 5–7 minutes until tender. Set aside a few tips for garnish. Transfer the remaining asparagus to a blender and process until smooth. • Cook the potatoes in salted boiling water until tender. • Drain and peel. Mash with the garlic, butter, asparagus puree, and onion seeds. Season with salt and pepper. • Make into 2-inch (5-cm) tortelli, following the instructions on page 70. • Tomato–orange sauce: Heat the oil in a saucepan with the bay leaves, basil, garlic, thyme, and orange zest. • Add the tomatoes and season with salt. Cook over high heat for 10 minutes. • Add the orange juice and cook for 1 minute. Remove the bay leaves, thyme, and orange zest and press through a strainer. • Cook the pasta in a large pot of salted boiling water until al dente. Drain and serve with the sauce. Garnish with the reserved asparagus.

Serves 4 • Prep: 60 min • Cooking: 60 min • Level: 3

Nests of tagliatelle

Nidi di tagliatelle

Two-cheese sauce: Melt the butter in a saucepan. Add the flour and stir to form a smooth paste. Cook, stirring, for 1 minute. • Pour in the stock, whisking to prevent clumps from forming. Bring to a boil and cook over low heat for 20 minutes, stirring occasionally. • Let cool and stir in the Parmesan, Swiss cheese, and cream. Season with salt, pepper, and nutmeg. • Glazed vegetable topping: Melt the butter in a large frying pan. Add the vegetables and water and cook over low heat for 10 minutes, until the vegetables are tender-crunchy. Season with salt and pepper and remove from the heat. • Cook the pasta in a large pot of salted boiling water for half the time indicated on the package. Drain and cool under cold running water. • Toss with the vegetables and the cheese sauce. • Preheat the oven to 400°F/200°C/gas 6. • Butter a large baking dish. • Using a large fork, make four nests of tagliatelle. Arrange them in the prepared baking dish and break an egg into the center of each nest. Season with salt and pepper. • Sprinkle with Parmesan and bake for 15–20 minutes, or until the eggs are cooked. • Arrange the nests in dishes and serve piping hot.

Serves 4 • Prep: 20 min • Cooking: 60 min • Level: 2

Two-cheese sauce
- 3 tablespoons butter
- 3 tablespoons flour
- 2 cups/500 ml stock
- 2 tablespoons freshly grated Parmesan cheese
- 2 tablespoons coarsely grated Swiss cheese
- cup/60 ml heavy/double cream
- salt and freshly ground white pepper
- teaspoon freshly ground nutmeg

Glazed vegetable topping
- 3 tablespoons butter
- cup/50 g zucchini/courgettes, chopped
- cup/50 g carrots, cubed
- cup/50 g asparagus tips, cut into lengths
- cup/30 g white mushrooms, cubed
- 3 tablespoons water
- salt and freshly ground white pepper
- 8 oz/200 g yellow and green tagliatelle
- 6 quail or duck eggs
- 2 tablespoons freshly grated Parmesan cheese

Making colored pasta

1. Beat the eggs with the vegetable puree (boiled until tender, then processed until smooth, such as red beets). Sift the flour onto the pastry board and make a well.

2. Turn the "colored" eggs into the well. Begin to mix the dough, taking flour from the interior of the well. Knead as usual (see Making pasta dough, page 64).

3. The pasta dough is ready when it is smooth and uniform in color, after about 15–20 minutes of kneading.

tomato and orange

Sauces

COLD SUMMER PASTA SALAD

Pasta fredda estiva

- 1 large eggplant/ aubergine (weighing about 1 lb/400 g), cut into ¹/₂-inch/1-cm thick slices
- 3 tablespoons salt
- 2 cups/500 ml olive oil
- 2 tablespoons salt-cured capers
- 2 yellow bell peppers/capsicums
- 6 tablespoons extra-virgin olive oil
- 1 medium onion, finely chopped
- ¹/₈ teaspoon salt
- 2 cloves garlic, finely chopped
- 2 tablespoons pine nuts
- 1 lb/400 g short pasta (such as ridged ditalini)
- 1 cup/100 g green olives in brine, pitted and coarsely chopped
- 1 small bunch fresh basil, torn
- 2 tablespoons finely chopped fresh parsley
- 1 tablespoon finely chopped fresh oregano

Place the eggplant slices in a colander and sprinkle with salt. Let drain for 1 hour. • Chop into ¹/₂-inch (1-cm) cubes. • Heat the oil in a large deep frying pan until very hot. Fry the eggplant in small batches for 5–7 minutes, or until golden brown. • Soak the capers in 1¹/₂ cups (375 ml) water for 1 hour. Drain and rinse under cold running water. If they are still too salty, repeat. • Broil (grill) the bell peppers until the skins are blackened. Wrap them in a paper bag for 5 minutes, then remove the skins and seeds. Cut into ¹/₂-inch (1-cm) cubes. • Heat 3 tablespoons of the extra-virgin olive oil in a small saucepan and sauté the onion with a pinch of salt over high heat until golden. Cover and cook over low heat for 15 minutes. • Add the garlic and sauté until pale gold. • Toast the pine nuts in a nonstick frying pan over medium heat for 2 minutes until golden. • Cook the pasta in a large pot of salted boiling water until al dente, about 6 minutes. • Drain and run under cool running water until the pasta has cooled completely. • Transfer to a large serving bowl with the fried eggplant, capers, bell peppers, onions, pine nuts, olives, basil, parsley, and oregano.

Serves 6 • Prep: 1 hr • Cooking: 20 min • Level: 1

PISTACHIO PESTO

Pesto di pistacchi

Sauté the onion in 2 tablespoons of the oil in a frying pan until softened. Remove from the heat and let cool. • Process the onion, pistachios, garlic, remaining 1 tablespoon oil, and Pecorino in a food processor or blender until smooth. Season with salt. • Cook the pasta in a large pot of salted boiling water until al dente. • Add 1 tablespoon cooking water to the pesto to achieve a creamy consistency. • Drain the pasta and serve with the pesto, adding more cooking water if needed. • Garnish each plate with a sprinkling of finely chopped pistachios.

Serves 4 • Prep: 45 min • Cooking: 30 min • Level: 1

- ¹/₂ onion, finely chopped
- 3 tablespoons extra-virgin olive oil
- ²/₃ cup/100 g peeled pistachios
- 1 clove garlic, finely chopped
- 4–5 tablespoons freshly grated Pecorino cheese
- salt
- 12 oz/350 g dried casarecce (small pasta twists) or penne pasta
- finely chopped pistachios, to garnish

Pistachio pesto

Sun-dried tomato pesto

SUN-DRIED TOMATO PESTO

Pesto di pomodori secchi

- 1 cup/100 g sun-dried tomatoes
- ¹/₂ cup/125 ml hot water
- 3 tablespoons red wine vinegar
- ¹/₃ cup/30 g peeled almonds
- 1 clove garlic
- Leaves from 2 bunches fresh basil
- 6 tablespoons extra-virgin olive oil
- ¹/₈ teaspoon dried oregano
- salt
- 12 oz/350 g dried short pasta

Soak the tomatoes in the hot water and vinegar in a large bowl for 10 minutes until softened. • Drain. Process the soaked tomatoes, almonds, garlic, basil, oil, and oregano until smooth. Season with salt and pepper, taking care not to over-season as sundried tomatoes are quite flavorful. • Cook the pasta in a large pot of salted boiling water until al dente. • Add 1 tablespoon cooking water to the pesto to achieve a creamy consistency. • Drain the pasta, reserving a little cooking water. Serve the pasta with the pesto, adding more cooking water if needed.

Serves 4 • Prep: 30 min + 10 min to soak the tomatoes • Cooking: 20 min • Level: 1

PASTA SALAD WITH TUNA AND OLIVES

Insalata di pasta

This salad can be prepared as much as a day in advance and kept in the refrigerator until you are ready to serve it.

Chop the tomatoes coarsely, season with salt, and place them in a colander. Drain for 1 hour. • Use a fork to crumble the tuna. • Mix the tuna, tomatoes, olives, scallions, celery, carrot, and garlic. Drizzle with almost all the oil and season with salt, pepper, and oregano. Cover with plastic wrap (cling film) and refrigerate for 1 hour. • Cook the pasta in a large pot of salted boiling water until al dente. • Drain and run it under cool water. • Transfer to a serving bowl and drizzle with the remaining oil. • Add the prepared ingredients and toss well. Garnish with the parsley and basil.

Serves 4 • Prep: 30 min + 1 hr to drain the tomatoes + 1 hr to chill the tuna mixture • Cooking: 15 min • Level: 1

- 8 oz/200 g cherry tomatoes
- salt and freshly ground white pepper
- 7 oz/150 g tuna packed in oil, drained
- 10 black olives, pitted and finely chopped
- 10 green olives, pitted and finely chopped
- 2 scallions/spring onions, coarsely chopped
- 1 stalk celery, coarsely chopped
- 1 carrot, coarsely chopped
- 1 clove garlic, finely chopped
- generous ¹/₃ cup/100 ml extra-virgin olive oil
- 2 teaspoons dried oregano
- 12 oz/350 g dried short pasta (such as penne, tortiglioni, or conchiglie)
- 1 tablespoon finely chopped fresh parsley
- 4–5 leaves fresh basil, torn

PASTA WITH DARK CABBAGE PESTO

Pasta con pesto di cavolo nero

- 1 lb/500 g young dark-leafed cabbage or curly kale, washed and stalks removed
- 1 clove garlic, lightly crushed but whole
- 1/2 cup/60 g freshly grated Pecorino cheese
- 2/3 cup/150 ml extra-virgin olive oil (new season oil recommended)
- salt and freshly ground black pepper
- 12 oz/350 g dried spaghetti

Blanch the cabbage in a large pot of salted boiling water for 3 minutes. Drain, reserving the water, and let cool completely. • Process the cabbage, garlic, Pecorino, and oil in a food processor or blender until pureed. Season with salt and pepper. • Cook the pasta in the cabbage water until al dente. • Drain, reserving a little cooking water. Serve the pasta with the pureed vegetables, diluted with a little cooking water.

Serves 4 • Prep: 20 min • Cooking: 15 min • Level: 1

FUSILLI WITH PESTO, CREAM, AND TOMATOES

Fusilli al pesto, panna e pomodoro

- 3 heaping tablespoons Genoese Pesto (see page 16)
- 2/3 cup/150 ml store-bought unseasoned tomato sauce
- 1/4 cup/60 ml heavy/double cream (you can substitute with 1/4 cup/60 ml Mascarpone cheese)
- 12 oz/350 g dried pasta, such as fusilli (or other short pasta)

Mix the pesto and tomato sauce in a large bowl. Stir in the cream until well blended. • Cook the pasta in a large pot of salted boiling water until al dente. • Heat the serving bowls with 1 tablespoon of the cooking water from the pasta. Discard the water. • Drain the pasta and transfer to the warmed bowls. Add the sauce, toss well, and serve hot.

Serves 4 • Prep: 10 min • Cooking: 15 min • Level: 1

FISH RAVIOLI

Ravioli di pesce

Put the garlic in the oil in a small bowl and let stand for at least 2 hours. Discard the garlic. • Pasta Dough: Sift the flour and salt onto a surface and make a well in the center. Break the eggs into the well and mix in with enough water to make a smooth dough. Knead for 15–20 minutes, until smooth and elastic. Shape the dough into a ball, wrap in plastic wrap (cling film), and let rest for 30 minutes. • Filling: Melt the butter in a saucepan over low heat. Add the fish and cook for 1 minute. • Increase the heat to high and pour in the vermouth and cook until evaporated. • Stir in the flour and cook it briefly. • Add the cream and fish stock and season with salt and pepper. Boil for 5 minutes. • Remove from the heat and let cool completely. • Process with the eggs, 2 tablespoons of the garlic oil, and parsley in a food processor or blender. • Transfer to a pastry bag and set aside. • Roll out the dough on a lightly floured surface until paper-thin. Cut into 3–4-inch (8–10-cm) wide strips and arrange small heaps of filling near one edge, about 2 1/2 inch (6 cm) apart. Fold each strip of dough lengthwise to cover the filling. • Use a 1 1/2-inch (4-cm) ravioli cutter to cut out ravioli. • Lay them on a floured surface to dry. • If the pasta is not too dry, knead the scraps together, reroll, and re-use. Continue until the pasta and filling are finished. Seal, after making sure no air pockets remain. • Tomato–Thyme Sauce: Heat the remaining garlic oil in a large frying pan. Add the tomatoes and thyme. • Cook the pasta in a large pot of salted boiling water until they rise to the surface, about 3 minutes. • Drain, reserving 2 tablespoons of the cooking water. Add the pasta and cooking water to the sauce and serve.

Serves 6 • Prep: 2 1/2 hr • Cooking: 30 min • Level: 3

- 2 cloves garlic, lightly crushed but whole
- 1/4 cup/60 ml extra-virgin olive oil

Pasta Dough
- 2 2/3 cups/400 g all-purpose/plain flour
- 1/4 teaspoon salt
- 2 large eggs
- 1/2 cup/125 ml lukewarm water, + more as needed

Filling
- 1/3 cup/80 g butter, cut up
- 1 3/4 lb/800 g white fish, filleted and coarsely chopped (such as sole or sea bass)
- 1/4 cup/60 ml dry vermouth or dry white wine
- 1/2 cup/75 g all-purpose/plain flour
- 2/3 cup/150 ml heavy/double cream
- 2/3 cup/150 ml fish stock or broth (made by boiling the fish bones in 1 quart/1 liter water with 1/2 onion, 1 clove garlic, 1 bay leaf, 3 sprigs parsley, see page 10)
- salt and freshly ground white pepper
- 2 large eggs
- 2 tablespoons finely chopped parsley

Tomato–thyme sauce
- 2 cups/500 g chopped tomatoes
- 1 tablespoon finely chopped fresh thyme
- salt

INDEX

Acknowledgments

All photos by Marco Lanza and Walter Mericchi and © McRae Books, except:

p. 8, Cape Mannu, Sardinia © Giuliano Cappelli, Florence; p. 12, Liguria © Diego Banchetti; p. 24, Piedmont © Diego Banchetti; p. 40, Lombardy © ; p. 54, Island of St. Giorgio dalla Riva degli Schia, Venice © Giuliano Cappelli, Florence; p. 68, Emilia Romagna © ; p. 90, Tuscany © Marco Nardi, Florence; p. 110, Umbria © Diego Banchetti; p. 126, Marches © Marco Nardi, Florence; p. 134, Lazio © ; p. 148, Porto Conte (Alghero), Abruzzo © Giuliano Cappelli, Florence; p. 162, Puglia © Marco Nardi, Florence; p.178, Basilicata & Campania © ; p. 194, Calabria © ; p. 206, Sicily © Diego Banchetti; p. 230, Golf of Orosei, Sardinia © Giuliano Cappelli, Florence; p. 244, Modern Classics © Diego Banchetti